Why I Remain a Gay Catholic

Why I Remain a Gay Catholic

A Spiritual-Sexual Journey

Paul F. Morrissey, OSA

FOREWORD BY

Sr. Jeannine Gramick, SL

Paulist Press
New York / Mahwah, NJ

Scripture quotations are from the New Revised Standard Version Bible: Catholic Edition, copyright © 1989, 1993 National Council of the Churches of Christ in the United States of America. Used by permission. All rights reserved worldwide.

Cover image by Benjavisa / iStock.com
Cover and Book design by Lynn Else

Library of Congress Cataloging-in-Publication Data
Names: Morrissey, Paul F., author.
Title: Why I remain a gay Catholic: a spiritual-sexual journey / Paul F. Morrissey, OSA; foreword by Sr. Jeannine Gramick, SL.
Description: New York: Paulist Press, [2025] | Includes bibliographical references. | Summary: "This book is an autobiographical work detailing the author's spiritual and sexual journey of faith"—Provided by publisher.
Identifiers: LCCN 2024040010 (print) | LCCN 2024040011 (ebook) | ISBN 9780809157259 (paperback) | ISBN 9780809188932 (ebook)
Subjects: LCSH: Morrissey, Paul F. | Catholic Church—New York (State)—New York—Clergy—Biography. | Gay clergy--New York (State)--New York—Biography.
Classification: LCC BX4705.M7244 A3 2025 (print) | LCC BX4705.M7244 (ebook) | DDC 282.092 [B]—dc23/eng/20250216
LC record available at https://lccn.loc.gov/2024040010
LC ebook record available at https://lccn.loc.gov/2024040011

ISBN 978-0-8091-5725-9 (paperback)
ISBN 978-0-8091-8893-2 (e-book)

Published by Paulist Press
997 Macarthur Boulevard
Mahwah, NJ 07430
www.paulistpress.com

Printed and bound in the
United States of America

Dedication

For Bob and all the others,
living or deceased,
beloved by God

And for Pope Francis's
"Who am I to Judge?"

Author's Note

To protect their confidentiality, I have given pseudonyms to people outside my immediate family and a few deceased Augustinian friars. For the same reason, on a few occasions, I have merged two persons into one or changed a few circumstances, especially in the interactions with the inmates. Other than these changes, the following is a true story.

Contents

Foreword

As I began to read Fr. Paul Morrissey's superb memoir, I thought of the late 1970s and early 1980s when the subject of gay priests and religious first emerged in the U.S. Church. I thought of Fr. John Harvey, who conducted retreats for priests and religious who were experiencing "difficulties with same-sex attraction." The word "gay," or even "homosexual," was avoided as it was believed that these sexual feelings were mere struggles of someone who was naturally heterosexual. Such feelings, Church leaders thought, could be overcome through prayer and avoidance of "near occasions of sin."

This approach was the sexual ideology of a large segment of the institutional Church at that time, and it persists to this day in some quarters despite the advances of modern psychology and other sciences. This approach was not the one advocated by Dignity, an organization for LGBTQ Catholics that began in 1969. Dignity supported the view that sexual feelings were not wounds but God-given gifts to be used in an ethically responsible way.

As I continued to read *Why I Remain a Gay Catholic,* I recalled fond memories of the Dignity chapter that I founded in Baltimore in 1977. I thought particularly of Father Harvey's visit to me at St. Jerome's parish convent; he listened intently and sympathetically as I spoke of lesbian and gay people as part of God's plan for creation. Although he acknowledged that, because he was a priest, he felt obliged to follow the magisterium, I was pleased that Father Harvey later invited me to speak about Dignity to his class of seminarians.

Some seminarians, at least, were hearing about newer understandings of sexuality. Religious orders such as the Jesuits, the

Christian Brothers, and the Xaverian Brothers discussed the acceptance of gay men in religious life in their internal publications. Organizations, such as the National Religious Vocation Conference and the Religious Formation Conference, and the journal *Review for Religious* published some commentaries about gay priests and brothers.

But the wider Catholic community came to read about the topic only a while later when the *National Catholic Reporter* printed three anonymous articles titled "I Am a Gay Priest with a Community Role," "Being Gay and Celibate," and "A Sacrifice without Growth." It was a tenuous time for gay priests and religious.

The spiritual advisors and formation directors who wrote about "the homosexual question," "counseling the invert," or "clerics with homosexual tendencies" did not inspire much admiration for gay priests and religious or much sympathy for the difficult path that they had to navigate. These writers did not help us understand the dilemma that gay priests and religious face in our homophobic Church, nor did they inspire acceptance of them as our brothers. By 1989, when I edited the book *Homosexuality in the Priesthood and Religious Life*, only three out of seven priests who shared their stories felt brave enough to use their real names. One was the Jesuit Fr. William Hart McNichols, a prominent artist and illustrator of books.

Only a handful of priests were publicly "out" or known to be gay. In those days, during the early Christopher Street Parades that would grow to become today's Pride Marches, Jesuit Fr. Bob Carter, who cofounded the National Gay and Lesbian Task Force, proudly marched down Fifth Avenue in front of St. Patrick's Cathedral in New York City. In the first years of my ministry for LGBTQ+ people, I joined those excited marchers and heard sidewalk cheers *and* boos as the militant chants went up: "Two, four, six, eight! Gay is just as good as straight!"

Also marching in those parades were Fr. Bernárd Lynch, SMA, and Jesuit Fr. John McNeill. Fr. Bernard Lynch endured many years of harassment from New York Church authorities and, in a highly publicized case, withstood vicious and false accusations of sexual abuse, of which he was later totally exonerated. Fr. John McNeill, a theologian, published his 1976 landmark book, *The Church and the Homosexual*, a critique of traditional Catholic teaching about homosexual ethics and a premier contribution to theological development about sexuality.

During these decades, Fr. Paul Morrissey was struggling with his sexuality. He was not out publicly, although he had shared his sexual orientation with some trusted friends. Paul's formulation of "in" and "out" in this book is unconventional; it is not related to being "in" or "out" of the closet. I find his use of these words quite thought-provoking. For Paul, "out" means estranged in some way from God or the Church. St. Augustine, as he was running away from intimacy with God before his conversion, is the classic example of being "out." For Paul himself, "out" means estrangement from the Church because of his sexual orientation.

Paul uses "in" to mean saved by God's grace, growing as a faithful Catholic in the Church and being close to Jesus and God. I like this conception of "in" and "out"—a truly spiritual way of using these words. He also coins a meaning for a third term, the word "with," which he defines as the actual experience of gradually reconciling or integrating "out" and "in," two apparently opposite aspects of oneself.

During his "in" phase, Paul absorbed the spirituality of his family. After supper each evening, his mother, father, and thirteen siblings gathered in the dining room to pray the rosary. It was here that Paul learned the meaning of faith and the belief that there is a plan for everyone in life. The family concluded evening prayer by reciting, "Dear God, please help us to find our true vocation and have the courage to follow it." This recitation was pivotal because only by discovering and fulfilling his vocation could Paul truly be happy. As he writes, "Whatever else you might accomplish in life—even if you become a millionaire, a movie star, or the pope—you would have wasted your life if you hadn't been true to yourself."

And being true to himself meant that Paul needed to struggle with sexuality, even when it led him to feel "out" and estranged from the Church. He needed intimacy with human beings as well as with his God. I do not use the word "intimacy" as a synonym for sexual intercourse, though, of course, it may sometimes include that. Intimacy involves openness, vulnerability, and a sharing that leads to a bonding between two individuals. Intimacy could, though not necessarily, include falling in love. To be fully alive, all human beings, even celibates, need intimacy with other humans, as well as with God.

Paul felt the inward tussle of being intimate and celibate. As Paul so honestly and heart-wrenchingly writes, "Somehow in this entire struggle to be whole, I never completely stopped believing that being a priest—including my desire for sexual integrity as a gay priest—was my lifelong vocation and the deepest fulfillment of my vows. Jesus had called me. Even though I was lost, I believed that you shouldn't leave someone you are sworn to just because you discover something new about yourself. What is God's desire for me?"

But how was Paul going to reconcile the two apparent opposites of "out" and "in" to become "with"? His entire spirituality was based on "laying down my life for others," as Jesus did. So, what was God's will for him? What was his true vocation, and how could he be true to himself and his need for human intimacy?

Paul's nascent fusion of his "out" and "in" phases can be credited to Dignity/Philadelphia, the outgrowth of the home liturgy group I helped to organize when I was a graduate student at the University of Pennsylvania. Paul began to preside at the weekly Dignity Eucharist celebrations, often speaking of Jesus's love and acceptance of all outcasts. He describes how "every Sunday I preached how God loves them no matter what. And all the while I realized that in God's mysterious way of healing us through others, the lepers were healing the priest." Dignity was teaching him to accept his own sexuality.

During his time with Dignity, Paul founded a group called Communication Ministry. While various priests, religious, and laypersons contributed to its growth, Paul was the main inspiration and a founding incorporator. Communication Ministry, Incorporated (CMI) was the outgrowth of a private workshop that he and the Dominican Fr. Richard Woods conducted during the 1977 Dignity convention in Chicago. The workshop, advertised for gay priests, brothers, and sisters, drew about a hundred priests and religious.

During its almost thirty years of ministry, CMI sponsored retreats, circulated a monthly newsletter, and published periodic journals on such topics as AIDS, seminary formation, and spiritual direction. It fostered supportive personal relationships, forged links across community lines, and gave hope to gay priests and religious, even beyond the United States. At its height, there were more than five hundred members, although most of the membership was male. But the membership would gradually erode, not due to the failure of the organization but to external events in the Church.

Clerical sexual abuse first became public during the mid-1980s, but it remained largely at the fringes of public attention until the mid-1990s. Salacious articles branding gay priests as pedophiles began to circulate. Author Jason Berry wrote about seminaries that spawned gay priests. The right-wing Catholic media railed that homosexuality was rampant in the priesthood. Sadly, the pedophilia crisis was laid at the feet of gay priests, who became convenient scapegoats.

After the *Boston Globe*'s 2002 reporting of the extensive hierarchical mishandling of a heretofore unknown immense number of clerical sex abuse offenses, the issue of priests' sexuality became widespread across the United States. But instead of looking at the scientific data or the administrative mishandling of these cases, the Congregation for Catholic Education, in 2005, issued a six-page instruction that said the Church cannot ordain men who are "active homosexuals," who have "deeply rooted" homosexual tendencies, or who support the "gay culture." Those who had overcome "transitory" homosexual tendencies, however, could be ordained. Basically, the bottom line was that gay men should not be accepted into seminaries or ordained to the priesthood. In the heat of the clerical sexual abuse crisis, the Vatican seemed to imply that gay men were the cause of the abuse; therefore, if gay men were not ordained, the crisis would go away.

Naturally, all these occurrences spawned fear in the hearts of diocesan clergy and men in religious congregations. Many gay clergy and religious feared that the hard drives of their computers that they used to stay in touch with one another could be used against them. A strong downward turn in CMI's membership base began in 2002. The organization canceled its national conference and retreat after attendance plummeted.

Because of this growing panic and alarm, the CMI board voted in 2007 to close the organization and asked New Ways Ministry to continue their mission as one of its projects. Since that time, New Ways Ministry has sponsored retreats and other supportive programs for gay priests, brothers, and deacons, together with a program of retreats for lesbian nuns and educational workshops for them and the leaders of their religious congregations.

During this crisis, only one brave bishop spoke out publicly to condemn the scapegoating of gay priests. In an essay in *America* in September 2002, titled "Yes, Gay Men Should Be Ordained," Bishop Thomas Gumbleton wrote,

> All this must stop: the scapegoating of gay priests for the sex abuse crisis, the demand to reject homosexual persons for the priesthood and religious life, the unchallenged suggestion that the ordination of a gay man would be invalid....
>
> I have worked with and come to know well many gay priests. They are healthy psychologically, and their committed ministry has been very effective. I am inspired by their love of God and of the people they serve so well and generously. I also know the struggle they now face as they see the bishops deal with the current crisis in the church.

As the twenty-first century developed, the average Catholic in the pew did not blame gay priests and religious for clergy sexual abuse. They did not confuse homosexuality with pedophilia. They could delineate between these two completely different categories. Most Catholics knew about the prevalence of child sexual abuse in families where adult heterosexual males molest young females. They knew, or assumed, that many of their pastors were gay, and that factor was immaterial to them. What mattered was: "Is my pastor a caring person? Is he a good shepherd to his flock?" They wanted to support the gay priests and religious who had served secretly and silently for years in their faith communities. These men had a rightful place at the table of God.

Soon after his election, Pope Francis spoke publicly about gay priests. On his flight home from World Youth Day in Brazil in 2013, his first papal trip, a journalist asked him about reports of a "gay lobby" of priests inside the Vatican. His answer "Who am I to judge?" stunned the world. Indeed, who are we to judge when we have not walked in the other person's shoes?

As Fr. Paul Morrissey perceptively points out, heterosexuals grow up learning that their sexuality is good. How does it feel to grow up being told that your sexuality is disordered? This was Fr.

Paul's predicament, and this is the quandary for all LGBTQ+ people.

This book is an example of the spiritual courage of one gay priest who struggled with his sexuality as he tried to find out what was God's will for him. Through vignettes, the author shows the reader that every human being needs friendship and intimacy. The real disorder in our Church is the fixation on sexual sin, an obsession with (and devaluing of) sexuality, and a fear of touch. All of this is dehumanizing. Human beings need signs of affection precisely *to be human.*

As I turned the pages of *Why I Remain a Gay Catholic,* I really fell in love with the main character depicted in this book—so vulnerable, so innocent, so giving, so longing to be himself, and so yearning to be one with his God. I loved his conversations with God, his sympathy for those who thought or believed other than he did, his philosophy that God reverences human freedom, urging us to do our best, yet "allowing us to go astray if we insist." I cried at some parts, especially when Paul described what happened after his father received the letter that he sent him.

While this book is an important piece of Catholic LGBTQ+ testimony, it is really a poignant and tender memoir about struggling with one's humanity and one's relationship with God. Fr. Paul Morrissey found his true vocation and has had the courage to follow it. We are indebted to him for sharing his journey with us.

Sr. Jeannine Gramick, SL

Acknowledgments

Recently, I picked up one of my journals from thirty years ago. The opening sentence reads, "If I don't finish this memoir soon, I never will." I want to thank God for all those people who helped and encouraged me to give birth to this book. Mostly, it is with the help of the Holy Spirit—guiding me, goading me on when I was almost giving up, even inspiring me in my dreams at times, and finally celebrating with me now.

First, I acknowledge my editor and dear friend, Judy Warner Scher, now deceased, who asked me once, "Paul, do you ever write? If so, would you let me read some of it?" When I did, it began a long career of writing and publishing with Judy's wise and loving guidance. I pray to her now, "Judy, can you believe this?" I thank you with all my heart.

Next, I am grateful for my wonderful family. They—including some of the in-laws and the outlaws—have read and given me challenging feedback about this memoir for many years as only a beloved family can. I could not be coming out so publicly today without their support. This certainly includes my mother, Nora, and my father, Tom. Like so many of our parents, they are saints. To all of you, love forever and *Slainta!*

My second family, the friars in the Order of St. Augustine, are also among those whom I wish to thank, especially four provincials—Jack Deegan, Donald Reilly, Michael DiGregorio, and Rob Hagan. We have wrestled over what is worth saying and what may be better left unsaid, and I appreciate their love and honesty. A few friars who have read and critiqued parts of my work are Joe Calderone, Kevin Dwyer, Jim McCartney, Richard Nahman,

Jim Paradis, John Shea, Bob Thornton, Luis Vera, and Bill Waters. Many thanks to all my religious brothers in our great community.

Wonderful friends have also encouraged me when I might have given up, including Fr. Bob Frueh, Brandon Williams, Mary McKenna, Sr. Alice Marie Badey, Sandra Boston, Phyllis and Dick Taylor, Andy McCaffrey, George Munyan, and George Lakey. Their love and belief in me keep me going at this special moment.

Many professional and religious colleagues have given me invaluable advice, without which I would still be searching for my way. They include Fr. James Alison, Sr. Joan Chittister, Fr. John Collins, Sr. Gail DeMaria, Stacia Friedman, Fr. Rick Fredericks, April Gagne, Sr. Jeannine Gramick, Dr. Patricia Kelly, Sr. Bernadette Kinniry, Fr. James Martin, John McNeill, and Sr. Andrea Nenzel.

My editors, so many and so great, include Elizabeth Benninger, Barbara Crawford, Cynthia Marmo-Obrien, Avery Rome, and Paul McMahon from Paulist Press. They are the midwives.

I must thank especially my "choir" of supporters, whom I recall every evening. When I kneel at my window and look at the stars, I hold a rock with the memory of Tom, Buddy, Aelred, Jim, Bob, and Marty and pray, "Help me, dear brothers, to listen to the Holy Spirit and finish this memoir." With them rooting me on, I believe I have done this. That is why I am confident.

The Augustinian brothers I have lived with during these years are especially worthy of thanks. They put up with my quirks and personality traits, and I with theirs. We sandpaper each other into love each day and so become what Augustine hoped for—"one mind and one heart in God."

Finally, my dear friend, Anne Gentile, with whom I have known and shared my heart and soul for thirty years. I thank you, Anne, for your love and hope, your faith and dancing, your belief in me and my writing, your hospital ministry and childlike love for everything and everyone, especially for children. "Unless you change and become like children, you will never enter the kingdom of heaven" (Matt 18:3).

Introduction

Through this book, I trace my spiritual-sexual journey from childhood to the present and discern God's action in my life. I want to share especially my experience as a gay person, including fifty-six years of priestly ministry in the Catholic Church. Can a gay priest really have a unique call from God today? As St. Augustine intended with his *Confessions*, I hope this encourages others to remember/discover their own evolving relationship with God so that they can experience his love for them more deeply and follow his call, no matter where it leads. My journey led me to stay in the Church and remain a priest, one who is open about his sexual orientation. I hope to demonstrate how this was possible with God's grace.

St. Augustine, and most others who wrote of their conversions, described it as a journey from "Out" to "In": from being estranged from God as a sinner (Out) to being found like a lost sheep and saved by God's grace (In). My experience was different. I discovered a pattern of being brought up as a faithful Catholic and entering the priesthood/religious life, "In," followed by running away from that intimacy with God and the Church as I discovered my gay identity, "Out." It felt like it had to be either/or, as many people feel today. Finally, I spent the next part of my spiritual journey trying to reconcile these two "opposites" in a path I call "With."

Through this personal soul-searching, I have come to accept and even enjoy my gay sexual orientation as a gift from God, not without pain and doubts. This faith journey has made me joust with the Church at times. I could have simply left the priesthood and the Church, but I didn't feel called to do so. At the same time, my conscience doesn't permit me to stay in the priesthood and participate in its marginalization of LGBTQ people, even in silence.

Since my entrance into the seminary in the early 1960s, the Catholic Church has changed. Change came when the Church had to wrestle with the voices of those on the margins, including LGBTQ people. Furthermore, disputes arose over the role of women, racial equality, and environmental justice. During these movements, the Church challenged "the world" by its historical emphasis on a divine and transcendent God whom we need to save us. As St. Augustine reminds us, we cannot save ourselves. We need amazing grace. Yes!

The Latin hymns and the altar against the wall at Mass emphasized this transcendent source of grace. But then Pope John XXIII called the Second Vatican Council. The document, *Gaudium et spes* (The Church in the Modern World) was issued. The altars were turned around so the priest could face the congregation, and the Mass was now celebrated in our own languages rather than Latin. These and other changes told us that Jesus is with us in his humanity as well as in his divinity. But did this identification with our humanity include our sexuality? We are still wrestling with that question.

Sexuality was the issue on which the Church would not budge. No sex before marriage. No sex with birth control. No sex with anyone other than your married heterosexual spouse. No divorce and remarriage. No abortion under any circumstances. Virginity is the primary way to sainthood. No married priests. No women priests. No gay priests.

The Catholic Church's teachings on sex have mostly remained black and white since the time of St. Augustine in the fourth century, even if a majority of worshipers may ignore the rules to make room for their personal choices. These personal and institutional conflicts are filled with blood and tears: from families divided, suicides, the catastrophe of sexual abuse by priests and its coverup, endless scrupulous confessions by some, and droves of people, especially the young, leaving the Church.

But many more stay because the Church is our Mother and our link with Jesus. This memoir is only one person's journey, but there are millions of Catholics today who persevere in our Church with their adult consciences. And tens of thousands of gay priests, religious brothers, and sisters who serve the Church faithfully. This story should not be forgotten and can make a difference.

After completing the manuscript twenty years ago, I shared it with my family. Some said that I should not publish it and warned me—because they love me—that I could get forced out of the priesthood. The parts that worried them involved aspects of my sexual journey. Yet I was heartened by the patron saint of my religious order, St. Augustine, who had shared his sexual struggles in his *Confessions*,[1] and after his conversion, asserted that he was still struggling with these things.

In writing his *Confessions*, St. Augustine took the unusual approach of addressing not readers in general but God. While this isn't my style, at various moments throughout the book I do raise my voice in prayer, praise, questioning, or wonder about where God is in my journey. For this reason, it is most important that I portray my way of relating to God not for its own sake but so that readers may get in touch with their own.

If we are ever going to be taken seriously, we need an honest discussion about sexuality and spirituality in the Catholic Church and beyond. My life struggle to integrate these might help others. Other members of my family encouraged me to publish my manuscript. They noted that it will help other people, including priests, be more real about their lives and their relationships with God. Through this book, I show the gradual evolution of my understanding of God and my sexuality. What does it mean to be both gay and a Catholic priest? I have wrestled with God my entire life about this apparent contradiction. This is my true vocation.

Part I
IN

For you created my inmost being;
you knit me together in my mother's womb.
I praise you because I am fearfully and wonderfully made;
your works are wonderful,
I know that full well.
My frame was not hidden from you
when I was made in the secret place,
when I was woven together in the depths of the earth.
(Ps 139:13–15)

1

The Church Versus the World

September 1963, Villanova University, Pennsylvania—

I headed across campus toward our church history class in my black habit. It was my first week at Villanova after a year at our Augustinian novitiate on the shores of the Hudson River. As I passed the library with its tall, dark windows, a familiar voice pierced my reverie. "Yo, Paul!"

It was my younger brother, Francis, a sophomore at Villanova. He looked cool in the olive-green suit I had left him. I was surprised that he recognized me in my habit with my hair clipped short, but his face lit up.

I halted in my tracks. My brother was a layperson. He was the world that I had left to become a priest. I hadn't seen him since that one visiting day at the novitiate six months ago.

Now, he huffed to a stop and grabbed me by the shoulder. "Hey, man! How ya been?"

"Francis, I can't." My hands went up as though to ward off the devil.

"What?" His face fell, confusion in his eyes.

"We're not allowed to talk...." I began to explain. I would have loved to hug him. Only four years apart, we had grown closer when he got into high school and the old battles were forgiven.

He searched my face. "You're kidding, right?"

"No, I'm not." I got my composure back. "Francis, we're not allowed to talk to laypeople."

"Laypeople!" His eyes flashed with Irish anger. "I'm your brother, you asshole!" His face hardened. "You're not gonna follow some damn rule when you see me, are you?"

Uh-oh! This was the test. Anyone could follow the rule with strangers. Anyone could follow the rule when it was easy. Only when it was difficult did it become a true challenge. Your clue to whether you really had the guts to make it or not to the end—ordination. It really was a choice between God and human love.

"I'm your brother!"

I felt my stomach flutter and drop. "Francis, we can't talk. Maybe when..."

But he became furious. One steamy look drilled me. Turning away, he headed back toward Dougherty Hall.

"Francis! It doesn't mean..." I shouted.

He wouldn't look back. And the wind whipped the religious habit around my ankles like a bunch of snakes, and the golden leaves drifted silently from the hundred-year-old trees with their ancient, gnarled roots, filling the space between us.

I recalled the last outing we had before I went into the novitiate. What a sendoff that had been! In Somers Point, New Jersey, the capital of college frolics across the bridge from Ocean City, the summer weekends were like bacchanals. Ocean City was a "dry" town. No alcohol. Somers Point loved that. Battalions of thirsty kids in souped-up cars sped across the bridge each night to worship at the altars of Tony Marts and Bay Shores, two raucous dance clubs across the street from each other next to the bay.

Before I left home for the Augustinian seminary, Francis and I headed down to the shore for a last weekend of partying. I had graduated from Villanova the year before; he was about to begin his freshman year there. I was twenty-two; he was eighteen. The drinking age in New Jersey was twenty-one.

After checking into the Pink Pussycat, a crash-pad type hotel for college kids in Ocean City, and grabbing a cheesesteak at the Chatterbox, we headed across the bridge to Somers Point. I had gotten my cousin Jim's driver's license from him so Francis could get into the clubs. Jim was my age. At a root beer joint up the road from Tony Marts, Francis and I role-played what might happen at the club entrance.

"Up against the wall, you two...show me your IDs. What's your name? Your birthdate?" When the two of us had the likely scenario down pat, we headed over to the club. What we role-played is exactly what happened, except for one additional question, "What color are your eyes?"

Me: "Blue."

The muscled bouncer thumbed me aside. He turned to Francis, squinting into his face, "And you?"

Francis: "Blue."

About to give him the okay too, he suddenly glanced again at the ID, then riveted his gaze back to Francis. "The ID says brown. This ain't you!" Suddenly, it was like we had defrauded his grandmother. The bouncer grabbed us by our collars and whistled for the cops in a nearby paddy wagon. They loaded us into the back seat like criminals as the other would-be patrons grinned at our plight.

Frightened and aghast at our stupid luck, I whispered through my gritted teeth as they drove us away, "Stick to your story!"

It was only later at the Somers Point Jail that we realized how bad our luck was. The judge who heard our initial plea that night had been sitting beside the root beer barrel at the place where we had rehearsed our lines! That night was a hellish one—droves of half-drunken St. Joe's, U of Penn, and Villanova kids screamed, cursed, and occasionally vomited through the night. A little after dawn, we were informed that we had one phone call to try and come up with the two hundred dollars each in cash for the bail.

Where could we come up with such money on a Sunday morning in 1962? There were no ATMs then. Eventually, I called home. Mama answered. "It's Paul, Mama. I'm with Francis, and we are in the Somers Point Jail. We need four hundred dollars in cash for our bail. I'm so sorry."

"What? Oh, my Lord!" The phone went silent. I imagined her distress, like when one of us got hit by a car or some accident.

"Oh Paul..."

"We—Francis—got caught for using a false ID to get into a club here. We are okay, but sad to have been such jerks." I knew she'd be thinking of my entrance to the novitiate in a week.

"Tom? Tom?" I heard her frantic call for Daddy. I can't recall what happened after that, except that it's the memory that arises now. Where else could you get a couple hundred dollars in cash on a Sunday morning but from the collection at the local Catholic parish?

I heard later that, as the pastor handed Daddy and Mama the envelope of cash, he mused aloud, "Isn't Paul the son who is going into the seminary next week?"

I shook off my musing on my past relationship with Francis and turned toward my church history class in Mendel Hall. It's odd the way these memories arise out of nowhere. What's the purpose of it? To find a meaning that allows you to let it go or maybe learn from the past to live the future better. That's what Mr. O'Grady told us in his class that day.

"Gentlemen and gentlewomen, if we don't learn from our history, we are doomed to repeat our mistakes." He paused for emphasis.

"Of course, of course! But I am sure you are thinking, 'What can this old geezer teach me? And what do I care about Church history anyway? I'm young and free. I want to live my life.' Hmph!" He scanned the room, holding our attention. "Let me tell you," O'Grady continued, "the Church you love—for good or ill—has influenced, even dominated your lives more than you can possibly imagine. If you don't understand this power and use this knowledge of history to transform the Church, you will spend your life reacting to it."

Transform the Church! This guy doesn't get it. The Church is infallible. It's us who need to be transformed.

"Go ahead and call yourselves Christians if you want to, but if you don't attempt to transform the Church into being more like Christ, and transform yourself in the bargain, you will have missed what it means to be baptized. You'll have wasted your lives in passivity, not to mention those of your children and your grandchildren. There! You've been forewarned!"

A lay student on my left glanced sideways at me with raised eyebrows. Together we grinned: *What is this guy, some kind of fanatic?*

In class, I began to daydream about the novitiate I'd just left and its beautiful setting. At times, happy to do crazy stuff to break my own will, I'd kneel with scissors to clip the grass under the wrought-iron fence that the mower couldn't reach. The more different it was from the world's ways, the better. I liked the challenge of how much we could take before our spirits cracked. My brother, Tommy, had it easier in the Marines.

"...three pages, double-spaced, and no plagiarism, do you understand?" O'Grady was giving an assignment. "I want your own thoughts on this. Do you think you can manage this assignment, Brother Morrissey?"

"Uh...yes."

"Good! That's all for today."

Something about this guy intrigued me.

2

A True Vocation

1940s, Upper Darby, Pennsylvania—

I grew up the second eldest of fourteen children in Upper Darby, Pennsylvania. We were as Catholic as the pope. By the time the ninth child, Kathy, was born in 1950, we had moved to a bigger house in the same parish, St. Alice's. My mother's parents, Maggie and Tom Harley, also lived in the parish. As they grew older (Granddaddy would die soon after the move), they sold their home and pooled the funds to help Mama and Daddy buy the new house, at the corner of Sansom Street and Copley Road, across from the parish kindergarten. A three-story duplex, it had three bedrooms on the second floor. Mama and Daddy slept in one, the younger girls in another, and our grandparents in the master bedroom. We kids ranged in age from Tommy, the eldest at twelve, to Kathy, the new baby.

On the third floor were two big dorm rooms. One became the girls' room, where Nonie, Anne, Mary, and Peggy slept. The other one was the boys' room, where Tommy, Francis, Joe, and I plotted against the girls. These rooms had no insulation, so we roasted in the summer and froze in the winter. But this was our space. Daddy and Mama almost never came up there, except once a month when Daddy would haul up a big vacuum. You had to be prepared that your socks and underwear might get sucked up for trash.

The first floor had an indoor porch with windows on three sides, where Mama grew plants. This opened into a large living room with a fireplace and a TV. The dining room was also large and had French doors that shut out the sounds of the television. Daddy had fastened together two tables—one from each set of grandparents—to make a long table with enough seating for a "Last Supper." Usually, we had a dozen people for dinner—even more as the family grew—and we occasionally brought home dinner guests. You had to guard your plate during these meals or the meatballs might disappear on someone else's fork.

A long, gilded mirror graced one wall. Occasionally, Daddy would tell Mary to stop looking in the mirror while we ate. This dining room was the center of our family life. At the daily meals, usually served by Mama out of a big pot, we shared stories from the day, jousting for attention and the biggest serving. We even did our school homework around this dining room table, asking one another questions if we got stuck on an assignment.

It was in this dining room that we learned the meaning of faith. After dinner each evening, we'd dash through a decade of the rosary in fifteen minutes, the dirty dishes stacked in front of us as though a reminder of our need to give thanks. To escape, we'd sometimes begin dancing in the living room until Mama ran in after us to grab the 45 rpm records and fling Fats Domino or Elvis Presley onto the carpet. We knew that the ritual must not be interrupted—dinner, prayers, clean-up (girls' night and boys' night in sequence according to Daddy's list), homework around the same table, and bed. When we got the chance, we danced anyway. It was all part of the game.

The prayers revealed a lot. Mama would begin by blessing herself with the sign of the cross, as we all did the same. Next, she would say the Our Father, which we'd all race through, then each in turn around the table leading a Hail Mary that again we all responded to until ten were said. The object was to get through your Hail Mary without the other brothers and sisters making you laugh because this would make Mama angry. Sometimes she giggled along with the rest of us.

After the rosary, we would go around the table and say a prayer uniquely our own, either a prayer to our own saint or a special variation such as Terry's "Little Flower in this hour show your power." Even our guests were unable to escape a test of faith. When their turn came, all eyes swung to them with the implied question, "And who is your favorite saint?" We loved it when they missed their cue or couldn't think of one while Mama nodded knowingly—*And you want to date my daughter!*

Through our prayers, we absorbed the belief that there is a plan for everyone in life. It was summed up in our closing prayer: "Dear God, please help us to find our true vocation and have the courage to follow it." We believed that God has a vocation for each of us in which we use our unique talents to the fullest potential. And it would be up to each of us to discover this vocation. No one could do this for you. Furthermore, God was counting on you to accomplish this, and it was the only thing that would make you really happy in life. We assumed that everyone else up and down our working-class block was praying for this, too.

The clincher of course was the last part: *"and have the courage to follow it."* It would be tempting to give up at times. I began to see that finding one's true vocation would be a lifelong adventure. The most difficult challenge was to be your true self. Almost everyone and everything would reward you for being otherwise. Whatever else you might accomplish in life—even if you become a millionaire, a movie star, or the pope—you would have wasted your life if you hadn't been true to yourself.

3

Being Special

1940s, Upper Darby, Pennsylvania—

Growing up, I always had a need to be special. In our tight-knit family, the newest baby got all the attention. Mama would come home from the hospital after a few days that seemed like forever. With much hoopla, Daddy would welcome her and the baby home with a kiss. We would all fuss over the little creature with the astonishing blue eyes and the tiny red fists, saying, "Oh, look at how silky her hair is! Look at her smiling at us! Be careful of the little soft spot on the top of her head!" All attention was riveted on this newcomer, while the "old" baby stared numbly from the highchair at the one who would soon usurp its place of honor. This was the first of many graduation days to come.

I was skinny and small for my age. Being so short, I was usually first in the procession lines that the nuns of St. Alice's arranged for us by height. At dinner, Mama would save second helpings for me at the dinner table. "Paul's your favorite," my siblings would complain to her, "you always save the extra dessert for him." I liked that.

In the afternoon, Mama would dress us all up even in the coldest weather and walk us around the neighborhood, our little hands clutching onto the baby stroller. People would stop and talk with her, looking down and counting us with their eyes rolling, asking us to tell them our names.

Everybody knew us.

When Daddy came home from work, Mama would greet him at the door with a kiss. She would have changed into a clean dress, with pearls and high heels. Sometimes she would work around the house dressed that way—making beds, cleaning windows, hanging wash loads out on the back line, cooking meals, all with her hair curled and makeup on as though she were going out on a date.

She needed to feel special too.

Mama started her day with daily mass and followed this homemaker regimen until she came down to the living room each night in her quilted bathrobe around 10:00 p.m. With her hair done up in pink curlers and Vaseline shiny on her face, she'd catch up on some last-minute sewing while watching the news with Daddy and then have a snack.

My father was a husky man with an infectious laugh. You could hear his booming voice a couple of blocks away whenever he called us to come in for dinner. When he came home from work, he would lift us off the floor. But he cried more easily than Mama, even when he spanked us, saying, "This hurts me more than it hurts you."

One of my earliest memories is wrestling on the living room floor with him when I was a toddler. He'd let me get him down on his back and groan in surrender when I knelt on his chest. Just then, he'd grab me by the ankle and roll me over. When he'd hug me against his cheek, I could feel the roughness of his day's growth of beard. Even though it hurt, I loved it.

When there were just a few of us, Daddy would take us fishing on a Saturday afternoon at Wissahickon Creek near Strawberry Mansion in North Philadelphia where he had grown up, though he didn't talk much about that. He taught us how to put a worm on a hook and how to watch for the popper to bob when the fish took your bait. I liked being out by the water and trees with him and Tommy, but I hated it when the slimy worm guts got all over my hands. Then I would wish I were home playing with my sister Nonie.

At that young age, I was mainly afraid of my father. Maybe it was this fear, or something else those days that didn't allow fathers to get close to their sons, but it was like there was a barrier in getting to know him. Once when he was spanking Tommy, I feared Daddy might kill him. Torn between defending Tommy and protecting myself, I ran upstairs and hid in the wardrobe closet as Daddy's powerful voice chased me all the way. "Paul? *PAUL!*" I can still hear that voice after all these years. Sometimes, it is softer now. Perhaps he wants to get to know me too. Maybe it is my own voice, or God's. It doesn't matter. It's something wanting to be healed.

Over a dozen nuns lived together in a convent that was a stone's throw from our house. Except for the superior whom we called Moneybags because she was always taking up collections, they all taught at the nearby parochial school. They would call our house for emergency altar boy help for funerals on Saturday mornings and for Stations of the Cross on Friday nights during Lent. Tommy and I had to stop whatever we were doing to respond to this need. We hated it and complained our heads off.

My sisters too were sort of servants for the nuns, accompanying them on shopping trips as "companions" because a nun was not allowed to go out on her own. We never questioned these rules that set the nuns apart, believing it was connected to their holiness. We did mock the way the same nuns, who screamed "You dumbbells!" at our class, sounded like angels when they spoke to Mama.

"Good morning, Mrs. Morrissey, would one of the boys be free to serve a funeral?"

"Why certainly, Sister, I'll send one of them over in a jiffy."

"Thank you so much, and God bless you."

Nuns had all sorts of mysterious rituals. For instance, contests between different rows of us to buy "pagan babies" in far-off lands like Korea and the Belgian Congo. Whichever row of students gave the most money would get to name these babies when they were baptized. I hoped to meet one of these children, but I never did. Never for a moment did we wonder why they were being baptized Catholics though, since we knew that this was how they'd get to heaven.

You always sat in the same desk in Catholic grade school. The bad pupils sat up front where Sister could keep an eye on them. I was good, so I was made a "row captain," Sister's representative in the back. It was the earliest form of creating a hierarchy among us that was easily translated into an understanding of authority. There was Pope Pius XII in Rome and then the bishops under him. After that, there was the pastor, Father Conway, and the other priests. Then Moneybags and the sisters. Under them came Mama and Daddy, then me and my brothers and sisters. My sister, Nonie, and I made an alliance. Only a year apart in age, we spent so much time together people thought we were twins.

On Saturday nights, Daddy would often gather a group of us into the bathtub together, including a neighborhood kid or two. He would sprinkle a box of Tide over us and soap us down, then have us jump into the shower in relays to wash off. Finally, he would towel us down. In those days, we'd hide our sexual differences behind a washcloth, giggling and protesting.

Nonie and I played with paper dolls together, and I wanted a leather schoolbag like hers with little compartments for pencils and books instead of an army bag like Tommy's. My parents let me be. I sensed that I was different, but we didn't have any words for it then.

Little capitalists that we were, Nonie and I would stage "shows" in the basement for the neighborhood kids, charging a nickel admission and selling them Kool-Aid at intermission. Nonie kept this money in her room. Most of the time, Nonie and I were like special assistants to Mama, wiping off the ten milk bottles delivered every few days before they were put in the ice box, scrubbing the linoleum dining room floor on our hands and knees on Saturday mornings, and feeding our baby brothers and sisters, who called us "Mommy Nonie" and "Mommy Paul." In those days, "mommy" was the only nurturing role we knew. I was good at that and was proud to be one of "Mama's little helpers" while Tommy was out fishing or hunting.

It was as though I was caught between Nonie and Tommy. I was closer to Nonie, but she was a girl. I liked being with Tommy, but I didn't like to do the things that he did. Because he was bigger, I learned to run faster than he could. When he was chasing me in the alley and just about to grab me, I would imagine a tiger about to chomp my head off and rev up with an amazing little spurt of speed. My brother was both a hero and a threat to me.

On Tuesday night, while the girls helped Mama do the ironing, Tommy and I had to put the trash out. It was a great chance for us to be on our own after dark. Once, I remember lying on my back next to Tommy over on Don's lawn; Don was already in high school.

"See that star over there, the one that's twinkling?" Tommy said.

"Yeah!"

"That's the north star."

"Really?" We watched in silence for some moments, hearing each other's breath, lost in the show overhead. The burning tail of one star blazed into nothingness.

"Well, one of my teachers said that stars are so far away that even though you can see them, they may no longer exist," Tommy said.

"What? I don't get it!"

"The light coming from them," he explained with authority, "could still be traveling toward us even after the star explodes."

My brain was too little to grab this concept, but it did make me wonder what was out there. After that, I would kneel at our bedroom window after turning the lights off and stare at the night sky. I was so small compared to all of creation, but God was out there somewhere and in control.

This private and quiet sense of God was different from my family's sense of God at the rosary. There, God often seemed like a football referee. It contrasted even more from the sense of God that I had in church. There, surrounded by the passionate reds, blues, and oranges that portrayed the life of Christ in the stained-glass windows and mesmerized into a trance by the bells and chanted Latin hymns—*Tantum ergo sacramentum, veneremur cernui*—I had no separate identity in this celebration of the mystery of God because the goal was to become one with it. I was intoxicated just to be one of the Lily Boys processing in front of the Flower Girls, who flung petals from their bouquets at the feet of the priest behind us who, clutching the Blessed Sacrament under a satin veil, was half hidden in the cloud of incense swirling around him—*Et antiqum documentum, novo cedat ritui....*

These rituals in the Catholic Church were our strong point as well as our Achilles' heel. No one could gain salvation without these sacraments of water, oil, bread, and wine. And there were all the other tangible ways that reminded us of our closeness to God—candles, statues, Masses, relics, rosaries, medals, holy pictures, nuns, priests, popes. And no one could gain salvation by themself. That was a Protestant thing. The individual interpretation of the Bible was a perfect example of the confusion that resulted if you didn't follow what the Church said, so we were never taught to read the Bible. We heard it on Sundays from the pulpit when the priest told us what it meant—and we never challenged this.

I suppose our parents swallowed this communal thinking whole because we were raised to know ourselves in the first place as a part of a family, before we dared to think of ourselves as separate individuals. The nuns and the Church taught the same thing. Selfishness was the worst sin, and a C in Self-Control on your report card signaled that you were on your way to damnation. I got a few C's. The communal baths and spankings we grew up with, the double beds and dormitories, the dining room table with its meals and homework and prayer rituals all reinforced this—God is in everything, but most of all in our togetherness.

The trouble with that is that a little kid can get lost in that togetherness and can spend his life searching for his identity.

4

A Space for Privacy

1950s, Upper Darby, Pennsylvania—

My separate sense of self evolved in the boys' room on the third floor. For the first time in my life, I was in a space where I had a measure of privacy. Tommy taught me how to make gunpowder there one day. I remember him carefully mixing the ingredients, some of which he had from a chemistry set, the other that he had procured at a drug store.

"Now after you carefully mix it together, you've got to make a long trail along the windowsill, see?"

Awed at such mysterious knowledge, I nodded my head, wondering what Daddy would think. But he and Mama were far away on the first floor, so it didn't matter.

"Now you make a little fuse with some toilet paper." He rolled it between his palms like an expert.

"What if it blows up, starts a fire or something?"

"Don't be such a worrywart. It only blows up when it's packed together like dynamite." Soon the experiment was all set. My brother's eyes glowed as he oh so carefully placed the fuse. I held my breath and licked my lips, proud to be included in Tommy's adventure. "Get me those matches over there," he pointed. Quickly I ran to get them, my heart racing with excitement.

When he tried to strike a match, it wouldn't light at first. But suddenly, the whole matchbook lit at once. He threw it on the windowsill next to the fuse. Both of us jumped back in anticipation, but it needed a push. Tommy looked at me. I hesitated for a moment, but just before the matchbook fizzled out, I grabbed a sneaker and nudged it next to the fuse. Whoosh! It lit. Sputtering for a second, it blazed along the trail of gunpowder as Tommy and I whooped like cavemen. As we cleaned up the ashes and hid the ingredients in a closet, we chuckled at how we would make a trail of it over to the girls' room some night to surprise them.

At this age, I began to face the question: How can I be accepted if it means always keeping the rules? Sometimes like with the gunpowder, I felt more accepted if I broke a rule. When Nonie and I needed money to buy treats for a show, I waited until my father took his nap after work to search in his trousers for a stray dime or quarter, my image deviously glancing back at me in the bathroom mirror. To avoid getting punished I learned to lie, or at least develop an innocent lamb face. I became an expert at hiding my feelings. At other times, I fought for my rights, especially among my brothers and sisters.

Even Nonie and I had our disagreements. Once when we were playing Monopoly, I was the banker. In the middle of the game, just after I had bought Boardwalk and Park Place and was preparing to sink all my money into hotels to bankrupt her as she passed by, out of the corner of my eye—*I couldn't believe it!*—I spotted her little finger inching toward a five hundred dollar bill. Boiling at her treachery, I swore, "If you do that again, I'll kill you." Naturally, less than three minutes later, she tried again. Immediately, I seized her by the hair at the temples and began to hit her head against the carpet—"You rotten little cheater, you…you…" I only came out of this blind rage when Nonie pulled the Dead Duck Trick, letting her head flop limp to let me know that I had won. In ways like these, we began to forge our separate identities in the family.

At times, Mama and Daddy would go out to a movie. Then the turmoil just below the surface would break out, and they'd always swear, "Never again!" Sometimes our older cousin, Nancy, who lived in the same parish, babysat us. We locked her in the basement bathroom once—it was very rustic—and listened to her scream threats and pound on the door for an hour. Finally, we heard her cry and one of us snuck down and opened it. She refused to come back after that, but we were getting old enough to watch ourselves.

During one of these evenings, it was calm enough at first with all of us doing our homework around the big dining room table. Tommy and I were left in charge. Before she had left, Mama had told me to make sure that Francis, four years younger than me, changed out of his clothes into his pajamas before going to bed. Of course, I took this responsibility seriously and proceeded to hit Francis with a pillow as he lay stubbornly in his street clothes on his bed an hour later, but that only increased his stubbornness.

"Put your pajamas on!"

"No!"

"Yes!" I swung the pillow.

"No!" he shouted, as his fist tried to deflect it.

"Yes!"

"No!"...and on and on until I realized it was hopeless. Besides, this was Mama's battle. What did I care anyway? Francis glared me out of the room with pure hatred, and I went down to join Tommy in the living room.

We made some popcorn and soon got to bragging about who was the strongest—an arm wrestle would settle it—and who had the biggest dick. Not to worry, he reassured me, mine would grow.

Later when I went up to bed, I noticed Francis asleep in his clothes and frowned. As I tumbled into my own sack, I almost hit my face on the four-inch penknife that was stuck into my pillow that must have had half a dozen stab marks in it and the feathers spilling out! And the little brat was sleeping or pretending to sleep.

At some point, it began to dawn on me that family life wasn't just a place of sweetness. Sure, the fighting and competing seemed natural. And yes, the occasional storm honed unbreakable bonds in us. But occasionally I spotted a devil, in myself or among us, and saw that someone could really get hurt.

During these years, I was a model student at St. Alice's Grammar School. I'd run home, clutching my honor card that was gold for first honors and silver for second. Unlike Tommy, who was only an altar boy, I was a choirboy too. I liked getting dressed up in my red cassock, with the white surplice that Mama had starched and ironed. I felt like a butterfly ready to take off.

At the end of the year, the choirboys were given a reward. "Boys, pay attention!" Rose Imelda, the choir director, demanded. "You can choose a group outing either to the Philadelphia 76ers basketball game or the Ice Capades."

Cramer and Simmons snickered. Rose Imelda shot them a glare. Most of the guys began choosing the basketball game. Closing my eyes, I imagined the skaters gliding gracefully to beautiful music, landing just a few feet away from me in their tight outfits, spinning and showering ice in my face.

"Morrissey?"

"Ice Capades," I blurted out. That night I lay in my bed on the third floor and pictured myself leaping with the skaters, *Shall we dance? Bump, bump, bump…on a bright cloud of music shall we fly?*

Living on a separate floor from the adults—a separate dorm for girls and boys, ice skating and basketball—it wasn't much of a separation, but it was an important start. As I forged my identity, I was posed with a challenge: How can I hold these things together?

5

High School

Spring, 1955, Upper Darby, Pennsylvania—

Throughout my high school years, I was a mass of raging hormones. Due to a wicked case of acne, I hardly recognized the face that peered back at me from my mirror each morning. I kept the Clearasil company in the chips, but no one had time to consider that I might be having troubles.

Eisenhower was the president, and everyone liked "Ike." I knew all the top rock and roll tunes by heart and lived and died for the Philadelphia Athletics, The A's, one of Philadelphia's professional baseball teams. After school each day, I worked in Daddy's restaurant. (He didn't own the restaurant; he was the manager of one of a large chain of them—the Automat.) When they gave the busboys a raise from seventy-five to seventy-nine cents an hour, we were overjoyed. The Everly Brothers twanged out "Bye-Bye Love," while Elvis wailed "Hound Dog" on the *Ed Sullivan Show*. When he swiveled his hips, everybody screamed, "Oh, my God, what are we coming to?" Yet even that seemed like a skit where we all played our parts. There was one little glitch in this play. Boys were only supposed to like girls, but I liked boys too.

I was leaning against the wall with my buddy, Nick, at the Saint Alice's Friday night dance the night I met Irene. Nick and I were sophomores at the newly opened Archbishop Prendergast High School, taught by Augustinian priests. We felt so cool with our pegged pants and our collars flipped up.

The dance floor in the auditorium under the church was half lit at 9:30. The girls hung in chattering packs on one side. The boys were in groups of twos and threes against the wall on the other side. Up at the front was a stage. There on Sunday mornings a priest celebrated Mass for the overflow crowd from the main church above. If you peeked behind the red velvet curtains that were drawn closed for the dance, you'd see life-sized statues of the Blessed Mother and the Sacred Heart of Jesus. In front of them was a bank of votive candles. You could light one of the candles for a dime and say a prayer. One was lit.

By this time, Nick was already shaving once a day and drove a '52 Plymouth that his father had bought him. Like most of my friends, he was Italian, and one of the rockier guys in our crowd who had no trouble getting dates. I felt happy when I was near him. We leaned together, trading evaluations of the girls across the room.

"See the one in the black sweater, the one with the big boobs over by the exit sign?" Nick confided. "She's hot!"

"Yeah," I agreed, watching him flick the toothpick across his shiny teeth. I leaned closer so my shoulder could touch his and watched his soft brown eyes roam the room.

"I don't see Angie yet," he murmured. They had been dating for a few months even though she was just a freshman. When they were in his car together, she practically sat on his lap.

"She'll be here," I assured him, figuring she would probably arrive with the crowd of Notre Dame girls who set the room in motion. The two of us kept watching the door.

"Uuh!" Nick grunted, stretching, and arching his back. "I feel like getting laid tonight. What about you?"

"I'm cool," I assured him, enjoying it when he talked sexily with me.

"Cool?" He elbowed me in the ribs. "Hey man, when are you gonna let that hot Irish blood come up? This could be the night!"

Oh sure! Having never gotten laid so far or really wanting to—the word *laid* sounded crude to me—I copied his style, rocking back and forth, letting my breath out slowly to suggest my pent-up feelings. I wondered at times like this whether Nick ever felt like I did. Nobody talked about these things. Meanwhile, to join his energy, I stared at the hopefulness and fear on the lipsticked faces of the girls.

Guys needed to muster up courage to stroll across that no-man's land and tap a girl on the shoulder and ask, "Wanna dance?" What if she said no? Oh God, you'd die inside because everyone would see you were rejected. The girls would sense there was something wrong with you and whisper to one another. The guys would see you were a loser and snort to themselves until it was their turn to try.

"Hey, there's my baby." Nick tilted his head toward a couple of girls who were checking their coats. A smile curled on his lips; then he licked them. Angie must have sensed this because she spun around and beamed back at him. Nick poked my arm and moved toward his girl. "Catch you later, buddy."

Standing by myself, I was like a small island. I felt like running—to a group of guys, to the bathroom, anywhere so I wouldn't be alone. At times like this, my sexual feelings were confusing, perking along at their own rhythm to help me break out of my aloneness, but I didn't know what to do with them.

"My prayer," the Platters' voices rose like velvet out of the gloom, weaving their magic, *"...is to linger with you."* My gaze wandered to the curtains and pictured the statues behind them. It was as though we always needed to be reminded of the dangers of "impure thoughts, words, or deeds." Yet the statues of Jesus often showed him pointing to his heart on fire. He must know about these feelings. Even though he was the Son of God, Jesus was human too. No one ever spoke about Jesus's sexual feelings. We never heard anything about his teenage years. When he got aroused, he must have had to figure out what to do just like we did. A prayer the nuns had taught us came back to me: "Sacred Heart of Jesus, I place my trust in you."

Glancing back to where Nick was standing, I noticed his arm twined around Angie's waist. Oh, he wanted her! What did I want? It wasn't yet clear to me. I did know that I wanted to be alive and in love as a young man, and not to be afraid to feel all my feelings. *I place my trust in you, Sacred Heart, but do you place your trust in me?*

When I looked up, I saw Nick joking with one of the girls who had arrived with Angie. A slim girl, not too tall, a little smaller than me. Even in the dimness, her eyes grabbed my attention. Flashing eyes, with long dark lashes. I watched her as she quipped something back over her shoulder to Nick. You could tell she was sort of wild, not the kind of girl who needed constant care. The long tight skirt with the flare at the bottom and white bobby socks showed off her figure. When she began to jitterbug with another girl and her hand flung back over her head to the music, it added to my intrigue. Once, I thought she might be looking my way. *C'mon Paul, take a chance tonight,* those eyes seemed to say. On the next fast number, I would try.

I was halfway across the gym floor before I realized I had made my move. Good thing, because now there was no turning back.

Having sensed an opening, Nick had strolled by a moment earlier and whispered into my ear, "Look at that cutey. You can see she digs you, man. Her name's Irene."

The crowd of girls were huddled together like a football team. Stealing up behind them, I could see Irene's wavy black hair, the side of her face, the long eyelashes. *Oh God, please help her say yes.* Just as my sweaty hand reached up to touch her pink sweater from behind, the girlfriend next to her screamed and laughed out loud at something. They all joined in the hilarity as I jumped back.

No way. I turned to head back in disgrace. At that very moment, Irene turned sideways and stared at me. Her smoky gaze met mine for a split second. *Well, what are you waiting for, honey?* she seemed to ask. That's all that a young heart needed.

Irene smiled when my hand reached for hers. The other girls clucked like hens. I felt crazy and happy as I led her onto the dance floor to try some of the steps my sisters had taught me. My body tingled all the way down to my toes. When I caught the beat and swiveled her sideways, her hand whipped back. I spotted Nick and the other guys grinning. My heart flipped for joy.

I felt good hanging out with my buddies and enjoying their friendship. In those days, I fell in love with girls like they did. At least it seemed like love to me. Irene was the first and the most enduring girlfriend I had—for seven years, on and off. I dated other girls through high school and college. It wasn't as if I knew some specific identity when I was sixteen that made it seem inappropriate for me to date or even marry a girl someday. Loving girls was the only affection you were allowed to show. I had to do something with all my feelings, or I would burst.

When I did notice any sense of sexual feelings toward guys, it felt like something extra, though secret, in my personality that I wasn't sure if other guys felt too. If anyone ever hinted at these feelings, it was in wisecracks about queers or homos. They were usually described as dirty old men trying to seduce young kids. I knew I wasn't like that. When my buddies made jokes about them, I didn't stand up for the queers, though I tried not to laugh.

If I could have grasped it, a clue about the focus of my passion at that time was in my approach to sex. Being a good Catholic boy, I didn't try to have sex with Irene. Our parents and teachers had drilled into our minds that we shouldn't get girls "in trouble." But I didn't even try to feel Irene up—what every guy bragged and lied about on Monday morning in the locker room as we grabbed our biology books and ran to class. I didn't *want* to feel her up, even though I noticed the bra straps through her sweater and Nick had told me how easily he could unhook Angie's bra with his very clever hand. When Irene's older sister, Trish, once called me "wholesome," I blushed with shame. I knew that they didn't want a boy who was wholesome. If Irene and I ever spoke about marriage, it was usually with humor and in the middle of a party or something.

"So, do you think we'll ever get hitched, Lafitte?" When she wanted to be playful, Irene would call me this nickname for some swashbuckling pirate we had seen in a movie.

"After we find ze chests of gold!" I'd crack, making a flourish with an imaginary sword in my hand.

On another occasion, she asked, "Do you think a hussy like me is the type to have kids?" Pushing her skinny chest out suggestively, she looked for a clue but gave me a way out by her humor.

I grabbed her and pushed her down on the couch, "A hussy like you will have many bambinos…someday." I didn't say that she'd do so with me. I was hedging my bets because I wasn't sure yet what my feelings for guys meant. Beyond this, Irene never pressured me.

It only vaguely occurred to me then that someday I might have to choose—that I'd probably have to relate sexually with either girls *or* guys, but not both. Emotional and sexual feelings weren't very distinguishable for me. When I loved Irene, I ignored the fact that we were more like dance buddies or friends. When my heart fluttered for Nick or one of Nonie's boyfriends, I didn't specifically think of having sex with them. Mostly I just wanted to be near them physically.

It did feel like I had already been a parent, having taken care of my little brothers and sisters as they arrived year after year. At least for a time, I needed a break from the responsibility that marriage would bring. I didn't consider what an eventual cost it would be never to have any children of my own. Maybe if there were someone for me and Irene to talk to about this topic, I wouldn't have hurt her so much in the end.

During these years, every spring my father took Tommy and me on retreats with the Men of Malvern along with our uncles—Lou, Gene, and Jim. When we arrived at the retreat center in the rolling hills of the Philadelphia suburbs on a Friday night, the robin redbreasts were usually hopping on the front lawn looking for worms at the same time Uncle Gene, who worked for RCA and was our wealthiest uncle, whipped out a bottle of Canadian Club whiskey from his suitcase and plopped it onto the table. "All right boys, the retreat has officially begun!" Laughing, they'd have a shot or two together. By the time of the first conference, their rosy faces could listen to whatever the priest might have to say.

Alcohol and prayer. For Irish Catholics, both helped us get into a good spirit. Roman Catholicism, at least before the Jansenists got their hands on it, was a very earthy religion. Since we were toddlers, we were taught that bread and wine became the Body and Blood of Christ at Mass. Food, drink, and God—they go together.

At weddings and funerals when we ate and drank, you could tell by the laughter and the dancing that God was present. Even the Bible stated this—"So I commend enjoyment, for there is nothing better for people under the sun than to eat, and drink, and enjoy themselves" (Eccl 8:15). The Gospels certainly showed that Jesus believed this when he turned a hundred and twenty gallons of water into good wine for them at a marriage feast (cf. John 2:6f). Maybe some Methodists or Baptists wouldn't understand, but we figured that God must have been happy when Daddy and our uncles got merry at the retreat after working so hard all year.

At one of these retreats, I noticed a pamphlet in the bookstore with the title "Why I Became a Priest." Glancing over my shoulder to make sure no one saw, I paid for it and slipped it into my pocket to read later. I would've been mortified to have Tommy notice my interest in such things. When I saw a young priest on the porch the next morning, I got up my courage and approached him.

"Um…Father…um, could I…uh, talk to you about something?"

"Sure, but could we do it later? I've got to get the Mass started."

With my blood pumping I turned away, though I was glad I had broken the ice. For the rest of the weekend, I didn't have the guts to ask again. I'm not sure what I would have said once I started, but when I eventually read the book, it planted a seed.

At the Holy Hour that evening before dinner, the men's voices rose in a deep crescendo:

Like a strong and raging fire,
In a narrow furnace pent,
Burns the Sacred Heart's desire,
In the Holy Sacrament….

We were singing of Jesus present in the tabernacle, in the consecrated Eucharist that burns with love for the world. I tried to imagine the Creator of the Universe, confined to this little box. Locked in with a key, in his own little prison, burning with desire for each of us.

All our sins, our slights, our coldness,
All our insults we deplore,
Pardon, Lord, our daring boldness,
We will never wound Thee more.

It felt so powerful to have my own voice swept up in the masculine sound of my father's, and brother's, and uncles' voices singing to Jesus, the Bridegroom of our souls.

Bending low in adoration,
All our sins are borne above,
Hear our hymn of reparation,
Heart of Jesus be Our love.

Combined with our family's strong devotional life—these retreats, daily Mass during Lent, the prayers after dinner, and the exalted way our parents, especially Mama, related to priests and nuns—these vocational seeds began to sprout a hidden space within me. Because my family seemed so spiritual, I didn't trust showing my interest in the priesthood to them yet. I knew I would have to cut off my sexual feelings if I went into the seminary, and I wasn't ready for that yet. I wasn't sure whether my need for independence from my feelings was a good thing or just fear of a commitment. My relationship with Irene during these years, without really speaking in depth about eventual marriage, kept me from dealing with commitment.

6

First Sexual Inklings

Summer, 1956, Upper Darby, Pennsylvania—

The summer I turned sixteen, I had further reason to wonder about where God was. It was the first time Mama and Daddy ever let Tommy and me stay home on our own overnight. The family had rented a bungalow in Sea Isle City for two weeks. Our parents believed that allowing their children to jump in the ocean would easily offset medicine bills in the coming winter. Daddy had gotten Tommy and me jobs at Horn and Hardart, the restaurant where he was the manager, so Mama and Daddy let us stay at home, make a small salary (seventy-five cents an hour) and fend for ourselves, while they piled into the big Chrysler with the twelve younger kids and headed to the Jersey Shore.

The freedom was so great. We could make our own curfews. We ate at the restaurant and slept whenever we wanted. Our friends came over and made a mess, but Tommy and I agreed to clean it before the family returned home. What a life to be on our own!

Tommy usually went out fishing at Springton Reservoir with his friends after work at four o'clock each afternoon. At first, I would just relax or take a nap before going out to a movie with friends. Soon that got boring. I was looking for ways to stretch my wings.

One Friday, I phoned Nick. "What's up?"

"Nothin'. Watching TV." His voice sounded cozy. "What's up with you?"

"Nothin'. Wanna come over?"

"I would, but Angie said she might call. We're gonna meet at the dance."

"I'm thinking of going too. Why don't you come over and we can go together." No response. I looked around the living room—at Mama's plants that I hadn't watered yet, at the pizza boxes scattered on the coffee table. So rare to have a space all to myself. "There's no one here, Nick. Except for Tommy, everyone's down the shore."

"Where's your brother?"

"Fishing, where else? He won't be back for a couple of hours."

"Hmm..." His interest perked up. "Okay. I've gotta take a shower first. Be over in half an hour."

"Cool."

"See ya." Click.

Wow! Nick all to myself. Cool! I hurried to take a shower too, but I couldn't find any clean jeans. I put on my cream-colored ski pajamas—it'd be easier to flop on the floor with Nick that way.

Thinking of Nick's bright Italian smile, I put on a record, *The Magic Touch* by the Platters. In a while there was a knock on the front door. It was Nick in khakis and a sport shirt. Running my hands through my hair at the mirror first, I flung open the front door. "Yo!"

Nick held up a quart of beer in a paper bag. "Compliments of my pop. He doesn't know, though."

"Dig it."

"You're goin' to the dance like that!" He pointed at my pj's.

"Nah...I just want to relax first. Here, gimme the beer." He thrust it at me, and our hands touched.

Nick followed me into the living room. "Make yourself comfy." I threw a small pillow at him.

"You're frisky tonight."

"When the cat's away, the mice will play. Ha-ha!"

Nick gave a sly look and slipped down onto the floor with his back against the sofa. "Hey, open the beer. I'm dying of thirst."

As I crossed into the dining room, I felt the pillow hit me on the back. A window fan made a whirring sound, but it didn't cool much. By the time I came back with the church key and some glasses, Nick had taken his shoes off and opened a few buttons on his shirt.

"Man, with this heat I'm gonna need another shower." He wiped his forehead as I poured the beer into Daddy's special pilsner glasses. *We're grown-ups at last,* I thought with delight.

Though Nick and I had hinted at it before, we had never done anything explicitly sexual. Once, the two of us had slept close to each other on a friend's floor when we stayed overnight. Another time, he jumped on my back as I lay face down by the fire on a camping trip. Nick shouted, "Ride 'em cowboy!" as I grunted, and the other guys snickered. Though I had fantasized about him, it seemed scary to do anything. Yet tonight something whispered within me, *It could be like the songs promised.*

When Nick took his shirt off, I challenged him with arm wrestling.

I felt strong and feisty. Quickly I got his arm down before his greater weight prevailed. I squatted then like a sumo wrestler, bouncing from side to side with my hands up to attack. Laughing, Nick grabbed my shoulder and whipped me onto the floor before we rolled onto our sides facing each other. Then I jumped on top of him. I wanted to pin his biceps down with my knees like Tommy used to do to me. A gleam sparkled in Nick's eyes. Without warning, one of his legs darted up from behind and forced me onto my back. Soon he had me pinned. I couldn't budge.

Nick glared down at me as his brown eyes taunted. "Okay? Okay? Do you give in?"

Straining against his weight, I grunted, "No!"

"No? *No?*" he mocked, though he was grinning.

I pushed back a few more times, enjoying our play.

"Give in," he demanded as his sweat dripped off his face onto mine.

"No!"

"Now Paulie, if you don't give in," he coaxed, "Nicky Boy's gonna have to make you."

"Make me! Make me *what?*" I dared, quickly arching to show him I wasn't a pushover.

"Make you...hmm...," he scowled down close to my face. "Make you my slave."

"Yeah, sure."

"Maybe you'd like that, huh?" he teased. Under his weight, my breathing only came in spurts.

"Okay, *okay!* I give in," I yelled.

"Atta boy, atta boy." He released his grip and rolled off me, sprawling flat on the carpet with his arms out.

Wow! Wow! My heart pumped happily. Exhausted but exhilarated, I lay down too, and listened to our breathing. In a while, we rewarded ourselves with long, delicious swigs of beer.

"You're stronger than I thought," said Nick.

"Yeah, next time I'll get you, man," I boasted, as I watched the rivulets of sweat on his neck and tried to think of a way I could still win. The clock ticked on the mantle as our breathing slowed. Nick looked across at me in silence. Soon, the beer was finished.

Nick seemed to read my mind. Reaching over me, he placed the empty bottle on the table and hesitated for a moment while I sat hushed as a rabbit, wishing him on.

"C'mere," he motioned at last, awkwardly pulling me closer.

Our seventh-grade nun's voice began to play in my ear, *A near occasion of sin! A near occasion of sin!* Yet I had never felt so alive. Nick was my friend; I had dreamed this dream forever, and it was vacation time. So, my sixteen-year-old heart cracked open like the Sacred Heart's, and all the fear and strangeness of finally being close to a boyfriend melted away.

A car door closing on the street broke this reverie. Concerned someone might see us from the window, Nick dragged me to the sofa. We lay tumbled in a pile of young arms and legs, laughing and unsure what to do next. The clock began to chime. Nick cocked his head to listen. Nothing. He turned back to me, and we just snuggled against each other like it was heaven. My lips reached out to kiss his throbbing neck.

BAM! Like an atomic bomb, the porch door suddenly flew open, and the light snapped on overhead. OMG, my brother, Tommy! I watched in horror as his jaw dropped along with his fishing rod. His eyes, wide with questions, soon tore into the two of us like daggers. Instantly, Nick and I leapt up and backed apart.

"Tommy! Tommy!" I pleaded. The beer bottle crashed to the floor as I fell against the table.

Tommy roared at me like I was some kind of traitor, while Nick scrambled to retrieve his shirt. "You stupid jerk! You idiot!" my brother yelled, while he chased me into the dining room, and I circled the table for defense, my erection poking my pajamas out. Finally, when my arousal and his fury had died down, I escaped upstairs.

From a second-floor window, I listened to Nick apologizing on the front steps before Tommy started to walk him home. "We were drinking, Tommy. We were wrestling and started fooling around. It was a mistake. It'll never happen again, I promise."

A mistake! It didn't feel so bad until Tommy barged in. Now I was all mixed up with guilt and grief. Would he have been horrified if he had found me making out with Irene? No! He would have been proud I was a real man. I wondered what he and Nick might be saying. Wanting to be asleep before Tommy came up, I pulled a sheet up over my head and escaped into a fitful dream.

The next day, Tommy and I didn't speak about it. A coolness rose between us, and we didn't look at each other. If Tommy told Daddy, I would be in big trouble. So, I hid my feelings, crammed them down into my soul with all the other memories of love and guilt, but my heart couldn't contain them. Tears came when I prayed, "Dear God, I'm sorry. I didn't mean to be so bad. All I wanted was to have a little fun after work. I thought you were supposed to protect the poor and the weak." *Geez, we work as hard as we can. We try to love our friends. And then, if we make a mistake, you kick us into the gutter like a piece of trash. Thanks a lot, Lord! Thanks a lot for my life!*

7

"Turn That Crap Off!"

Therapist's office, Autumn, 1983—

Rarely had I been able to be honest about my sexual feelings, especially toward guys. It took a few years of therapy in my mid-forties to trace my efforts to do so.

For the past few months, I had been receiving professional counseling from Phillip, a pastoral psychotherapist. He was also an Episcopal priest, which made it easier for me to relate to him. He was pushing me to address an area that I was reluctant to explore.

"So, tell me about your sexual history," Phillip asked from his chair behind me as I stretched out on a couch.

"How far back?" I asked.

"As far back as you can remember."

I lay there in silence for some moments. "When I was growing up in our large family, whenever we'd be watching a TV show in the evening that seemed to be somewhat risqué in Daddy's eyes"—*or was it Mama's? Maybe she gave him a signal and he had to do the dirty work*—"he would announce to us abruptly, 'Turn that crap off.' No arguments were allowed; we simply had to go to bed. At other times, you might be reading *Life Magazine* and suddenly find certain pages missing."

"You say, '*You* might be reading.' Do you mean yourself?"

"Yes."

"It would be better if you use 'I' then. Saying 'you' keeps you at a distance."

You *or* I, *what's the big deal?* Phillip kept trying to get me to take more responsibility, not hide in a group.

"What happened to these pictures?"

"Daddy's censorship system had ripped the offending pages…usually photos of Marilyn Monroe…out of the magazine. I guess he wanted us to remain innocent."

"Hmm. Were you innocent?"

"To a certain extent, yes. I remember standing in line once during my sophomore year in high school. A few of my classmates began talking about abortion. I looked confused, I guess. One of the guys asked me, 'Do you know what an abortion is?' 'No,' I admitted. My face turned hot when they told me and laughed."

"So, you were naive?"

"When I was about thirteen and my brother, Tommy, was a year older, Daddy read us sex information from a book called *Modern Youth and Chastity*. I can still remember the color of that book—pink and white—as though it were a clue to how the Catholic Church wanted us to relate to sex."

"Pink and white!"

My jaw clenched. *Is Phillip mocking our upbringing?* "We were up on our third-floor bedroom and could tell that Daddy was nervous. For one thing, the book was written in weird language: 'A sperm is invisible to the naked eye…under the microscope it is shaped like a tadpole, with a head and a tail.'"

"Paul, what are you feeling?" Phillip asked.

"Tadpoles?" I went on. "Tommy and I looked at each other and giggled."

"You were feeling amused?"

"Not exactly amused. I think it was embarrassing, for Daddy and for Tommy and me."

"Embarrassing. Are you feeling embarrassed now?"

"No."

"Your hands are covering your crotch."

"What?" Leaning up, I quickly pulled my hands back. With Phillip behind me, I felt exposed. *I want his help, but I'm not ready to be so vulnerable.* "I guess I am embarrassed."

"Paul, let yourself feel whatever. It's all right. That's what we're doing here, helping you get in touch with your feelings."

With Phillip's help, I was discovering the difference between my religious self and my worldly self. I needed to integrate these two if I was going to be whole. "I feel vulnerable, but I want to continue," I said. As I lay back down, I made sure to keep my hands at my side.

"Go ahead."

"As Daddy kept reading to us, it was all about how sex is so holy. It didn't seem especially holy to Tommy and me. I guess we sensed Daddy felt this way too, but we were stuck with this little pink and white book that Mama must have picked up in some rack in the vestibule of the church. The three of us—a father and his two sons—could hardly look at one another because we felt somehow ashamed."

"Ashamed...of what?"

"Y'know, Phillip, despite our parents' and church's attempt to make them so separate, I often had trouble sorting out the difference between God and sex. In the first place, our Roman Catholic tradition had all sorts of things in which the two were mixed. During the month of May, we had a May Queen. Usually, the prettiest eighth-grade girl would dress up like the Blessed Mother. At the end of a procession of the school kids around the neighborhood, she would crown Mary's statue in our church with a wreath of roses. Since the nuns so easily mixed beauty and holiness together, they never picked an ugly girl. As a thirteen-year-old, it was natural for me to be drawn the same way."

"You wanted to be the May Queen?"

"Ha-ha! Very funny!" I became quiet. "Well, maybe a little part of me did...and I think now, why didn't they have a May King? Basically, it was like girls and sex became so holy you couldn't touch them."

"No. They were split off." Phillip cleared his throat.

"Well, we got conflicting messages. On the one hand, we were taught that Mary and Joseph didn't have sex to conceive Jesus. Rather than seeing sex as too lowly for conceiving Jesus, our fertile little minds imagined—mine did anyway—that the Holy Spirit somehow did it. If that was the case, it had to be good, didn't it? In some ways, it seemed that, for Catholics, sex was *too* good, so holy and wonderful that you could go crazy with it if it wasn't controlled."

"So, you tried to control it."

"I guess so. We tried to pray it into submission. On Mother's Day and other secular holidays, the nuns would encourage us to give 'spiritual bouquets' to our mothers. These were greeting cards with holy messages on them that the nuns sold. On the inside cover was a space to write in how many 'ejaculations' you had accomplished for your mother. Ejaculations, we were taught, were little prayers such as 'Jesus, have mercy!' or 'Sacred Heart of Jesus, I place my trust in you!' You could say these a thousand times a day whenever you got distracted, especially when you were thinking of sex. When you did so fervently, under your breath on your way home from school or before you went to sleep, whomever you offered these for would get many blessings from God. Maybe even get out of Purgatory and go straight to heaven when they died."

We fell into silence. The clock ticked on the mantle. I realized how much like a child I sounded, but I wanted him to understand the feelings I had back then.

"So, Catholics spiritualize sex?"

"Well, our prayers weren't always successful. And you can imagine how we laughed when we got to the seventh grade and some wise kid described another meaning for ejaculations."

Phillip and I laughed together.

"For us, sex was hidden and exciting and confusing all at once. Guys rarely talked about it except to brag about how they felt girls up. My three other brothers had their army beds situated at strategic places in the boys' room on the third floor. I had commandeered a little alcove on one side with an old chest of drawers set up as a barricade. With its little window peering out onto the alley, I could gaze at the stars after the lights were turned out and imagine what God might be like."

"God…up in the sky?"

"Not only." I wondered about Phillip. He seemed so sure of himself. I didn't want to jump to his conclusions though. Could I trust myself to him?

"It might have been in this little alcove that I first began to write. Gradually, it dawned on me that I could create a private world in my writing. Many of the things I longed for but couldn't speak about to anyone—not even to my brothers or father—I could at least talk to myself about in a journal."

"Yes. Maybe that part of you is what we are trying to get in touch with here." His voice was now warm and inviting.

I pondered this, then continued: "There was this whole inner world that I began to get in touch with, one where I could let my true feelings out. My sense of sexual difference started to appear then, along with my awareness of God."

"So, your sexual confusion got you in touch with God?"

"Yeah. In some ways." I realized that I was clutching my crotch again.

"Paul...Paul! Why don't you sit up so we can bring this to a conclusion for today? You've gotten in touch with some very important memories. We can hold onto them together until the next time."

"Okay, Phillip." I pulled myself up to a sitting position. "I'm feeling all these emotions again," I said.

"That's good. That's what you are here for."

I felt grateful that he had listened as well as challenged me, though I wasn't ready to tell him this yet. "Okay."

We stood, and he ushered me into his well-appointed waiting room. As I got my coat, he looked at me with his gray eyes. "Write down these feelings if it helps, okay?" His gaze held mine. "Whatever you do, don't censor them too quickly. They are your feelings."

"All right. I'll see you next week then." *Maybe I can let him in....*

When I try to go back into these memories now, they seem so far away. The actual feelings seem almost inaccessible. Certainly, the sense of awareness of who I was becoming—either a little priest in the making or a little gay kid making telltale choices—doesn't seem very clear.

You wonder if it is clear for anyone, or whether we just tumble or stumble into our future identities and wake up at some age and wonder in amazement or dread, *How did I get this way?*

8

A College Crush

Winter, 1958, Upper Darby, Pennsylvania—

"I don't want to lose my faith," I explained to my parents and myself when I turned down the Horn and Hardart scholarship to the University of Pennsylvania. Penn was an Ivy League college with no specific religious identity. In my twelve years of education so far, I had only known schools that were staffed by Catholic religious teachers. I decided that I needed the sense of religious familiarity that a Catholic college would provide.

It seems odd that I was so spiritually minded at the age of eighteen, and that my parents were willing to go along with this given our financial situation. With fourteen kids to support, they weren't going to be able to send many of us to college. By then, my parents' motto was mine too: *Deus providebit—God will provide.*

Situated on the beautiful Main Line of Philadelphia, Villanova University was a half-hour train ride from my house and was staffed by the same Augustinian priests who had taught me in high school. Its School of Engineering was one of the best on the East Coast. When I was accepted with a half scholarship and began my college days as a "dayhop" (commuter) that fall, I figured my faith was being rewarded.

Engineering was a strange career choice for me. Although I had excelled in algebra and trigonometry in high school, another whole side of me was spiritual, even poetic. I knew all the Latin hymns from church and had memorized some of Shakespeare's sonnets. That side got buried in college. Back then, it seemed to me that you had to choose between the sciences and the arts.

There were so many required science courses that very few liberal arts courses were offered to the engineering students. These "humanities" courses, like history and literature, would take lots of time away from the more important ones for us. Yet in a required religion course, where a crusty old priest, "Bunky" Dunne, informed us that the three theological virtues were faith, hope, and the Brooklyn Dodgers, you could at least count on getting an A or a B to help your grade average.

Unlike the liberal arts majors who had the freedom to choose all kinds of unusual courses, the engineering students knew that we were getting a whole system of thought that held together like a brick building. Who cared if we spent half of our time in labs and carried slide rules stuck in our belts like members of a secret tribe? The arts majors got lost in essay exams trying to articulate the difference between Aristotle and St. Thomas Aquinas.

When spring came and flowers poked their heads through the frozen campus ground, I mocked the English majors along with the others. "Ooh, look—a daffodil!" we'd goof, pretending for a moment to be excited about nature like they were. Even though I didn't show it, I was.

Since Tommy had entered the Marines, I was the oldest child living at home. Instead of the phosphorescent stars Daddy had put on the ceiling when we were younger, the third-floor boys' dorm now had engineering formulas written on the ceiling: $E=MC^2$, $F=MA$, along with an occasional quote from some philosopher—*"The Moving Finger writes: and having writ, / Moves on: nor all thy Piety nor Wit / Shall lure it back to cancel half a line, / Nor all thy tears wash out a Word of it."*[1]

At night, we all still did homework together around the big dining room table. The younger brothers and sisters in grammar school were trying to live up to the older ones' reputations. The high school kids were taking phone calls and planning their weekend dates on our one phone that hung on the dining room wall.

It was a chaos of sorts, but our family didn't know any other way. For us, studying didn't mean retreating to a private space like a library nook or a desk in your own room. We got energy from one another, taking turns helping one another with homework. If you got stuck with a problem, you could ask a question of someone from grade one through college. Through the French doors, we could see Mama and Daddy sitting in their rockers and munching on Oreo cookies as they watched *I Love Lucy*. Who cared if Ike liked Nixon or not? There was a handsome Irish Catholic guy from Massachusetts, John Kennedy, who might be running for the Democrats, and we were rooting for him.

Irene and I had one of our breakups. In fact, we sort of drifted apart. Upper Darby and the Friday night dances seemed too small for me after I started college. I began to date one of the Villanova nurses who lived in our parish. When spring came, I decided to pledge to the engineering fraternity, Phi Kappa Pi. They were famous for throwing great parties on weekends at a club in Norristown where you could drink all you wanted. There were always a few inches of beer on the floor by the end of the night.

Nick had joined the Navy. It was new for me to get letters from a guy, even if he just talked about the midnight drills that he had to put up with at some boot camp in Texas. I saved these letters, my hands turning warm when I reached the part where he would sign off, "Your buddy, Nick." I started to sign mine the same. We never mentioned the night in my living room.

In one of my classes at Villanova, I got friendly with a guy from Cape Cod. His hazel-colored eyes were easy to look at. When he flipped his scarf jauntily over the shoulder of his nifty tweed jacket on chilly days, you knew he didn't have a care in the world. I loved hearing him drop R's in words, saying "pahty" or "pahk the cah" the way Kennedy did, or add them to other words that had none. It seemed so free to pronounce your words differently. It was like New Englanders just made up their own world. Soon, I was throwing my scarf over my shoulder the way Kevin did.

A few months after I met him in the lunchroom at Villanova, I invited him home for dinner one night. Usually, when one of us brought a guest home unexpectedly, Mama would get a spare plate and make each of us give some of our food to the guest before we ate. Naturally, you'd hear lots of grumbling about this, and the guest would start to cringe. By the time dinner was over, they'd forget it though. With the hoopla that went on at our table, it was like they had just been to the circus, and they were one of the stars.

The night I brought Kevin home, I had called ahead of time to give Mama a heads up. We were lucky because she had made one of my favorite meals, roast pork with all the trimmings. After a few introductions, Nonie arranged a place for Kevin across from her and next to me. Suddenly, just as we sat down, thirteen-year-old Joe bragged to Kevin, "I spit in your milk." A devilish grin lit up his face and ours, recognizing the game he and the younger kids played to get the biggest glass of milk if it wasn't at your place.

"What!" Laughing nervously, Kevin pulled back.

"Joe!" Mama shot him a glare over her glasses. With her sense of humor, I looked for a clue that she was enjoying a little of the predinner sparring anyway, and how our guest would show his colors through it. But Mama kept her composure.

"Well here, you can have it then." Kevin inched the larger glass toward Joe.

Quickly, Joe grabbed it and took a sip. He flashed a smile at the rest of the brothers and sisters, all aware that Kevin had passed the first test because he hadn't been completely grossed out. Everyone quickly dove into the meal: "Yummy! Pass the gravy!"

"Wait! Wait!" Mama called from her place at the head of the table. "What do we do next?"

"We forgot to say grace," Terry volunteered, a string bean dangling from the corner of her mouth.

"Yes."

Mama sat down and folded her hands reverently. Even a guest would not upset our ritual. All of us, including Kevin, followed her example, putting our forks down and folding our hands in prayer. With her eyes closed, Mama began, "Thank you, dear Lord, that we have such a good meal to eat, and that we have such a wonderful family to share it with. May everyone else in the world have as much as we do. And thank you for our guest, Kevin, tonight."

There were a couple of seconds of silence while we all drooled at the luscious meal steaming on our plates.

"Amen!" Mama said softly.

"Amen!" we all chimed in, happy to dive into the feast.

"Oh, please!" Mama wrinkled her nose. "Kevin will think you never get a good meal." But the one who always served herself last was happily chewing a morsel now too. *Who cares what Kevin thinks? We gave him the treatment so he's one of us now,* I thought.

"Mmm." Kevin let us know he was enjoying the whole event as much as we were. As usual, before we could run into the living room to dance after dinner, we had to say the rosary. I didn't mind until we began the hymn that we always sang to end it. Mortified along with the rest of the older ones at how Kevin might react to this childish devotion of ours, I glanced at him for a sign as the Morrissey Family raised up our voices to the Lord in the syrupy hymn Mama had taught us:

> Good night, sweet Jesus, guard us in sleep,
> Our souls and bodies, in thy love keep,
> Waking or sleeping, keep us in sight,
> Dear gentle savior, good night, good night,
> Good night, dear Jesus, good night,
> Goo-ood Night.

Kevin's face was blank when he glanced over at me. Dying to know what he was thinking, I found out later as I drove him back to school. "Wow, Morrissey, what a family you've got!" He offered me a cigarette. "It's terrific the way they compete and still get along. Even the spit trick—ha-ha!"

I crunched up my nose. "That's sick. To do that to a guest…" I feigned concern while I cracked the window to let the smoke out.

"No, no!" he laughed, "It made me feel accepted."

"Really?"

"Yah. And your sisters are cute. Did you notice the way they made sure I got seconds?" He made a circle with his lips and blew a smoke ring toward the ceiling.

"Yah," I copied his accent. A realization dawned: I'm gonna have to compete with my sisters for his attention.

At a red light, he looked at me and said, "It's amazing how your ma can control all of you. Even the prayers. I almost feel like I've been to a Mass." Rolling my eyes, I didn't want him to think that we were some kind of religious fanatics. "Well, a different kind of service," he said while he held the smoke in, then blew it out of the side of his mouth. "Maybe that's the way it's supposed to be, and your ma's the priest."

"Hmph!" I considered his idea, picturing Mama with the big stew pot in front of her, ladling out her version of the Eucharist to us at our Last Supper table. "Y'know something? I bet Mama would've been a priest if she were a guy. She did tell us once that she knows she could've run a corporation."

"Well, she is running a corporation." Kevin looked over at me as I rounded a corner and blew another smoke ring.

I thought of how Mama managed the family finances, squeezing the most out of Daddy's paychecks so the clan could survive through the years. How the milkman left off his extras at our house when he had some left. How she wasn't ashamed of the care packages the neighbors and relatives left at our house with clothing their kids had outgrown even though we hated it.

Not used to bragging about my mother with others, I mentioned, "Her faith is unbelievable, too. Once when she was folding a basket of laundry on the dining room table, one of the younger kids asked her what she'd do if the end of the world came that day. Mama just looked up with the diapers in her hands, 'The end of the world?' she asked as though they were referring to a ball game, 'I wouldn't run over to church. I'd just keep folding the laundry.'" Both of us considered this kind of faith, even while it revealed some home-based spirituality alongside my mother's deep devotion to the Church.

"That would be a different kind of priest, wouldn't it?" Kevin said.

"I guess." Both of us blew smoke rings up toward the roof that flowed into each other and disappeared. We drove along in silence for a while. When we reached the traffic light before his apartment, I turned toward him. "Well, you'll have to come again, Kevin. Just let me know so we can get an extra pork chop for you."

"Whenever. I'd love it."

When he closed the door and I gunned our family car out of the driveway onto Lancaster Avenue, I glanced into the rearview mirror. The corners of my mouth had curled into a grin. "Me too, Kevin," I murmured, "Me too."

These and other events drew the two of us closer. Kevin was a good student like me, and we often studied together. I never really stopped and asked myself: Is engineering what you really want to do in life? Even when we had to stay up late and cram for exams, I was just happy to be with my friend. Except Kevin was heterosexual. These were the kind of guys I was attracted to in college. Not wanting sex so much but rather to be close to them, and in the closeness feel I was one of them. What a strange bind to be in: needing to be close to them physically, and yet, if I showed that I wanted to be closer than a friendship, it would drive them away.

You had to watch yourself. Only get so close. Hide your deepest feelings. Don't show your friend that you would die for him. The trouble is that you do die. Day by day as you hide your feelings, you hide them from yourself too. Everything gets buried except the shame.

Most of the time, I hardly thought of this. Yet in the English class that I thought was a waste of time, a poem spoke of this to me:

When, in disgrace with fortune and men's eyes,
I all alone beweep my outcast state,
And trouble deaf heaven with my bootless cries,
And look upon myself, and curse my fate,
Wishing me like to one more rich in hope,
Featured like him, like him with friends possess'd,
Desiring this man's art and that man's scope,
With what I most enjoy contented least....[2]

When I first tried to memorize this sonnet for class, I was sitting in Falvey Library. Some students were around me at the long tables, copying sections of books, others whispering to one another and laughing, and others looking bored. I was anxious to get back to my math notes. We had a big test scheduled on differential equations the next day. Just another strange poem, loftily describing somebody's emotions from a time in the past...*and trouble deaf heaven with my bootless cries.* Something in my chest tightened. I swallowed a lump in my throat. Tears welled—*what's this?*

I reread it slowly, *When in disgrace with fortune and men's eyes.* Yes, it had to be. Shakespeare knew what it's like! Glancing up, I searched the room to see if anyone had noticed. I pretended to pick up my slide rule so I could brush away a tear. The second part of the poem was mysterious, though it seemed important to understand. It spoke of someone who, if you just thought about them, could change you from feeling like an outcast into a bird chirping for joy.

Yet in these thoughts myself almost despising,
Haply I think on thee, and then my state,
Like to the lark at break of day arising,
From sullen earth, sings hymns at heaven's gate....

"I think on *thee....*" Who could *thee* be? A man? A woman? How great it would be to get to know someone like that! Oh, I'd give anything to feel that way. And then it concluded,

For thy sweet love remember'd such wealth brings
That then I scorn to change my state with kings.

But how could this be for someone like me? Any sweet loves I remembered brought up the very feelings I had to hide if I wanted to survive in the world I knew. That night, I wrote in my journal:

Sometimes I wonder what's going on with me. I feel really alive, like I can be anything, do anything. But I don't feel exactly normal. All kinds of things are percolating in me—sexual feelings and then religious feelings and then back to sexual feelings again. It is like there are two sides of me and each of them wants to own all of me. Sometimes I imagine myself building fantastic bridges, but then I ask myself why. What is the long-range good of that? I want to do something really great, but what? Maybe build a bridge between these two worlds.

If someone asks me today how I decided to become a priest, it is usually easy to respond with some pious thoughts: "I wanted to serve God, to help people, to bring more love and peace into the world." These motives are very good, and much of the time these have been my goals during my many years of ministry. Yet when I look back on my journey, it is difficult to separate what Roman Catholics understand as a vocation to the priesthood from my search for human love, and even from the frustration of my search for human love.

I believe that God calls us by our human longings into whatever path we eventually take. I presume that he was calling me then—at least in part—by my longing for a human relationship with someone I could love fully. As the 1960s grew near, it was hardly possible to accept that I could love another man and be happy, let alone be aware of any role models of how to do so. It was as though I was yearning for something I could not yet find, and that God used this frustration of my young hopes to lure me into searching ever more deeply for that which promised to fill the emptiness.

9

"You Should Be a Priest"

May 1961, New Jersey Shore—

"I'm horny. I hope we meet some chicks," Kevin announced as we headed across the Walt Whitman Bridge. It was Memorial Day weekend, the kickoff for all the New Jersey summer resorts a hundred miles from Philadelphia. We were excited. It was our last big getaway before graduation when we'd go our separate ways—he to the U.S. Department of Interior in Utah and me to Sikorsky Aircraft in Connecticut as a junior test engineer. On Friday after our Descriptive Geometry lab, the two of us were driving down to Ocean City, New Jersey, in his blue-and-white '56 Chevy. We had rooms in the Pink Pussycat, the college crash pad, where you could rent a room for twenty-five dollars a night.

His remark reminded me of our differences. As much as I cared for Kevin, I couldn't plan a future with him like I could with a girlfriend. I didn't want that thought to mess up our special time together though. A whole weekend stretched ahead with my friend. Nothing was going to spoil that. "Yeah. We'll have a blast!" I laid my head back on the seat and watched the pine trees glide by.

Ocean City, founded by the Methodists as a religious family camp eighty years before, was a popular seashore town for families now because it was alcohol free. Anyone who wanted a gin and tonic at dinner could drive across the bridge to Somers Point where there were lots of drinking joints. In some, like the Dunes, the bartender might yell "Last call!" on a Sunday morning as a sloshed college kid hollered, "Anyone going to Mass?" Three or four of us would squash into an old Volkswagen and barrel over to Our Lady Star of the Sea where we'd pray.

At another club, Tony Mart's, you'd find hundreds of dancing, drinking, party-loving college kids all through the summer, especially on weekend nights. Around 10:30 p.m., Kevin and I arrived with a cooler of beer in his trunk.

"It's gonna be a good night, Morrissowitz," Kevin prophesized. "We'll meet out here for a beer around midnight, okay?"

"Okay."

From a stool by the door, the club's bouncer checked our IDs. Finally, he gave a nod and waved us through the heavenly gate and into the crowd's frenzy. *"A-wop bop a-loo bop a-lop bam boom!"*

Wreathed in smoke were two huge horseshoe-shaped bars that you could almost imagine were altars. Surrounding them like acolytes were bleach-blonde girls in jeans and halters and glassy-eyed guys nursing beers. The crowd quickly swallowed up Kevin as I watched. Dancing was so much fun. Everyone was built so differently, yet somehow everyone's body seemed beautiful when they were dancing. I let the music get inside of me.

When Tony Mart's got too crowded, they had a unique solution. Every so often, without warning, big-shouldered bouncers would surround a few dozen or so guys and girls and sweep them out into the parking lot. Then they'd slam the doors shut. Everyone would be in shock at first. It was all part of Tony Mart's scene. Separated from your friends and the music, you'd mill around briefly. But all you had to do was go to the end of the line and wait your turn to get back in again. Unaware as I watched the dancers, I suddenly got caught up in one of these tactics and swept out through the doors. *Damn!* A girl spilled her beer on my shorts. "Sorreey," she called out as her boyfriend pulled her through the crowd. Brushing myself dry with a handkerchief, I checked my watch. 11:15 already.

I glanced at the sky. A half-moon shone over the bay. I could walk along the shore until it was time to meet Kevin. I turned in that direction. There is something scary about the darkness of the ocean at night, and I feel so small compared to its vastness. Yet the relentless crash of the breakers is comforting too, coming from that great unknown that says, "We are here. We will never leave you." You can't see the waves in the dark, not until the foam surges over their tops, almost like a row of teeth, smiling but a little fierce. A little like God.

The bay is calmer, with only an occasional lapping of a small wave from a speedboat stirring it. My father came to mind. He had taught me as a kid to float, his hand supporting my back. "Don't fight it. Just look at the sky and breathe calmly. The water will hold you up if you trust it," he'd say. Then he'd slowly take his hand away and I'd be floating. I wanted so much for him to be proud of me. But my college years only seemed to pull us further apart. And as far as telling him about my sexual interest in guys, I thought my working-class father would never understand. Maybe I was just chicken to talk to him in need. Well Dad, the tadpoles are kicking up tonight!

I reached the beach behind Bayshore's. The moon, now pale, had some wispy clouds floating across its face. In the distance, I soon noticed a guy and a girl walking toward me. Every now and then they stopped to embrace. They glanced toward me as I approached but looked away as they passed by. How great it would be to walk with someone arm in arm like that. A twinge of loneliness struck my heart. I wondered how I looked to them, a man strolling by himself on the beach at midnight?

Walking on into the darkness, I murmured, "Lord, what do you want from me? Why did you create me this way? All these feelings and nowhere to put them...no one to share them with."

Silence.

"How can I use them to love? I need you to show me, Lord, what should I do with my life? I've graduated, gotten a job with an aircraft firm. Is that what you want me to do, build helicopters?"

I wandered on in silence before I suddenly stepped into a pool of water, soaking my shoes. *Damn!* "Okay, that's it! You'll have to give me a better clue. Tonight, I'm on vacation!" Though frustrated, I felt glad to have articulated some of my real questions to God. And to myself. Turning, I sloshed back to the parking lot to meet Kevin. I saw his square head in the front seat of his car, nursing a beer. I knocked on the window and got in.

"Hey, where've ya been? I was wondering if you got hooked up with someone and were standing me up," he smirked. "Grab yourself a beer. There's plenty of them."

I reached back for a cold one while he began to jabber about a girl he had met. "Dina...she could be Greek, maybe Jewish. Long dark hair, a terrific tan, and what a body!" He stretched languidly. "Mmm....Can't wait to see her on the beach." I smiled at his lucky night.

Noticing that I was silent, Kevin asked, "What about you? Did you meet anybody?"

"No. Would you believe I got shoved out the door in one of their bouncer sweeps?"

"You idiot! I told you to watch out for that."

"Yeah, so I took a walk on the beach."

He looked sideways at me. "By yourself?"

"Yeah."

We sat quietly sipping our beers. The moon had disappeared. It was our last weekend like this for who knows how long, maybe even the rest of our lives if one of us got married. I wanted to say something, but the right words wouldn't come.

"Y'know, Morrissey, I've been thinking." He took another chug of his beer and looked sideways at me again. I held my breath. Mellow like me now from the night of drinking, my friend might be ready to say something about our future before I did. He took a long chug and licked his lips.

"Paul, have you ever thought of becoming a priest?"

I choked on my beer. "A priest! Are you kidding?" I frowned at this bizarre question, as though I was being herded into a bunch of eunuchs.

"No," he pressed on, as though we talked like this all the time. "I mean you've done just about everything else."

Crushed that my friend was thinking about me on another level entirely, I searched for some distraction, something to push this idea away. Even so, a spark had been lit. "Everything else?" I gawked. "What do you mean?"

"Well, you've dated. You've been in plays. You've worked in a restaurant. In a week, you'll be graduating as a civil engineer. You've got a good job at Sikorsky." He rattled off my history like an obituary. "You've got your terrific family that keeps you down to earth and some good friends."

Yes. Yes. As affirming as his view of my life was so far, I wasn't ready to hear my path connected to the priesthood. Not now. It wasn't the first time I had thought of the priesthood myself, but it felt like every word that Kevin said took his friendship away from me. I certainly didn't want to think of the priesthood if it meant he and I had to say goodbye. "Well yeah, I have thought about it. Doesn't everyone?" I gulped my drink to get a buzz.

We sat for a brief time in silence, staring ahead. The muffled sound of the music pumped from the club. I remembered my questions to God on the beach, "What do you want from me? What should I do with my life?"

"Everyone might think about it," Kevin blurted out, "but not everyone'd be good at it. I think you would...hey, you want another beer?"

"No, I'm still working on this one." With my heart sinking, I remembered the times through our college years when he had seen me expressing my religion—our family rosary after dinner, the Good Friday service at his home parish in New England when I got up to go to church and he didn't, the ashes on my forehead on Ash Wednesday, the Celtic cross I wore around my neck.

In that parking lot at Tony Mart's, by the bay, with both of us kind of sloshed from drinking beer, I began to see myself through Kevin's eyes. And because I loved him, I could hear him like no one else. *Haply I think on thee....* Maybe God sees me this way too.

As though waking from a deep sleep under all my physical longings, I felt something like my soul stretch inside...*like to the lark at break of day arising.* "What would I do as a priest?"

"Oh, I dunno. You could teach, hang out in bars, and counsel people like us!" Both of us laughed until we fell quiet. Kevin finished his beer and threw the empty can into the cooler on the back seat.

"Someday, maybe...." I considered...*whether I could be the kind of priest he's talking about.* "Thanks Kevin." My heart began to skip. I couldn't tell Kevin that his asking me to think about being a priest in the parking lot at Tony Mart's had made it seem almost normal. And though I would have given anything for him to pull me close for a hug, it was my very love for him that allowed me to hear his words like God's voice, pulling me in a different direction.

We got up and went back into the club.

10

Leaving Home

Therapist's office, Autumn, 1983, New York City—

"What was it like," Phillip asked me, "when you first left home, Paul?"

"I've always had problems with leaving places I know, people I love or who love me." Closing my eyes, I let my mind wander back to then.

"It was very difficult for me when I graduated and got my first job with Sikorsky Aircraft in Connecticut. My sister, Anne, and a friend drove me there with all my belongings. When they left, I cried myself to sleep in the Bridgeport Hotel. And I was already a college graduate!" I grinned sheepishly.

"So, it was difficult for you to leave home."

"Yes. I was all alone for the first time in my life."

Phillip jotted something on a notepad. "How did you cope there?"

"At first, when I'd go to the beach or a mall, I kept looking for a face I could recognize, but there were none. I make friends easily, though. I moved into a house with a group of guys from Sikorsky."

"You didn't want to live by yourself?"

"No. It would've seemed odd to me then. Now I enjoy solitude. I was probably afraid of it then." I thought of how Phillip lived in his apartment by himself even though he was a member of a religious community.

"What happened when you decided to become a priest? How did you break the news to your family and friends?"

A sore memory surfaced of my sister, Nonie, and her husband, Harris. "I tried, Phillip, but I don't say goodbyes very well. I think it has something to do with not wanting to reject or be rejected."

"Mm-hmm."

"In the spring of 1962, the year after I had graduated from college, Nonie and Harris announced their plans to get married. Harris was Jewish, so theirs was considered a 'mixed marriage.' Everyone in our extended family had always married Catholics up until then. The only way our church would allow it is if the non-Catholic party signed a promise in front of a priest to raise the children Roman Catholic. Harris made that promise, and they got married that fall, but I wasn't there."

Phillip looked surprised. "Why not? Did you disapprove?"

"I was in the seminary by then. In fact, I was glad to find a way to beat Nonie out of the house."

"Oh?"

"I would rather have seen her marry one of the younger guys she had dated through high school. Besides, it seemed that whomever Nonie married, she'd somehow be leaving me and our old childhood partnership behind. Even though I had moved away to Connecticut, I wasn't ready for that."

"Go on." Phillip scribbled on his notepad.

"One of the few places you could get any privacy at our house was in the basement. I could see from Nonie's face that Harris wanted to speak about something important. Maybe it was time to talk to them about something going on with me too. So, the three of us trooped down into the basement catacomb. We pushed our way past stacked shelving into the room where Mama did a couple of loads of laundry every day. Harris's head almost scraped the ceiling pipes. Amid the cobwebs and smell of Clorox, Harris blurted out, 'Paul, your sister and I are getting married in two months.' Holding her hand, he looked toward Nonie for encouragement. 'I would be very honored if you would be my best man.'"

Nonie beamed and turned for my reaction.

"All I could do was stammer, 'Oh, Harris, Nonie…thank you, thank you.'"

"Slow down a moment," Phillip said. "What were you really feeling then, Paul?"

I thought for a moment, then said, "I felt trapped."

"Trapped?" I heard him scribbling.

"Any happiness I felt for them, particularly Nonie, struggled with another feeling. It may sound odd, but I wanted to leave my sister before she left me."

"She was abandoning you by getting married?"

"In a way it felt like that," I grimaced. "It just wouldn't be the same again with her and me."

"No. Harris would be her main man from then on."

"I know it sounds pathetic, but…"

"She wasn't leaving you out. She found a way to include you in her big day."

"I told Harris, 'I can't be your best man. I won't be here.' I turned to Nonie. 'I won't be at your wedding because I'm entering the seminary. I'll be leaving the second week of August.'

"Nonie lurched as if she had been stung. 'Whaaat?! When did you decide this?'

"Relieved to have it out now, I began to ramble...'I've been thinking about it for almost a year...'"

Phillip cleared his throat, jarring me back into the present. "Paul, you say Nonie was hurt. How so?"

"Yes. Months earlier, she had shared with me her hopes about getting married, confiding that there was no one she loved more than Harris. 'Except maybe God,' she had quipped. By not telling her until now, it seemed, I had treated our childhood bond all through the years like it wasn't that special. But she said, 'I'm glad for you, Paul,' and hugged me, 'if that's what you really want.'"

Phillip interrupted, "Was it?"

"Well, I had been wondering about my long-range future since I began working at Sikorsky. I had finally decided I needed to be doing something bigger and went to talk to the Augustinian vocation director.

"'It became clear to me about two months ago,' I explained to Nonie and Harris, 'but I didn't want to tell anyone because I felt too easily influenced. I'm so sorry to tell you this way.'

"'I'll miss you,' Nonie said, reaching for my hand. *Miss me*. Her smile showed me our old bond would continue, and our rivalry too. 'You really did want to beat me out of the house, didn't you?'"

"So," announced Phillip, looking at his watch. "Leavings are tough for you. And for all of us, I might add. But we need to stop now, all right? We can pick up here the next session."

"Okay." I was pleased to get back in touch with such pivotal memories, believing they could help me be more grounded in any leavings I was struggling with now. I just wished I had stopped before Phillip had to stop me.

Spring, 1962—

I found Daddy in the bathroom, reading the evening newspaper. Other than the basement, it was the only place in the house where you could get some privacy.

The second-floor bathroom brought back memories. Here, Daddy had provided his homemade remedies, such as a horrible mixture of sulfur and molasses on the day after Halloween because we had eaten too many sweets. Here, I was in that same space now, needing my father's blessing.

"Hi, Daddy."

I imagined what he saw—the skinny second son out on his own now, gone before we really got to know each other. He had the power to reward or ruin me with a glance. How was it that I had come from him and yet was so different? Even the college education he had encouraged only made us grow more distant.

We were like travelers who reach a fork in the road too soon in our journey, and realizing we are going in different directions, flick a look of resignation and nod goodbye before hurrying down paths that lead us forever apart.

He cleared his throat. "So, what's on your mind?"

"Daddy, I've been wanting to tell you something for a while." He looked older, and his wavy gray hair needed a trim.

I continued, "Do you remember those retreats you used to take us on with the uncles? Well, once I picked up a pamphlet there with the title *Why I Became a Priest.*" *I can tell him about the vocation part, so now I don't need to tell him the other part.*

"I felt shy about it, but I couldn't get the idea out of my head." Please believe in me, Daddy, I hope it's not too late. The feeling of his hand supporting me as he taught me to float returned.

"Well, what I want to tell you is that I am going into the seminary."

The comics tumbled to the floor. My father took it all in—the mysteriousness, the sensitivity, our distance through the years, perhaps finally making some sense. His eyes filled up as he searched for the right words, "Well, we always hoped we might have one of you become a priest. I never thought it would be you, though. Does Mama know?"

"I just told her." I explained how I would be leaving for the Augustinian novitiate at the end of the summer. "Francis can have my clothes and my car. All I'll need is a black suit." A grin crept onto my face at the thought of my younger brother's reaction.

"A black suit, huh? Does that mean you'll be one of the bad guys or the good guys?"

"The good guys, I hope."

"Congratulations, Paul." Rather than a kiss or hug like the Italians do, his big hand reached out to shake mine—the Irish blessing.

When I finally told Irene, screwing up my courage at the end of June, I wanted to share the clearest expression of my feelings. Though we had often kidded over the years about getting married, something always held me back from discussing it seriously. I used to think it was my attraction to other guys. Now I could tell her what I hoped was the real reason—a vocation to the priesthood.

So, on this night, parked at 12:45 a.m. in front of her house in my second-hand '52 Plymouth, I reached to hold Irene's hand.

"So, what's up? What's on your evil little mind tonight?" she teased as usual.

With all my heart, I hoped that Irene could hear my plans and accept this awesome call from God.

"Irene..." I began, "I've had something I've been wanting to say to you for a while." On the radio, Elvis was panting the words of the song, "I Want You, I Need You, I Love You."

She flirted at me through a strand of her hair. Her voice was low and velvety, "Well, go ahead."

I began to stroke her hand.

"So many years we've known each other, so many incredible things we have done together..." She moved closer to me under the streetlamps. "Irene, occasionally we've said some serious things about our future."

"What's up?" She drew my hand to her breasts.

It was too late to falter. Elvis kept moaning the words of his song.

"Irene, I've not always been as honest as I could have been with you." I pulled her against me for an embrace, but my other hand got stuck between us.

"I'm going away to become a priest, Irene...."

Suddenly Irene looked like she was a million miles away. I wanted her to know how much she meant to me, how I would always miss her.

"...but if I ever loved anyone..." I searched for some thread of meaning, "...I loved you."

As I tried to hold her close, she growled into my shoulder, "Paul, you have never loved anyone but yourself."

As I write this, I think Irene may have been onto something. But she didn't know, as I couldn't then, that I didn't really love myself yet. I had to learn to do so before I could really love another. Instead, I ran away from myself into the priesthood.

Part II
OUT

You duped me Lord, and I let myself be duped.
(Jer 20:7)

11

Celt's Kiss

Autumn, 1964, Washington, DC—

A*nima una et cor unum in Deum* (You shall be one mind and one heart in God) (*The Rule of St. Augustine,* 1.2). This was the motto of the Augustinian Order to which I had vowed myself. Once a week, the Rule of St. Augustine reminded us: "To the extent that you prefer the good of the community to your own good, you know that you are advancing in charity" (8.3).

This was the understanding of the vow of poverty we took. Nothing we had was to be considered our own; everything was held "in common." We even wrote *ad usum* (for your use) inside our books to remind us that we didn't own them. They belonged to the community.

You could call this a religious form of communism. Naturally, I jumped right in. Submerging my own welfare in the larger, and supposedly greater, good of the community was a breeze for me, having grown up with thirteen siblings. "Who do you think you are?" still rang in my ears from back home. Christianity—the 1950s Roman Catholic version of it anyway—glorified community over the individual. If you sometimes felt oppressed by this, you were rewarded by a wonderful sense of belonging.

By going into the seminary, I had jumped into a scene even more communal than my family that let me put off the human development challenges of dealing with ownership, power, and especially intimate personal relationships. That wouldn't last.

Donning a religious habit didn't protect me from adult responsibilities for long.

Our community was suspicious about "particular friendships." At first, I didn't know what they were talking about. Wasn't every relationship particular? But this approach to the perils of intimacy was constantly reinforced: no visiting one another in private; common recreation times, so we were always in groups; and all our walks taken in threes rather than twos.

Oh, it wasn't all bad or I wouldn't have lasted. We did learn to value community, and that is no small feat in our individualist American society. Even the sense that our affections could be channeled beyond our own good became part of our experience and would help us minister to God's disadvantaged ones in the future. But this community building also had a downside.

We, at least I, drank in a more insidious message: friendships between two men are suspect. You had better be wary when you started to feel fondness for another guy.

This wariness of deep friendships included women, of course. In fact, they seemed to be the real threat. No one ever mentioned the word homosexuality. In fact, no one ever taught us about the goodness of *any* of our sexual feelings in the seminary, either heterosexual or homosexual. It was as though we should, and could, spiritualize all such urges. During these formative years, I thought that if I loved someone else deeply, I could no longer be a friend of God. *Anima una et cor unum in Deo*—oh yes! But the heart of this God seemed to be so jealous, so insecure, that he couldn't bear to have me love anyone else.

All the young men around me—my ninety-six classmates in the Augustinian Theology School in Washington, DC—were a joy and a temptation at the same time. Many of them were straight guys in their early twenties, who used up their sexual energy plowing into each other in touch football games every afternoon. Celt Dougherty was one of these men.

He wasn't especially handsome or big. In fact, he was built like me, a sprite, wiry, and strong. I loved the way his face flushed when he got angry. He usually played quarterback, and his self-confidence drew me to him like a magnet. A thrill ran down my back when he sidled over to me during a break in the game one day.

"So, what's up, Paul?" Sweat poured down his face and neck, soaking his T-shirt.

"Nothin' much." I smiled at him, this ruddy-faced popular upperclassman from the West Coast. Yet, when he wore his habit, he seemed a little out of place.

"Watcha doin' tonight?" Celt spoke out of the side of his mouth, glancing quickly at me for a response.

"Studying for our sacraments exam…what else?"

"Sacraments? Shit! Take a break from that stuff. Come down to the boiler room after night prayers. We're having a card game… and there'll be some beer. Yo, Mike!" He suddenly shouted across the field to another guy as he hurled the ball, "You pussies ready?"

I knew a few seminarians lived by another set of rules, holding beer parties after midnight and catching movies downtown when they could. Someone said that Jerry Keller even had a car. But I never let myself get into that stuff, figuring it would get me thrown out. At the very least, I wouldn't know where to draw the line.

"I don't know, Celt."

"C'mon! Let your hair down for a change. Right after night prayer, okay? Be there." He shoved his sweatshirt at me. "Here, hold this for me." His words stayed with me later through the lasagna dinner the nuns had prepared.

A little later, in the chapel, we chanted back and forth to one another in our facing pews.

How very good and pleasant it is
when kindred live together in unity!
It is like the precious oil on the head,
running down upon the beard,
on the beard of Aaron,
running down over the collar of his robe. (Ps 133:1–2)

It was Night Prayer, my favorite time. The day was done. Stars sprinkled across the purple sky outside. The world could relax in the sense that everything was okay. God was in charge. Any struggles you were caught up in could be given over to him, "That's it for the day, Lord. It's all yours. See you in the morning."

As we bowed for the *Gloria Patri*, I heard the burner click on below us. The boiler room! Remembering Celt's plan, I imagined myself sneaking downstairs with him and the other radicals to play cards and have some fun for a change. All around me, the strong young male voices echoed beautifully in the cavernous chapel:

Salve Regina, Mater Misericordiae,
vita dulcedo, et spes nostra salve.
Ad te clamamus exules filii Hevae,
ad te suspirantes gementes et flentes
in hoc lacrimarum valle....

Hail Holy Queen, Mother of Mercy,
our life, our sweetness and our hope,
To you do we cry, poor banished children of Eve,
to you do we send up our sighs,
mourning and weeping in this valley of tears.

In the flickering candlelight, we chanted to Mary. God was weaving one voice out of many. I spotted Celt and caught his gaze.

Be there, sport! But Celt...Be there!

I couldn't bring myself to disrupt such unity, so I didn't go down to the boiler room. Instead, I went back to my room and memorized my class notes on the sacraments one more time: "A sacrament is an outward sign, instituted by God to give grace." While slipping into my pajamas, I noticed Celt's sweatshirt hanging over my chair. I wanted to be close to him. No one would know. I put it on. Pulling the covers up around my shoulders, I fell asleep like a little saint.

It must've been around dawn. I awakened to a soft click. My door had opened quietly. Like a mouse, a shadowy figure drew close to my bed. It was considered a big no-no to be in another guy's room, so the sight of Celt's face in the dim light above me was like a visit from an angel, longed-for but frightening. I held my breath and leaned up on my elbow.

"Celt!...What?"

"Paul," he whispered, "I waited for you. What happened?" He sat down on the side of the bed.

"I'm sorry. I just couldn't." My voice was louder than his and shaking.

"Shh! Be quiet or someone will hear." A car pulled away from the curb outside and I jumped. "Don't sweat it. The others are going out for some breakfast." He smoothed the hair back from my forehead. "I wanted to see you."

Wow! How unbelievable to have a guy I cared about sitting on my bed and saying he needed me. I was terrified though. At any minute the Master could come crashing through the door and expel us both for forbidden activity. My hopes of being a priest would be over.

"I'll only stay a minute. Okay?" Like a cello, his voice stroked the fear from my trembling heart. I leaned back down.

For a few moments, we remained like that, his hip pressed against mine as we breathed in unison. My legs quivered but I didn't dare move. *Oh, God!* "I better go." I wanted him to stay but remained silent. Soon Celt stood, his face receding into the shadows like a dream. About to open the door, he suddenly turned and asked, "Paul, is it okay if I kiss you…on the cheek?"

What!? Caught between desire and fear, my eyes widened. Never had anyone, let alone a man I admired, shown me his strength and need so mixed together. I nodded, and he bent down to me. All these many years later, Celt's kiss still tingles on my cheek.

12

Suavissimo

Spring, 1965, Washington, DC—

Because his style was so smooth, we all dreamed of being like Fr. Jack Burke. We called him "Suavissimo." With his wavy salt-and-pepper hair, Irish good looks, and athletic physique, noticeable even underneath his habit, Burke was one of the "new breed" of priests emerging from the Vatican Council's effort to renew the Church. He taught moral theology at Augustinian College.

Pope John XXIII, who had succeeded the triumphalist Pius XII, was trying to drag the Church out of its Counter-Reformation fear of the world. He wanted to "open the windows of the Church," let a little air in. Under his pontificate, the people, whom we had grown up avoiding because they were heretics, were to be called "separated brethren." Pope John wanted to make the Church a participant for change in the modern world. To do so, we had better get our own house in order, he believed. Well, he opened the window, and the Holy Spirit flew in. Or, depending on your ecclesiology, flew out!

In the sixteenth century, Martin Luther had demanded, among other things, that the liturgy be conducted in the language of the people and that priests be allowed to marry. The Roman Catholic Church, sensing a loss of the transcendent sense of God, had circled its wagons and defined itself in contrast to the world—continued celibacy for its priests, a hierarchical authority structure with a subordinate role for women, and an emphasis on the sacraments rather than on the Word of God in Scripture. Of course, priests conducted these sacraments in the universal language of Latin, which helped emphasize the Church's otherworldly realities. It also guaranteed that priests, the mysterious celibate men who understood Latin, would continue to be the primary keepers of the faith.

These signs of identity of the Church of Rome were all being challenged anew at the Second Vatican Council, five hundred years after the birth of Protestantism with its emphasis on individual conscience, almost a thousand years after celibacy was made a requirement for Roman Catholic priests. In the first five hundred years of Church history, many priests were married.[1] Only after a lengthy bitter struggle did the celibacy faction win. Now this battle was going to be fought all over again. This was the contentious atmosphere in which my classmates and I prepared for ordination.

How could we get close enough to the people to offer them anything, the progressives like Jack Burke argued, if we were so removed from the world that we couldn't understand its everyday problems? "God is *with* the world and its concerns, not out there somewhere above and beyond them," he taught us. In contrast, the conservatives argued that familiarity—with God and priests—breeds contempt. "How can we offer them ideals to strive for beyond themselves if we are just like them?" they insisted. The battle lines were drawn, and the fight went on in our heads, groins, and hearts.

According to Father Burke, a priest communicates God best through his humanity. The people may venerate a spiritual icon, he explained, but they aren't drawn to imitate it. He stressed the humanness as well as the divinity of Jesus. "Look, Jesus got angry, wept over lost friends, had sexual feelings, and really suffered like you and me," he explained in his mellow voice. "If the Lord felt these emotions, then they are holy." Eyes wide, I imagined being a disciple of this human, loving Jesus. The priesthood began to feel more real to me, though I couldn't imagine Jesus being sexual.

By my second year in theology, I was beginning to change. My own sexuality drew me more to the progressive side of this struggle within the Church. No longer could I ignore this human part of me. I started to see that God is in the world with us, and that this is the message of Jesus Christ's humanity. "The Word became flesh and lived among us" (John 1:14). I discovered how to pray to a

God who resides in the hidden struggles of our lives, pushing up like spring flowers through the frozen ground.

I began to listen to the evening news differently as well. When Martin Luther King Jr. compared the civil rights struggle in America to Israel's being set free from the Egyptians, his dream became my dream too. Yes, this is what the psalms are talking about, the psalms that I chanted every day with my brothers:

> O Lord, you will hear the desire of the meek;
> you will strengthen their heart, you will incline your ear
> to do justice for the orphan and the oppressed,
> so that those from earth may strike terror no more.
> (Ps 10:17–18)

With seminarians of various churches, I found ways to take my faith out of the chapel and classroom and into the streets. I took part in night vigils for civil rights at the Lincoln Memorial. I was happy to be involved, even when a carload of young guys drove by yelling, "Faggots!" Soon, I discovered the peace movement when people all over the country began to protest the daily bombing of Vietnam. I prayed aloud for these people at our liturgies even when I got strange looks from classmates. Beneath all this, I was wrestling with the role of Church authority, especially in sexual matters. What did I believe? And how could I represent a Church that condemned who I was? My sexuality was still a secret because I knew it would cause trouble. Underneath my religious habit and the idealized role of the priesthood, a caterpillar began to stir in its cocoon.

One day, as I was returning from a St. Patrick's Day celebration, I spotted Father Burke in the driveway by the priest's house. Feeling light-headed, I didn't want to meet anyone just yet.

Like me, Burke was dressed in his habit. "Paul!" he called out. "So, what's up with you on this fine day?" His Irish eyes sparkled, blue as the sky.

"Nothing much. What a beautiful day, huh?" A brisk early spring nip was in the air. Suddenly, a jet's exhaust plume streamed out from behind it and pulled our gaze upward.

As I turned back to him, Burke was chuckling, making a series of low conspiratorial snorts through his nose. "Hmph, hmph, hmph!"

"What? *What?*" My heart raced. *Oh no! The Phantom knows something. We called him this as well as Suavissimo because he wasn't around on weekends.*

"How was the party?" He kept snorting.

"Party?" I feigned my best innocence.

"Yeah. And you didn't invite me." He sounded hurt, his voice as smooth as silk.

Caught, I snorted too. "We had a little St. Pat's gathering at a friend's house." A sheepish look came on my face.

Burke gazed at me like a father toward his wayward teenage son. "Next time wash the green beer off your lips before you come home, okay?"

We laughed together at the discovery. "Okay!"

Even if he later told the Master, I knew it would be with the Suavissimo touch, helping people to laugh at their foibles. When I got ordained in a couple years, I sure wanted to have a human touch like Suavissimo.

In recalling that occasion, I realize that my green lips said it all. They symbolized that hidden part of me that was trying to come out, the part that is visible to others even if I think it is hidden. The hidden secret part where both God and Satan dwell, but if you don't shine light there, you can hardly distinguish between them.

During the next few months, the Roman Catholic Church did something simple and extraordinary. The priests would turn around and face us at Mass. It was to emphasize the communal nature of the Eucharist, the "holy meal," and the laity's active involvement rather than being passive spectators. Father Jack Burke was a natural to celebrate the first Mass facing the people in the Augustinian seminary. Unintentionally, this liturgical change began to expose the shadow side of the Church and the priesthood, a side not always pretty. No wonder some in the Church today fight tooth and nail to return to the old ways. There was a price to pay for change. The congregation might really get to know us.

A few years after we were ordained, my classmates and I were shocked to hear that Father Jack Burke had been forced to resign from the priesthood. It had been discovered that he had a wife and family he was supporting—and living with on the weekends!—during those years that we were mesmerized by the human face of his priesthood in the seminary. I wondered how he dealt with the different needs: the need to be a priest with a partner to love, or the need to speak the truth while protecting himself from people who would never understand. I wished I could talk to him now. *Suavissimo!*

We heard later that Burke became a successful Baptist minister and, more recently, that he had died. What a tough life to straddle two worlds. I wonder how his wife and children dealt with the situation, and how they regarded his expulsion from the priesthood. Maybe they were finally glad. Yet I wonder: Would those of us who sympathized with Father Jack's plight and possibly cut him a little slack feel the same if it were discovered his lover was gay? At least we know how he got his compassionate heart—from the suffering of juggling two callings.

13

Finding My Voice

Autumn, 1965, Washington, DC —

Suddenly, we were thrown into the world of modern theology. Up until this point, our studies were taught in Latin and based on the philosophy of St. Thomas Aquinas. Now we received the latest Vatican Council II deliberations each week. It was as though we were being chopped in two.

This type of learning required more than the memorization and logical thinking that had powered me through engineering school, and more than the almost literal understanding of the Bible we had received up to then. Now we were required to wrestle with the teachings ourselves, to ground them in history and our own experience. Losing the secure base of reading the Bible literally would be the biggest challenge.

Rather than always being suspicious of personal feelings, we were now encouraged to get in touch with them and to develop a personal conscience. What could you do if your personal conscience was at odds with Church teaching? How could the "bottom-up" theology of a personal conscience fit with the "top-down" theology of an infallible pope? My poor brain began to bend.

One day, in Old Testament class, we were studying the origins for the Catholic teaching that Jesus Christ was born in Bethlehem. Our teacher, Fr. Roland Murphy, a renowned expert on Old Testament prophets, had written books on the Wisdom Literature, which included the psalms and the Song of Songs.[2] Father Murphy was a member of the Carmelite order, an ancient order like the Augustinians. His dark brown Carmelite habit had a band of cloth material, a "scapular," worn in the front from the shoulders to the floor. The Carmelites, with this symbol of chastity, were especially devoted to Mary, the Mother of God.

Murphy, a great strapping man maybe six feet six inches tall, with a thick shock of white hair and blazing eyes, had a rumbling voice that made us call him "Yahweh," the Hebrew name for God. One day, he was explaining an obscure verse from the Hebrew prophet Micah: "But you, O Bethlehem of Ephrathah, who are one of the little clans of Judah, from you shall come forth for me one who is to rule in Israel" (Mic 5:2), he intoned. Then, ever so carefully, he began to show us that this prophecy in the Old Testament that was traditionally used as a proof of Jesus being the Messiah wasn't necessarily about Jesus or even needed to be for us to believe.

"The New Testament authors, Matthew, in particular," he explained, "often wrote in ways in which they sought to make Jesus fulfill everything that was written about a messiah in the Old Testament. And so, we have Matthew's story about Jesus being born in Bethlehem. From all the new evidence we have, it seems to be the case that Jesus was born in Nazareth rather than in Bethlehem," Murphy continued, his bright eyes roaming the room. "It really isn't important, except for symbolic reasons, that he had to be born in Bethlehem."

Eager to understand, I had been listening intently. But when Murphy seemed to me to break away from a literal interpretation of reading the Scriptures, it was like a platform dropping from underneath me: the platform of my childhood religion, the Christmas hymns about angels and shepherds, and the stable at Bethlehem. If Jesus wasn't born in Bethlehem, what else in the Bible could be just a story? My hand shot into the air with a question.

"Morrissey!" Murphy's voice drilled me. "You have a concern?"

With the adrenalin of my fundamentalist understanding of Scripture surging through me, I couldn't help but stand up to face my opponent. The black of my habit contrasted with my white knuckles as I gripped the desk. "Yes, I do." My heart began to pound.

Murphy put down his Bible and waited. The rest of the class turned around to watch. *This could be good—David and Goliath!*

"Are you telling us," I began, my voice rising with righteousness, "that, even though it says in the Bible that Jesus was born in

Bethlehem, that he *wasn't*?" Oh, it felt good to punch out the truth with such force, something I was unaccustomed to do. My eyes blazed with all the indignation of a Philadelphia Catholic defending the true faith to a heretic. *Go ahead, Yahweh. Talk your way out of this one!*

Pausing, Murphy surveyed the class, seemingly unfazed. Maybe he was hunting for words. I almost felt sorry for him. Mumbling about the heat, he strolled over to the windows and pried one open. Then turning in a single scorching movement, he swept up his scapular with both hands and threw it back over his shoulder. His eyes shone like a demon's.

"MORRISSEY!" He roared through bared teeth. Only when he had us in his hot grip did he drop his voice to a whisper and plow on: "If you were only going to be here for a weekend, I wouldn't waste my time telling you this." He paused and dropped his head. When his voice began to ratchet up again, my temples started to pound. It felt like someone was punching me in the stomach.

"But you are going to be here for *four years*!" Yahweh boomed from his mountaintop. My breathing stopped. "And that's exactly what I'm telling you!" His scarlet face, as he finished, showed a tiny smile.

The class let out a gasp. No one stirred. Shaken, I crumpled back into my seat.

"Look, if you don't understand this, give it some time," he cajoled, his voice now a gentle breeze floating over a wrecked shoreline. His fiery eyeballs dimmed their voltage. "It's the symbolic meaning you've got to look for, okay? It's what the author wants to tell us, what the words mean, not just what they say."

I didn't understand, but my head wagged slowly up and down anyway to show him I would try. I hated him for bullying me with his brilliant mind. Yet a warm feeling began to rise in my belly and spread to my trembling hands.

Glancing sideways at my friends, Tom Vitello and Bill Ferguson, my chin tilted up a notch. I had done something new, something revolutionary for me. *Hey, you guys, whether I'm right or not isn't necessarily the main point, is it? For once, I didn't just give my voice away. My feelings do matter. So do yours. I had the guts to stand up to Yahweh. And damn, does that feel good!*

14

A Secret Between Me and God

Winter, 1965, Washington, DC—

Fundamentalism, I've discovered, has a problem with sexuality as well as biblical literalism. In fact, the Bible's teaching about sexuality seems equally unable to learn from discoveries.

One day in pastoral practice class at Catholic University of America, we were assigned a book with the strange title, *Counseling the Invert*. It happened to be written by our professor, Dr. John R. Kavanaugh, a Roman Catholic psychiatrist. Our professor wrote a book! Wow! We were impressed. But, with growing curiosity and dread, I read in the preface:

> Sex is a little understood subject. In recent years, an effort has been made to overcome this difficulty in regard to heterosexuality....Some of the serious writing has been very good, some of the romantic writing very poor. There has been, however, no lack of good material.
>
> In regard to homosexuality, this has not been true. In fact, there has been very little serious effort to illuminate this area of deviant sexuality. Clergymen who wield so much influence over the lives of others have not been well informed. Problems of the marriage of

inverts, their entry into seminaries, and their employment have blind spots…

Gulp! The sweat on my palms began to stain the pages. Dr. Kavanaugh was pointing out his hopes for those who read his book, "The invert himself may find it helpful to have some information about the development of his disorder, not only what is necessary to eliminate it but also the knowledge that it can be treated." He smoothed the lapels on his outdated tan suit.

"So, what's he pushing?" Bill Ferguson whispered to me.

Wanting some levity, I joked, "Something about perverts…or inverts, or some kind of verts." I was anxious to hide my feelings.

"Tell you what, if he gets into any real sexual fantasies instead of his nice safe clinical categories—you know, the crazy kind we all have but no one talks about?—" Bill dug his elbow into my ribs, "let me know, will you?"

Kavanaugh droned on. The use of the word *invert* instead of *pervert* was actually a breakthrough, he explained. *Invert* described homosexual *tendencies* in a person. Only if they *acted* on them were they perverts. "It is important to have psychological tests before sexual deviants are accepted into the seminaries," he warned, "not to punish them, but because we honestly care about them. It would be extremely difficult for an invert to be a chaste and happy priest."[3]

Really? I flattened myself back against the seat. My world was opening and collapsing at the same time. *An invert. A sexual deviant. He's talking about me!*

Bill and I decided to get some lunch at the cafeteria. A burly bombastic Bronx Irish guy with a reddish pockmarked face, Bill loved to quaff beers in a tavern and slap you on the back while laughing at his own jokes. Even though he had majored in psychology at St. John's College, he didn't usually discuss feelings.

He was striding fast, both of us in our habits, and I had to hustle to keep up with him. Suddenly, he asked, "You seem quiet, Paul. Did he say something that threw you?"

"No, no…not really."

Ahead of us, the blue and yellow eggshell dome of the Immaculate Conception Shrine glinted brilliantly in the afternoon sunshine—the Golden Tit, we called it. Hovering alongside it, the Knights of Columbus bell tower thrust itself skyward like a big phallic symbol. *Everything's so heterosexual! Do I really want to open this up? But how will I ever know the truth unless I talk?* "Bill, I know a guy who's...struggling with homosexual tendencies." My voice sounded frail and tentative. "What would you advise him?"

"Well, I gotta admit, girls will always be my main squeeze." He laughed happily to himself. "Is it someone on campus?"

"Yeah." We walked straight ahead, neither of us looking at the other.

After a while Bill said, "Well, I get angry when I hear that stuff we heard just now. Y'know, Kavanaugh's views aren't the only ones on homosexuality. There are other approaches. I'd think twice before I'd send someone who wanted to deal with that issue to him." He glanced over at me. I nodded, taking in his words.

Then, as though he were considering variations on a football play, Bill mused, "Y'know, I'd probably tell him to talk to the campus minister first. Even if it's a nun. Yeah, that's what I'd do. Nuns are easy to talk to. They don't judge you. If I felt comfortable with her, I'd ask her if she knows of any good psychiatrists to refer me to."

Psychiatrist. The word froze me. You had to be crazy to see one of them. I didn't feel crazy, just confused.

Bill noticed my reserve. "I mean, a modern, savvy shrink, someone who isn't trying to jam everyone into a clinical category." He stroked his fat dimpled chin. "They wouldn't have to be Catholic. No, in fact, maybe it'd be better if they weren't. Someone who doesn't have an investment in the system. Do you get what I mean?"

"Yeah." My mind was doing flips at the drift of our conversation, but at the same time I was constructing my own game plan. "My friend is studying for the priesthood," I said. "How could he afford a psychiatrist?"

"I'd tell him to ask his diocese or community to pay for it. He belongs to them, right? He's one of them, and he probably needs help if he's gotten this far. He shouldn't let anything get in his way of this help either." His voice dropped. "But he doesn't have to tell them the particulars. I mean, whether he is homosexual or not is his business." His bulging brown eyes rested on me. "And tell him he has the right to have a doctor of his own choice."

I started to crack inside, not from sadness but from deep gratitude for him. "Sounds like good advice, Bill. You're gonna be a great psychologist someday."

"You better believe it." He slapped me playfully on the back with his big paw. "Whaddaya say we grab some cheeseburgers now? I've got an appetite that could devour a horse."

I punched his arm. "Me too!" As we hurried to the cafeteria, I memorized the pieces of his game plan in my head like they were treasures. A little giddy with hope and fear, I promised myself: You need to run with this soon, Paul, no matter what. *No matter what.*

Later that week, I went to see the Master, Father Perkins. New at the job and in his early forties, Perkins was jovial and personable. He was a refreshing change from the previous Master's strict style, and he represented the new thinking coming out of the Vatican Council. But whenever he relaxed a rule, the old-time priests on the faculty whispered, "He's ruining the seminary, you know."

"Come in, Paul. What can I do for you?" Perkins's office was bright and cheery.

I zoomed right to the point. "I'm having some problems."

The welcoming smile faded. "Oh, I'm sorry to hear that, Paul. Do you want to talk about it? Have a seat." I continued to stand.

Earlier that morning, I had role-played Bill's strategy. "I want to talk with a psychiatrist," I said.

Perkins surveyed me as though for the first time. By voicing what I wanted and risking conflict, I had created distance between us and between the community and me. Both of us knew it.

"Very well, Paul." He glanced down for a moment, before assuring me with the kindest voice, "I know a fine doctor, a good Catholic psychiatrist whom I can recommend. He has seen some of our other men over the years and has been very helpful to them. I am sure he can be helpful with you."

Oh, I wanted so much to please him, to reassure him that even though I had some problems I was not off on some wrong-headed path. An image of Dr. Kavanaugh at his rickety podium came to mind, reassuring us that inverts could get help to change their disorder.

Perkins leaned forward, his hand reaching for a small red booklet. "I can give you his phone number. You can call for an appointment." I could feel his concern, but in my bones I didn't see how I could trust Kavanaugh or any other Catholic psychiatrist.

They'd all have the party line. *No. I don't want help to change it! I want to understand it.*

Picturing Bill's bulging eyes with their challenge, I said with the greatest confidence, "I want to speak to someone who isn't connected to our community. Someone of my own choosing."

Perkins leaned backward. "Paul, I...I'm not sure we can do that. We don't have any precedent for this. What would the purpose of this be?"

"I need someone I can trust," I said. I didn't add my fear that a doctor of the community might not be able to protect my confidentiality. Maybe the seminary authorities would want progress reports on me. Maybe any hint that I was struggling with homosexual feelings would make it difficult for them to approve me for the priesthood. The openhearted honesty that I equated with the truth began to retreat into a secret place within me.

"You can't trust our doctor?"

"Maybe I can, but I'd prefer someone else."

He paused to search my face. "Do you have a name?"

"I do." I produced the crumpled card of a Jewish psychiatrist that Sr. Bernard Mary had given me earlier that week. "One of the campus ministers at the university recommended him."

"Sheldon Feinstein?" Perkins adjusted his glasses and frowned before saying, "All right, Paul. Give him a call. See if you can make an appointment for a consultation."

"Okay," I nodded.

Smiling across the space between us, Perkins added, "You surprise me sometimes, Paul, but you have my support. Let me know how it goes, okay?"

"Okay." We shook hands before either of us could change our minds.

Quickly, I phoned Dr. Feinstein's office in downtown Washington. His secretary gave me a 9:00 a.m. appointment for Monday the following week. Trembling with fear and excitement, I ran to my room.

That appointment was so pivotal for me that I can still hear the hum of that building's elevator, see myself opening the doctor's office door in slow motion, hear the cheery normality of the receptionist's voice, "Come in, have a seat please, fill out this form and the doctor will be with you in a moment." *Sure, as though I'm just getting a cavity filled!*

The picture on the wall, jumbled figures—Picasso?—I closed my eyes and thought of Monet's water lilies instead. Soon, I was shaking the psychiatrist's hand. The warmth and firmness of it gave me a flicker of hope.

"Please, have a seat," he said, "tell me what the problem is." I sat on a sofa across the room from him.

I heard my own voice, as though outside of me. It was as though I were talking about someone else, telling him such personal things. "Yes, my mother and I are quite close; my little brothers and sisters used to call me Mommy Paul because I took care of them; no, my father and I don't have a very close relationship; I had a girlfriend for seven years, but we never had sex; I've had a few playful sexual encounters with guys, but not since I've been in the seminary."

When he summed up at the end of the session, my mouth had become dry as a desert. "It seems to me that you are homosexual, but you are basically okay with that. And if you feel you can be celibate, as the priesthood requires of you, I don't see any need for you to come back. Just give me a call if you have any problems, okay?"

What is this? A tremendous relief came over me! The first time I had ever told these things to anyone, and I had been accepted without judgment. Also, it was the first time I had ever heard someone professional say those clinical words, *It seems to me that you are homosexual....Oh God, this is me!*

Now it wasn't just a matter of having certain feelings. It's a category, an identity that forever holds me in its frame. On the one hand, I was relieved. I wouldn't just be floating uncertainly underneath the robes of a priest, underneath the sexual neutrality of celibacy that implies that it doesn't matter what your orientation is as long as you don't act on it.

On the other hand, I was terrified. *I'm one of THEM*. Those people whom others snigger about or hate. People I have shunned and despised. And how would God feel about this? I needed to know. I couldn't bear to devote my life to God if he despised who I am.

Later, when I returned with this awareness to the seminary at lunchtime, I saw my brother Augustinians seated elbow to elbow at the long dining tables, all dressed in their flowing habits, happily chatting because it was the feast of St. Rita, the Patron of Impossible

Causes, and we were allowed to talk. Finding my seat across from Celt, I tried to join the conversation. My head was numb, though, and a deep pit began to open in my belly.

Celt, at first engrossed in his hamburger, soon asked, "Paul, your face is chalk white! Is anything wrong?"

"No, no...nothing's the matter."

Though quite a few were like me, as I have learned since, there was no one among the nearly one hundred of my religious brothers with whom I felt I could share this knowledge about myself. All of us were sworn to "share all things in common." Yes, but this secret would have to be between me and God.

15

New Year's Eve

Winter, 1966, Washington, DC—

On New Year's Eve, Augustinian College threw a party. I was in my third year of a four-year theology and spiritual formation program leading up to ordination. After night prayers, the seminarians were given special permission to stay up until midnight and have some Pepsi or Budweiser in the common room. Another opportunity to experience that elusive dream of the Augustinian Rule—community life.

Two sides of me were fighting each other: the old Paul who loved a party, and the new holy Paul who had left that world behind to become a priest. If I relaxed too much, who knows what I might do? Get up and dance? Hah! Sit too close to someone like Celt? In either case, eyeballs would roll, and my secret would be out to everyone.

Celt and I had become friends over the past year. We weren't sexual partners—we had never talked about our orientation. There was that kiss on the cheek, and once when I had snuck into his bed in my pajamas as a joke to greet him when he got back from the shower.

"What the hell are you doin'?" he said as he quickly closed the door. His sly grin told me he was glad, though.

With the covers pulled up to my chin, I grinned back, "I just thought I'd surprise you." I wasn't consciously trying to seduce

Celt. Yet my skinny body tingled with happiness. *To be so close with my friend, oh, this is heaven!*

"You'll get us both thrown out." He hung his towel behind the door and came a step closer, his gray pajamas damp from the shower.

"Okay, okay, I'll go." But my bravado had touched him. Besides, I was certain my feelings for him were pure friendship and would have righteously told Perkins so if he somehow found out, "Oh, give it a break! Everything's so serious! It's just a joke!"

Nevertheless, I had those homosexual feelings deep down. Everything I read in Scripture and Church teaching told me these were wrong. Passages in the Old Testament said you should be put to death (see Lev 20:13). In our modern psychology course, homosexuality was considered the result of a stunted sexual development, a mental illness. A life of celibacy could hide this from others, but not from me. And not, I guessed, from someone I loved either.

Half consciously, I was trying to show this to Celt with my antics. I needed him to love all of me, not just the polished part that society and the Church considered good. After peeking out to see if I could return to my room undiscovered, I glanced back and saw the love in his eyes. Barefoot and beaming, I ran to my room.

Now, on New Year's Eve, as the Catholic University bells chimed 11:30, I gulped the last dregs of my beer. Bart Lomax drained his second beer and raved on about Villanova's lousy football season. "I'd fire him," he spat out about the coach as though he were God.

Across the room, I watched Celt. He seemed equally animated, but I was bored, and then a deep loneliness rose in me. Quietly, as Lomax described a botched play, I slid off the vinyl chair to leave.

"Hey! Morrissey, where ya goin'?" called Lomax. "It's almost the magic hour. You're not gonna leave us alone at midnight, are ya?"

"I'm going to the bathroom," I said.

He wasn't buying that. "You're probably going to pray."

"Yeah," I couldn't resist the dig, "I'm gonna pray for Villanova. Hah!"

I eased away as the rest of them laughed. I needed a breath of fresh air. I needed someone I could talk to honestly. The only place I could think of was the chapel.

Except for the red sanctuary light that flickered shadows off the walls, it was dark. Even the stained-glass windows were black. Good. I didn't want anyone to see me like this. Slipping into a long horizontal pew, I knelt, and words tumbled out silently in my heart:

Lord, are you there? I feel so alone in this place. There is no one on earth to share my heart with. No one to love me for who I am.

Incense and candle wax aroma hung in the dark air. I felt like crying. I waited. Nothing. Then across the campus I could hear bells, deep and melancholy, strike midnight. Bong! Bong! Bong! Bong!

Lord, I'm sorry for having all these mixed-up feelings on New Year's. I want to be happy, but I feel like shit tonight. Bong! Bong! *Should I pretend to be different than I am? Even if that gets me accepted, do you think that is good? Up there in that tabernacle as another year ends, supposedly as Bread for the Poor, do even you love me for who I am? for my whole being…my real self?* Bong! Bong!

Up front at the sacristy's entrance, I heard a door close. In a moment, a shadowy figure rounded the corner and stood still by the organ. My heart stopped. Embarrassed at being caught in prayer like some holy roller, I remained perfectly still, hoping to stay hidden. Bong! Bong!

"Paul!" A voice whispered, "Is that you?" Bong!

Celt! Quickly I brushed some tears away. He was the last one I wanted to see me like this. Well, maybe the only one.

"What are you doing up here? It's midnight!" His voice, low and sultry with its Western twang, echoed along with the bells as he moved next to me.

"I don't know. I guess I needed to be alone." A hint of his aftershave floated between us.

"I was looking for you. I missed you." He tugged at my sleeve. "Let's get the hell out of here. C'mon. It's not too cold out. We can take a walk outside. It'll do you good."

Maybe that's what I really needed, to be found by Celt. To be alone with him, not lost in a crowd. I nodded my head and followed him out, glancing back toward Jesus in the tabernacle.

Once outside, we started down the path that led past where the priests lived. Hearing voices, Celt steered me toward the ball field off to the right. As we stepped onto the grass, I remembered his kiss on my cheek that night and felt hope.

"Look! The Big Dipper!" I pointed. Though we weren't supposed to smoke, Celt produced a pack of cigarettes from under his capuche and lit one up. He looked like James Dean.

We walked for a bit. "So, what's going on, Paul?"

Now that I was with my friend, I wanted to forget any heavy stuff. It was New Year's. In just a few hours, back home in Philadelphia, friends would be gathering for the Mummer's Parade, kicking up their heels to the "Golden Slippers" and celebrating. *How often will you be alone with Celt like this? It's now or never.*

"Celt?"

Though we were far from the priests' house now and invisible in the shadows, a man's voice screeched across the field and alerted us that a group of our guys was walking over there. I sure didn't want Lomax and that crowd to see us and cringed. Celt didn't pay them any mind. He just kept dragging on his smoke, occasionally bumping into me.

"Yeah?"

I thought back over the times I had felt disgusted at myself, and the times when I had heard someone snicker at a joke about queers. Even though I hadn't laughed at those moments, I had never defended them either. The Bible condemned queers, though Jesus never said a word about it. I thought of how the soldiers had stripped him and spat in his face when he was arrested. I wished I could've stood between them to protect him.

"Celt, I need to tell you something...." Something began to crack inside me. It was like bile coming up out of a dark place inside, a poison that had trapped me in its grip for as long as I could remember. It just started to erupt, and nothing could stop it. "Something that might make you want to spit at me."

"What?" He turned to look at me squarely. We both froze in our tracks. Off in the trees, an owl hooted.

"Celt, you're my friend." My heart thumped, and my breath came in short spurts. "I need you to know me as I really am, or else you're loving me for something I'm not—"

Though I couldn't clearly see his face, he lifted his hands in a bewildered, helpless fashion.

"—and I just couldn't bear that."

I couldn't take him looking at me so directly any longer. "Celt, I'm a homosexual."

For a few horrible seconds, a silent void hung between us. The muffled voices of our classmates drifted from far away. Suddenly, chilled to the bone, I felt an old ghost shiver itself out of me and fly away into the darkness. Then, a wild growl rose out of Celt's guts.

Oh God, please, please....

Celt could have punched me or spat at me, and I would have barely flinched. Instead came something else from my friend that to this day I realize was my blessed salvation. Around my shivering shoulders, he placed his wiry arm, pulling my self-hatred close, melting it by his acceptance, showing me at last the love of God for which I had been longing my whole life.

...Oh God, oh God...like to the lark at break of day arising!

The two of us walked back and forth on that field for a long time. The moon floated up behind the evergreens as a witness. With Celt's arm draped over my shoulder, I was the lost sheep finally found. I don't even remember what we said before parting. It didn't matter. I was a long way from fully accepting myself, but for the first time in my life, I felt loved for all of me. I was twenty-seven, nine months from ordination.

16

Ordination Day

September 9, 1967, Villanova, Pennsylvania—

Talk about a whole new life! It was ordination day. Everything during my six years in the seminary had led to this. My whole family was there at Villanova University, along with relatives, neighbors, and friends through the years. During the ceremony, nine classmates and I, dressed in white albs, lay face down in the middle aisle of the church as a sign of our total surrender to God. All the while, the choir chanted the Litany of Saints over us. At one point, I realized my ankles were crossed. Did I really surrender?

By then, I had silently accepted the fact that I was homosexual. Although the visit to the psychiatrist a year before was a key coming-out moment, even more so was my friendship with Celt. We weren't sexual with each other, but I loved him more than I had ever loved anyone up to that point in my life. More important, I knew in my bones that our friendship was good.

But Celt left the seminary before ordination. I never got to say goodbye, to tell him how much he meant to me. And there wasn't anyone I could speak to about this, so I went to his empty room that night and looked around. I wanted to feel his presence before it was all gone. In a drawer, I found his leather cincture, the belt worn around our habits at the waist that hung to the floor, and switched it for my own. I spotted his crucifix on the wall and brought it to my room. For a month after he left, I slept on the floor by my bed having heard that African people mourn this way, holding onto the suffering for a while so they don't forget their friend. I still have that cross and pray with it.

My mind couldn't stay on my studies. In Scripture class, we explored the biblical passage from the Book of Samuel about how much David loved Jonathan: "I grieve for thee, my brother Jonathan: exceeding beautiful, and amiable to me above the love of women. As the mother loveth her only son, so did I love thee" (2 Sam 1:26). *That's what I felt for you, Celt, but now you'll never know.*

When it finally sank in that he was really gone, I realized that, despite all the talk about "community," I was going to have to take the step of ordination on my own. There wasn't any "Buddy Program." I considered leaving too, but my sense of vocational call was even stronger than my love for my friend. In those days, there were no public models of two guys living together as lovers. If there were, I might have left to seek that as my life's meaning. Instead, I went ahead with ordination, hoping that God could help me to sublimate my sexual longings into deep caring for the people I would serve as a priest. True, it was only a fledgling feeling then, but a glimmer of a more radical thought stirred too: maybe I can do more for homosexuals inside the official Church than outside.

There is a key moment during the ordination ceremony when the formal sacrament takes place. It is when the bishop or cardinal places his hands in silence on the ordinand's head. We had been prepared for this "ontological change" that we believe stamps an indelible character on the new priest's soul. I wondered if I'd feel it inside as I knelt before Cardinal Krol, the conservative bishop of Philadelphia, seated on an exquisitely carved throne. Slowly placing his surprisingly strong hands on my head, he stared down at me with a withering look to receive my promise of obedience. Against my perspiring forehead, I felt the cold metal of his bishop's ring. Little did the cardinal know how in that moment of pregnant silence, while my family and the whole congregation craned their necks to see, the Holy Spirit swooped down, gathered me and my gay history up in a flourish, and sent me on my mission.

I didn't feel any physical change inside me then, but soon after, when Father Perkins proclaimed the Gospel from St. Luke, I heard it in a new way. It was like the words were being spoken directly to me:

The Spirit of the Lord is upon me,
 because he has anointed me
 to bring good news to the poor.
He has sent me to proclaim release to the captives
 and recovery of sight to the blind,
to let the oppressed go free,
 to proclaim the year of the Lord's favor. (Luke 4:18–19)

How I longed to proclaim release to captives of all kinds, in the name of Jesus Christ—including myself.

To have a priest in the family was a great honor then, and my Irish family celebrated in grand style. In my home parish of St. Alice's in Upper Darby, Pennsylvania, my parents had invited several hundred people for my First Mass, the day after ordination, to be followed by a sit-down dinner. There was one major glitch, though. I wanted to celebrate Mass facing the people. I couldn't imagine doing it in the old pre–Vatican II Council style, facing away from the people, "toward the wall and God," as we used to say. When I told this to the pastor who had previously been the spiritual director at St. Charles Seminary, the bastion of orthodoxy for the diocesan priesthood of Philadelphia, he listened intently before explaining politely, "If you wish to celebrate Mass facing the people, there is an altar for this in the school hall." He seemed certain that I would balk at not having the main church for the event.

Equally sure that he would relent for a new priest and his family, I eagerly countered, "I could bring in a portable altar to the main church."

But two stubborn Irishmen had met. "There will be no portable altars in the main church," he responded, his velvety voice rising ever so slightly and muffling my hopes.

"Oh! I'll have to talk it over with my parents," I said to save face. But I had already decided. For me, the Eucharist was a sacred meal for the people. God was in our midst, as we shared the bread and wine that we believed was Jesus's Body and Blood, not up in the sky like some judge as we crouched in fear. I was determined not to be a priest who fostered this fear. No way was I going to be seduced by the stained-glass windows and marble columns of the church. Already, I was wrestling with religious authorities just like Jesus had done, and I was glad.

At first, Mama was stunned. Her clenched jaw showed her anger at the pastor, and probably at me too. But in the end, she took my side. Now, the pastor had to rustle up a crew to polish the floors in the hall and try to explain to the parishioners why we weren't celebrating such a major event in the main church. Determined to make the rite something to remember, I hired a cantor who would lead the congregation in singing new English hymns. Excited about the new access to the ritual, my sisters flung themselves into decorating the stage with flowersand draped a big banner over the altar that proclaimed a phrase they had found in the Psalms: "This is the day that the Lord has made. Let us be glad and rejoice in it" (118:24).

Oh, we were going to rejoice! I had insisted on having a rock and roll band so we could dance after the dinner. That plan was quickly dashed when everyone wanted my blessing, a tradition for a newly ordained priest. There was no way that I could bless the long line of people, including many relatives, old friends I had grown up with, even non-Catholic employees of Daddy's from Horn and Hardart's restaurant, while the band pounded out "Blue Suede Shoes." It broke my heart, but we had to send the band home.

Grabbing a mic, I invited everyone back to our house for a party afterward as my parents gaped at each other. We packed our living room and dining room and danced and partied for eight hours. Exhausted but happy at 2:00 a.m., I pulled the light switch on the lamp and started up the stairs. Half-looped on the excitement and beer, I gazed back on the darkened living room where so many events of my life had taken place. The hurtful ones were all dim memories. The good ones were all swept up in the vision of my nine sisters, singing and kicking their legs like chorus girls to the anthem of the night still ringing in my ears, "You're just too good to be true, can't take my eyes off of you…."

17

Father Potsy and Conscience

Summer, 1968, Queens, New York—

After my ordination and my graduation from Catholic University, I was assigned to St. Nicholas of Tolentine parish in Jamaica, New York, as a parish priest. This was supposed to be a warm-up. At summer's end, I was scheduled to go to Biscayne College in Florida to be the chaplain to young male students, live in the student dorm as a counselor, and teach theology. My brother, Tommy, drove me to St. Nicholas parish in late June. I showed up in Bermuda shorts, excited about my future.

Rev. Patrick "Potsy" Kenny, a scowling bear of an older priest, met me at the front door in his habit. "What the hell are you doing showing up here late for dinner?" he growled.

"Don't worry. I intend to work...but I want to relax too." Crinkling up my eyes and smiling, I held up my tennis racket. "Wanna play?"

"Is that what this new theology is teaching you?" sputtered Kenny. "No wonder the Church is going to hell!"

But I had managed to claim my space. After a delicious meal of lasagna, the two of us had made an initial bond of mutual respect. Tommy enjoyed our sparring. When I walked him to the car to say goodbye, he gripped my hand like a vise.

"Don't let that bastard get you down. Keep your head down, you hear?" He winked.

"Hey, Tommy, say one for me, will ya?" It was as close as I could get to ask for a blessing.

"Sure. No sweat." An emptiness rose within me as I watched his car disappear, but I was ready to give up everything for Christ's sake. Rushing by the dining room, I almost missed Kenny with a sheet of paper in his hand.

"You have the seven o'clock Mass tomorrow morning. Get a good night's sleep. You wouldn't want to be late for your first duty now, would you?"

"No, I wouldn't." He was such a target; I couldn't resist it. "By the way, do you have an alarm I can borrow?" I wiggled my nose to show him I was kidding. As he glowered like a madman, I turned and ran cackling to my room.

That week, the Vatican issued a long-awaited encyclical on birth control, *Humanae Vitae* (On Human Life), which created a firestorm in the Roman Catholic Church. Its main message was to prohibit artificial contraception for Catholics, even if they were married or if they had as many children as they wanted or could afford. The Pill was a no-no for Roman Catholics.

The fateful decision was made by Pope Paul VI, supposedly a liberal and intellectual, when he realized a papal commission set up by his predecessor, Pope John XXIII, was about to relax traditional teachings against contraception. He reversed the commission's findings.

In Pope Paul VI's mind, "every act of intercourse must remain open to the transmission of life." A couple could restrict lovemaking to the non-fertile periods of the wife's menstrual cycle (Natural Family Planning), but they couldn't actively use "artificial" means such as the birth control pill or condoms to prevent fertilization. They had to leave that decision to God.

This teaching on the unbreakable connection between intercourse and childbearing (and thus marriage) has been the basis of the Church's sexual theology for almost 1,500 years.[4] It sought to protect the sacredness of sexual intercourse, showing that God intended sex only for those in a committed, lifelong bond of love that the Roman Catholic Church considered a sacrament. Even if renowned moral theologians such as Bernard Häring and Charles

Curran urged that procreation of children and conjugal love be considered "coequal" goals of marriage, according to the pope, these two goals could never be separated.

If the Church changed this teaching, all hell would break loose, Pope Paul apparently believed. Most bishops seemed to agree with him. They feared that people would have intercourse and swear it was for "love"; sex would become like a handshake, something you might do on a first date; women would be taken advantage of; abortions would increase; and even homosexuality could be justified. No, the Roman Catholic Church would not let these things happen, even if it were the only one to stand its ground before the onslaught of modern liberal thinking.

Regarding many of his fears, the pope was proved right. Over fifty years later, the Church is still fighting this battle, holding its ground, banning the use of any contraceptives, including condoms, even if you are married, or even if one of the parties is infected with the AIDS virus. In 2009, on a trip to Africa, Pope Benedict stated that condom use is not the answer to the spread of HIV infection; rather, he said, it may spread it, because condoms aren't 100 percent effective. Once any exception is made, it is believed, the entire sacred ideal around sexuality will come tumbling down. The world needs ideals even if it doesn't follow them. The problem here is that this is not where the Catholic people stand.

Soon after this encyclical's appearance, I drove home to Philadelphia for a visit one afternoon. Mama was happy to see me, especially because I wore my black shirt with the Roman collar. Daddy was at the restaurant, and the rest of the clan were either working or at school. So, Mama and I had some unusual space to ourselves. The two of us sat at the long dining room table, enjoying hot tea and toasted Vienna bread smothered in butter, her favorite treat.

I got the urge to raise the ticklish subject. "Mama, what do you think of the pope's new encyclical?"

She sipped her tea slowly. "Well, I'm certainly glad he isn't letting himself be influenced by some of those theologians who want to change things." Contentedly, she smiled, secure in the truth of her lifelong commitment. At fifty-seven, she and Daddy were about to celebrate their thirtieth wedding anniversary. During those thirty years they had fourteen children and four miscarriages. Eight of the kids were still living at home. Oh yes, Mama and Daddy had kept the pope's rule. No upstart theologian was going to upset that conviction now.

We had never talked about these things before. Certainly, our parents' sexual choices were out of bounds for discussion, even when we became adults. Whose idea had it been, though, to have so many children, Mama's or Daddy's? And was it connected to a drive for sexual pleasure? My father seemed to have that, but Mama? She could almost have been a nun the way she was so religious. Who would ever know?

I hadn't really shared much with my family either, how the Vietnam War and the Vatican Council, as well as the growing awareness of my own sexuality, were changing me. I decided to tell her where I stood, at least regarding birth control. With all my newly emerging authority, I said, "Mama, what if someone doesn't agree with the pope?"

Gazing back at her priest-son, now an official representative of the very Church she'd bet her life on, Mama's blue eyes turned a steely gray. At that moment, years of sacrificed desires strengthened her voice into a riveter's hammer. Mama announced to me, and to the pope if he were listening, "If-they-ever-change-that-rule, I'm-going-to-write-the-pope-a-letter!"

A rush of childhood fear swept over me. As her face slowly reddened, I glimpsed the woman in her, more than just the self-sacrificing mother. Underneath the religiousness and the thrift shop dress appeared Nora, the sexual woman, the fun-loving girl with the mirthful eyes, whom Daddy dipped to the floor when they slow-danced at our parties. I realized that this mother of fourteen, this sexual woman—*my mother!*—was ready for war now with anyone, including her son the priest, who would insinuate that we might have a choice about these things.[5]

"But Mama, should we never change things just because it'll make us be right about our past choices? What about Nonie and Nancy, Anne, and Mary? Your daughters and daughters-in-law? Do you think they can manage to have as many children as you did?"

The hairs on my neck quivered. I realized that if the pope ever did change the Church teaching on birth control, Mama's letter would be scorched with centuries of women's sense of betrayal, of being used by the Church. *You're going to change the rules now?*

"If they have strong enough faith," she said, "God will provide."

God will provide, but he needs our help, I wanted to argue. But the debate was difficult for her, because I was using the very faith that she had taught me to challenge her most basic beliefs.

I saw myself mirrored in those piercing blue eyes, as righteous in my progressive beliefs as Mama was in her traditionalist ones. She seemed to sense this surety could cause me trouble. "You better be careful," she said softly, "whom you say that to."

Mother and son. So alike and so different. It wasn't just in private conversations that these tensions showed themselves. In the immediate aftermath of Vatican II, it was like you had to take a stand on everything.

As priests, we heard confessions every Saturday. One Saturday, I slumped down at the table across from Father Kenny.

"Now, what's the matter? You just got here, and you look like you're ready to bail out."

Feeling drained, I didn't want to get into a discussion with him. I knew he'd have the party line and would be angry if I didn't. But this ministry made me feel isolated. There was no one with whom I could let out my frustration. The "Seal of Confession" required us to hold all confessions as confidential.[6] I blurted out, "Did you ever get sick of hearing people confess things they really don't think are sins?"

"What's that supposed to mean?"

I took a swig of water. "If someone confesses to you that they missed Mass because they were sick, what do you say?"

"I tell them to try harder the next time and give them three Hail Marys for a penance." His voice was calmer, and he was grinning. I began to relax.

"But why wouldn't you tell them that if they are sick, it isn't a sin? Why have them feel guilty about something they can't help?" Sure of myself, I stared straight into his beady eyes.

"Jeanne!" He bellowed toward the kitchen for our meal. "We're ready." Then back to me. "Did you ever think that people... *need to feel guilty*?" He almost blew me off my chair with his bombastic outburst.

"Need to? What?" I squinted in confusion as Jeanne arrived with the main course on a cart—baked ham, mashed potatoes with gravy, and cabbage.

"Look," he said, leaning close as if we were hatching some plot, "when they tell you an excuse for a sin, whatever it is, that's probably not the real reason." He forked ham onto his plate and handed the platter to me. "Otherwise—do you want some mustard?—they wouldn't be bringing it up in confession in the first place, right?"

I considered his words.

"Usually, there isn't enough time to get into the real issues. You gotta get 'em in and out fast. Most of the time, they don't want you to delve into anything either." He cackled as if only a dummy wouldn't get it. "So, in your kindest voice, just tell them to try a little harder and give them absolution. That's what they want." He popped some cabbage into his mouth.

I remembered that Kenny had received his theology training at the University of Louvain in Belgium. He must've been one of the brains of his day. Even so, at Catholic University, we had learned from Charles Curran that it was important to help people develop their personal consciences. Earlier in the confessional, when a married guy had confessed to using condoms, I heard the pain and embarrassment in his voice. I wanted to help people like him, not just treat confession like an assembly line. With all Kenny's street-talking roughness, I couldn't believe he didn't hear this pain from people too.

"So, what do you say when someone comes in and says, 'Father, we have four kids. We can't afford any more.'"

"What's your problem?" he said. "Don't tell me you want to talk to people about their sex lives!" Below the table, my hands squeezed my napkin. *It's not* their *sex lives, dummy. It's* all *our sex lives!*

"Look," I pleaded, "I'm twenty-eight years old and unmarried. What do you want me to say to these people? If I absolve them for what they simply can't do responsibly—have more kids if they want to have sex—they'll only show up again in a month distraught over their sin."

Kenny's eyes were on his plate. "You've got to understand," he explained the traditional understanding of our role, "that priests are here to represent what the Church teaches, not to make up our own rules. No, even if they gripe about it, the people want it that way too. That way, they've got a clean slate after they confess. They are right in God's eyes, even if it is just for a while. What would happen if everyone did just what they wanted?"

"But don't you think we should talk to them about it? And if they seem sincere, encourage them to follow their own conscience in the future and not confess it? Why should priests be caught between some impossible ideal and the reality of people's lives?"

"Conscience?" He sneered at the crazy thought. It was as though I had questioned the Blessed Mother's virginity. "Conscience! If people follow their conscience,[7] there will be no such thing as sin anymore, don't you get it? They won't come to confession."

The guy was so angry that I decided to shut up before he had a heart attack. For the rest of the meal, we ate in silence. From that evening on, Potsy Kenny and I began to treat each other like we were in different camps. To try to bridge this gap and keep me as a child, I suppose, he took me for a ride each evening to show me the parish and buy me an ice-cream cone.

At the time, some priests publicly disagreed with the pope. The Canadian bishops and the Dutch bishops issued challenging alternative interpretations. In Washington, DC, over fifty priests signed a public statement that said they would leave the matter of birth control to people's individual consciences. The whole debate may have started as a moral issue, but it soon became a battle over which direction authority comes from in the Church—from the pope and bishops down, or from the people in the pews up. Priests were caught in the middle.

Feeling his authority on the line, Cardinal Patrick O'Boyle, the crusty old East Coast defender of the pope, along with Cardinals Krol, Spellman, and Cushing, demanded that his Washington, DC, priests retract their statements or be immediately suspended from their ministry.[8] Shockingly, many of these priests left public ministry, the large majority of them vibrant young guys who had been educated with the new theology of the Second Vatican Council. I began to wonder if this was my future.

Thousands of priests left the ministry during this time and the immediate years thereafter. As well as the teaching that conjugal love and procreation were coequal—though inseparable—goals in marriage, the Vatican Council also taught that the vocations of marriage and religious life were coequal in honor. Before this, the teaching was always that anyone who gave up the right to have a spouse and family to take the vows of religious life was leading a "life of perfection" that marriage didn't quite match. Yes, human sexuality was created by God, and yes sexual intercourse was good—"it is better to marry than to be aflame with passion," wrote St. Paul (1 Cor 7:9)—but we had been taught that a life of consecrated celibacy was holier than marriage. Now they were considered coequal.

Priests, who may have thought a promise of celibacy at ordination settled our sexuality issues, now had to wrestle with what our motivations were in making such vows. Most of the canonized saints were celibate. *Yeah sure!* we complained, *but only* after *they gave up a wild life, like Saints Ignatius, Francis, and Augustine did!* Making marriage equal in honor to religious life gave many young priests just the impetus they needed to leave the priesthood and get married. Now, more than fifty years later, the priesthood has yet to recover from this exodus, mostly of heterosexual priests. In 1968, gay priests hadn't even been heard of yet.[9]

I sat on the front steps of St. Nicholas Church in my black religious habit on a gorgeous July afternoon. Covering "house duty" meant being ready to jump and answer the phone if someone called with an emergency. Enjoying the warmth of the sun on my face, I was only slightly aware of how odd a priest hanging out on the church steps may look. I got to chat with kids walking past, a young priest who seemed to talk their language. I figured it was worth Potsy Kenny's wrath to get a friendly nod from someone passing by, even be asked questions about the Church by someone who hadn't been to confession in twenty years.

I was reading the *National Catholic Reporter*, a liberal-thinking monthly Catholic newspaper out of Kansas City.[10] A full-page spread on the birth control debate caught my eye. At the center of the debate was Fr. Charles Curran, one of the brightest and best teachers I ever had, Charlie always carefully traced for us the historical turns of moral doctrines that the Church taught, especially its sexual teachings. Despite the Vatican mantra "the Church has *always* taught this," we had learned that all of our teachings had evolved through history, influenced by scientific discoveries and human questioning. "As theologians, you should carry a Bible under one arm and a *New York Times* under the other," Charlie used to implore us. Even though I had resisted this historical consciousness, it felt like history was being made all around me.

I wanted to be a part of this. In a burst of affection for my teacher, I had sent Charles Curran a postcard a few weeks before. "I agree with you on human life," I had scribbled to him. Absent-mindedly, I now began to gaze down through the list of names under the banner headline: "Theologians Differ with Pope on Encyclical." State by state, listed in small print, it covered a whole page. With growing emotion, I scanned the list, searching for people I might know. Under the state of Florida, where I was headed in August to teach at Biscayne College, there was only one name.... It was mine.

18

"You're Screwed!"

August 1968, Miami, Florida—

I arrived at Biscayne College, reeling along with the rest of the country from the assassinations of Martin Luther King Jr. and Bobby Kennedy earlier that year. Many cities had been set on fire; street intersections manned by the US Army; machine guns set up on the steps of the Capitol. When I walked down toward the center of Washington, DC, in my Roman collar to see if I could be of help, a Black guy leaned out of his car window and shouted, "What are you doing down here, whitey?" It was not an ordinary time to be setting out on your first major priestly assignment.

The president of Biscayne, Fr. Ralph Schuler, and I were on opposite sides of the division in the country and the Church. Schuler was a traditionalist canon lawyer while I easily identified with the "new breed" of Vatican II priests. We each disdained what the other stood for, and we both knew it.

When we met for the first time at his office, I noticed the *National Catholic Reporter*, with its list of errant priests, spread open on his big glass desk. "What does this mean?" His stubby manicured finger pointed at the offending page. "Well?" He waited.

My classmates, who had been forced to take sexuality courses from this droll medieval guy at Augustinian College before they mercifully kicked him upstairs to this job at Biscayne, would laugh if they could see this scene. Beneath his hooded eyelids, I sensed fear as well as anger, fear my free spirit sometimes stirred in others. *Is there no way we can coexist?*

There wasn't. Within the year, I was transferred to our college in Massachusetts. "They need you at Merrimack," our personnel director told me over the phone. I knew that was just a cover, that Schuler was the problem.

"You should get rid of him, Bob," I blurted out, "everyone hates him." But that is not the way it works. They don't get rid of presidents.

When I broke the news to the students after Mass on a Sunday in May, they were ready to fight. Young bravado. I was touched. Regardless, I knew the decision wouldn't be changed. I had to cut my losses and move on. Someone else could take my place. I was learning.

Father Mike, my friend and fellow classmate, who had started with me at Biscayne, strummed his guitar and led the students in song at the liturgy before I left. "How does it feel, to be on your own?..." I began to choke up, but if I began to cry, maybe I wouldn't be able to stop. "...Like a complete unknown, with no direction home?"

Closing my eyes, images of Celt came to mind, and further back, of Irene and my family. My bond with the religious brotherhood had been stronger than my love for any of them. But was it now? I went back to my room and began to pack my belongings. The last thing I crammed into my suitcase was my religious habit.

September 1969, North Andover, Massachusetts—

It was late afternoon, and I was lying on a lawn near the tennis courts. Since the students wouldn't be arriving for a few days, the campus was eerily quiet. Scheduled to teach the Old Testament course to three freshman classes, I would also be serving as a prefect and living in the boys' dorm along with other young priests.

Exploding social issues that year dwarfed even the Church battle over *Humanae Vitae*. Earlier that summer, America had landed the first man on the moon. *Anything we set our minds to we can do*. The Woodstock Festival and its theme of "free love" were emblazoned on young people's brains. At the same time, Nixon and Kissinger were escalating the war in Vietnam even while they denied it. A lottery was being set in place to draft kids by their birth dates. The war had invaded the campuses.

A major national conflict over the role of authority was emerging on every level of society. Particularly in academia, it played itself out in everything from debates about core course requirements to who sits on the board of trustees. Fearsome things seemed to attract me. For me, fear was the doorway to freedom. Every time I had faced fear in my life, it had built up my courage. Why stop now?

I was gradually beginning to accept myself as a gay person as well, even though I couldn't talk to anyone about it. This identity seemed to be at the root of my fears and my need to face them. I wasn't supposed to be myself in society or the Church. My anger at this abuse of authority was looking for a release.

I didn't know then that the Stonewall Revolution had already begun, that drag queens and queers had fought back at the police raids of their bars in Greenwich Village that June, building the Gay Liberation Movement. I didn't take a stand with gay people. I was too afraid then of any public connections to my deeper feelings. I was a celibate priest. What did gay rights have to do with me?

But supporting *Humanae Vitae* was really the same issue—sexuality. To stand up for the right of heterosexual married Catholics to use artificial means of contraception[11]—even in private—was risky enough for a new priest, but at least it was "normal." Yet in the Roman Catholic Church, all sexual teachings depended on each of the others. The Church leadership feared that if one teaching changed, everything, even the pope's authority, would come tumbling down. The bishops would do anything to prevent that. *I'll have to choose sides between the faculty and the students. It can't be both.* Laughing teenage voices bounced merrily across the lawn. *I'm only twenty-nine, barely ten years older than most of them, even though I'm their teacher.* Sitting up, I looked for a clue for the right direction to go. "The students," I shouted to the wind, "I'll stick with the students!"

Life is full of choices, decisions that affect us for the rest of our lives. If we ever saw the consequences, we would probably run screaming in the opposite direction. Yet, even if we don't choose, we have still made a choice. We take one path with whatever savvy we have and forge ahead. Life is short. It keeps moving through us like sand through an hourglass. All our later choices build on the ones we make now. Day by day, we build our identities and write our histories. No one can make the decisions for us.

May 1972, North Andover, Massachusetts—

I stayed at Merrimack for three years. With another professor, Peter Ford of the History Department, I started a draft-counseling center. We showed students and guys from the local towns how to apply for conscientious objector status if they wished.[12] With some radical students, I formed a group called Concerned Students for Social Change. One day, we wheeled a movie projector into the student cafeteria and beamed onto the walls a film of the atomic bombing of Hiroshima. The Marine recruiter watched with a stony face. He was there to sign kids up for Vietnam.

This all sounds so bizarre when I think of it now, but by 1970, there were already forty thousand dead American soldiers from the war, not to mention a million Vietnamese. Beginning in October, "moratoriums" were staged across the country on the fifteenth of every month to bring the country to a halt until the war was stopped. With groups of students, I went to these demonstrations, running down alleys behind Harvard Square in my priest collar while holding a coed's hand as we tried to escape the tear gas.

A civil war was going on in the country over the war. You had to choose. Most of the priests at Merrimack were pro-war. When a Spanish Augustinian hissed "Communist!" across the dinner table at me one night, I thought of my brother Joe who had been drafted earlier that year and was somewhere in the swamps of Cambodia. When Joe wrote that he and his soldier buddies had painted "Make love, not war" on their helmets, I began to write him everything. His letters back to me deepened my feelings that the war was all wrong.

Since I was assigned to teach Old Testament, the Jewish Scriptures, I wanted to bring it alive for my students on its own terms, not just as a forerunner of Christianity. I wanted it to say something about our country's present turmoil.

Browsing through a bookstore in downtown Boston, my eyes jumped hungrily on a text, *You Shall Be as Gods: A Radical Interpretation of the Old Testament and Its Tradition* by Erich Fromm.[13] It seemed to be just what I was looking for. "The Old Testament is a revolutionary book," read its introduction; "its theme is the liberation of man from the incestuous ties to blood and soil, to the submission to idols, from slavery, from powerful masters, to freedom for the individual, for the nation, and for all mankind."[14] Yes, I thought, and from a Church that stifles our exhilarating call to freedom, that hides us in our habits from fear of our God-given human passions.

Wow! This was terrific stuff. Every morning at 8:30 a.m., I encouraged my thirty fresh-faced eighteen-year-old students to reflect on this revolutionary step described so excitingly by Fromm:

> The Christian interpretation of the story of man's act of disobedience as his "fall" has obscured the clear meaning of the story. The biblical text does not even mention the word "sin"; man challenges the supreme power of God, and he is able to challenge it because he is potentially God. Man's first act is rebellion, and God punishes him...because God wants to preserve his supremacy...
>
> Man has to yield to God's superior force, but he does not express regret or repentance. Having been expelled from the Garden of Eden, he begins his independent life; his first act of disobedience is the beginning of human history, because it is the beginning of human freedom.[15]

So, what I had grown up calling "original sin"[16] was, in Fromm's view, humanity's first step for freedom. In a demonstration that fall, I breathed in the euphoria of the banners and shouts, the sheer energy of this roiling sea of humanity—men, women, children on their parents' backs or pushed in strollers. Everyone could march for peace. Only when I saw the pink-and-white banners of the Gay Liberation Front did I shrink and wonder: Why do they have to make a spectacle? Don't they know they'll give ammunition to the pro-war people? I could see the next day's headline in the *Boston Globe*: "Gays March in Peace Protest!" *Damn!*

Still, the war went on. Daily massive bombing of North Vietnam continued for months. Two Catholic priests, the Berrigan brothers, broke into a selective service center in Catonsville, Maryland, and destroyed government records.[17] They poured their own blood over them to protest the killing. "In the name of Christ," they said. For months afterward, they hid in the homes of Catholic protesters as the FBI searched for them, and Cardinal Spellman, the Archbishop of New York and Chief Military Chaplain of the US Armed Forces railed from his pulpit about this abuse of government property. The Church and the country were splitting apart at the seams.

In Vietnam, Buddhist monks began to set themselves on fire outside their pagodas as a protest. A young peace activist, a friend of the Berrigans, did the same in New York City. People were horrified at such desperation. Still, the war and the bombing and the deaths went on.

"Peace with Honor," kept insisting President Nixon. "There can be no peace through violence," countered the demonstrators—Yippies, Black Panthers, and other "radicals." This stalemate might have gone on forever if the war had not reached into middle-class homes. The government's draft lottery and the protests hit the campuses and the country big time. Now you had to vote with your flesh and blood. The ones whose birthdays were called first would be the next ones to go and fight for "Peace with Honor."

"Faddah Paul! Faddah Paul!" I heard the pounding on my dorm door. It was after 2:00 a.m. I shook the sleep away. I had been waiting for this moment. My students needed me.

"Hey, Padre! Where ya been?" It was Ted and Liam, two guys from my religious studies class. Wild-eyed, they stumbled into the room. Liam's chubby baby face was flushed. Had he been crying? Ted, a tough guy from South Boston, had often regaled us with stories about fights he'd had. I couldn't imagine being involved in such physical brutality, but I felt a masculine bond when Ted shared his street life with me.

"You said we'd have choices, Padre," Ted blurted out. "I'm gonna be a soldier! Now, whaddaya think of that?"

They had been drafted. A father's heart stirred in me. *Oh man, I'll protect you. I won't let them hurt you!* I made some coffee in big mugs. In a while, they calmed down and were making sick jokes about the "gooks" they'd soon be fighting in 'Nam.

"I wanna talk to you when I get some sleep on this, Padre," said Ted as they left a while later. "My call-up date's in a month." He leaned into my shoulder as he shook my hand. "Me too," echoed Liam. "Thanks for being here." We hugged too.

The special moment of closeness had passed. I watched them shuffle down the corridor. Just kids. *My* kids. Their plight got to me.

The Church kept praying for peace, yet still the bombing and killing continued. Sure, the bishops said that Catholics could be selective conscientious objectors, but the government wouldn't buy that. You had to be against *all* wars to be a CO. Most of my students didn't have the spiritual savvy to come to that decision anyway. What should they do? Refuse and go to jail? Escape to Canada? What would I do? I fell asleep picturing one of them or my brother Joe coming home in a body bag. I imagined myself lying in a coffin in my habit. *Lord, help me do something while I can.*

At the end of the 1972 school year, I left Merrimack College. They said I didn't have a doctoral degree to teach theology. My department chair didn't either, but that didn't matter. I was brokenhearted, but I didn't have the strength to fight it anymore. I had lasted three tumultuous years, the best years of my life until then, because I had been the most real.

It felt like I was being kicked out of the Garden of Eden, but Erich Fromm's words about Adam's choice gave me hope: "It was the beginning of human history, mankind's first step toward freedom." Actually, my Augustinian community was glad to let me study nonviolence with the Quakers at a place called the Life Center in Philadelphia. As I drove onto the Massachusetts Turnpike with all my belongings in a U-Haul, I remembered Ted's last words to me before he left for Vietnam: "You're gonna get fucked, Father Paul, but keep it up."

19

The Quaker Life Center

Autumn, 1973, Philadelphia, Pennsylvania—

Why didn't I give up the priesthood and religious life when I left Merrimack? On some level, I sensed that living out the gospel as a priest and religious would lead me, like Jesus, into conflict with authorities. I wanted to live and study for a time with people who seemed to have a stronger calling than even my fellow priests and Augustinians. I wanted to be rejuvenated by a common belief rather than always being seen as a renegade.

Leaving the priesthood and the Augustinian brotherhood isn't just like leaving a job. Your friends and family might feel that you have failed. "You are a priest forever," the bishop proclaims during ordination. Forever. Like marriage. Not just when you feel good about it, not just when everyone loves you, but even when you're struggling and feel tempted to quit. You don't. You can't. You won't. You would die rather than do this.

Ordination changes you "ontologically," in that you are another Christ now. With your whole being you have accepted responsibility for everyone, not just yourself. Priesthood becomes your identity and once you have accepted this, there is no other way to live. But, what about my internal conflicts? Wasn't I aware that my sexual orientation would fuel problems wherever I went? Did it never occur to me that I might need therapy? Well, no. My Irish Catholic family and my Augustinian community didn't think therapy was normal. Only crazy people went to shrinks. My soul belonged to God. I wasn't ready for that yet.

After being ordained for a while, a priest might have a doubt about his vocation and be allowed to live apart for a period of discernment called a "leave of absence." To see if you could commit for the long haul, you would work at a regular job and live a normal life for a year or two. Many guys on a leave of absence used the time to question their vows by dating, saving money, and seeing if they could live on their own. Many eventually left; some got married. So, instead of formally leaving the priesthood, I got permission to leave the structure: of living with fellow religious priests, of wearing a Roman collar or habit, of teaching at a Catholic college, and of being called "Father."

After I left Merrimack, I lived at the Life Center, an organization of households, communes, in West Philadelphia devoted to promoting peace and nonviolence on all levels, internationally and nationally, in community decision-making and interpersonal dynamics. Oh, and especially regarding environmental concerns, down to what we ate.

The Life Center was founded during the Vietnam War by Quakers and was an extension of their retreat and study center at Pendel Hill near Philadelphia. By the time I arrived in 1972, the Life Center comprised ten mixed communities of men and women. I lived with seven others at the Stone House, a rambling three-story house that was our headquarters, on 43rd and Spruce Streets.

Our diet was vegetarian. Not only was this healthier, but according to the articles we read in the "macroanalysis seminars" that we attended once a week, a meat diet required an enormous amount of grain for the cows, a tremendous waste of protein. Instead, this grain protein could be used to feed droves of people in the Third World who would otherwise starve.

Amazingly, these meals cost us about a dollar a day per person. We had combinations of grains I had never heard of before—lentils, bulgur, wheat germ, tofu, homemade "stone-ground" whole wheat bread—as well as vegetables of all kinds, yogurt, honey, fresh cider, dates, pomegranates, nuts, and seeds. Most of these were purchased at a local co-op where the members of the Life Center traded time at the register and as shelf-stockers in exchange for cheaper prices. I was thrilled to be part of this grass-roots movement that was going to change the world.

On my first night cooking for everyone, I almost freaked out. So, I called my mother. "Mama, it's Paul. I'm cooking dinner here tonight for eight of us and I'm going nuts!"

"Oh Paul, how good to hear from you. What's the problem?" I missed her.

"Mama, this is what you've been doing all these years!" We laughed, but I could tell my latest adventure concerned her. "I just wanted to say thanks for all those meals you cooked for us. And say *hi* to Daddy for me, will you?"

"Thanks, Paul. I really enjoy it when you call. Come in any-time for a visit, even at the last minute. I'm having roast pork, potatoes, and lima beans this Sunday." I was off meat now. "Okay, Mama. Bye."

When my provincial, Harry Cassel, came for a visit to check on me, I prepared lentil soup for dinner. I'd learned that lentils, brown rice, and a big salad made a hearty, well-balanced meal.

"Lentil soup, Paul? It's good. And nutritious, too, I bet." He grinned, and I thought of the roast beef or chicken cordon bleu they'd be serving back at the Villanova monastery.

One late summer morning, after I'd been at the Stone House for a week, I was thinking of my fellow priests and brothers. My door was open to catch a breeze, and I saw my housemate Blair's pink and white breasts as she sauntered stark naked to the common bathroom. *Ohmygod!* But why not? I brushed off my prudery. *But how can I explain this to my Augustinian brothers?*

The Life Center was an interfaith community, open to people of all faiths as long as they practiced nonviolence. Its emphasis on community and simplicity was what our Augustinian brotherhood was sworn to, but the Quakers did it even better. They believed that each person is a Light of God who speaks to them in the deepest silence of their hearts. The inviolability of each person's conscience was a core tenet, so all decisions were made by consensus. Only if every person supported a plan did it go forward. I imagined my church trying this. Maybe we could make up sexual rules by consensus. Ha!

I hoped I could learn to feel comfortable with my sexual orientation in the Life Center here, far from the Church's black-and-white thinking about sex and homosexuality. With the Quakers,

I figured I would be less locked in by peoples' expectations of a priest. So much of our Roman Catholic identity focused on sex: from the Virgin Birth of Jesus to the rule against artificial birth control, from insisting on a celibate priesthood to our not-too-subtle discrimination against women. In contrast, the Quaker identity seemed to value ecology and equality issues. I needed this balance.

The people at the Life Center used the barter system to pay for skills. Constantly, I had to rethink basic suppositions. There were bricks in the toilet tanks to save water. Thermostats were turned down. Everything was recycled. I joked that our compost pile had become a religious shrine to our reverence for the earth. And when I looked out my window at night to pray, I could hear rats genuflecting before the altar.

Childcare for the kids living with us was a communal responsibility, even if you didn't have children. There were about twenty kids, from age one-and-a-half to seventeen. During an evening discussion, when we were preparing for an antiwar demonstration near Fort Dix, Judy, a nurse in her late twenties, chaired the meeting in a long denim skirt and peasant blouse. Her boyfriend, Toby, in jeans and sandals, lolled next to her, admiring her presentation. "It's important for everyone to take a turn caring for the children," Judy explained. "This way the parents can participate in the demonstration."

I surveyed the room of twenty-five people of all ages. Quite a few married pairs, and some couples like Judy and Toby. Others were unattached, like me, and Sandra and Gerry, single moms with a few kids each. Busily, they signed the childcare sheet. A question stirred in my mind. I love kids, but I didn't have any of my own, and I'd paid my babysitting dues long ago. I raised my hand.

"Some of us don't have children," I began tentatively. "Some of us might even be celibate"—heads swiveled; I hadn't mentioned celibacy before—"...to free us up to do things we couldn't do if we had a family. You know, like traveling at a moment's notice, or"—(I threw in the Quaker "sacrament" for a punch line)—"being arrested."

Silence.

I felt myself on a roll. Judy and Toby's closeness stirred up my own need for a companion. "If the married members feel it is important to share the care of their children with us," I paused for effect, "I wonder if they are open to share the intimacy of their marriage relationship with us?"

Even the egalitarian Quakers dropped their jaws. I kept a straight face.

"I mean, the one goes with the other, doesn't it?" When I smiled, they got the joke and the place exploded with laughter. "I'm kidding, I'm kidding," I protested. Well, not completely. In ways like this, I kept chipping away at the barrier my Catholicism and the priesthood represented to them. After a few of these discussions, we could talk about anything.

Everything was up for discussion: our diet, sexuality, gender roles. I had never encountered the feminist energy that I found in the Life Center. Even back at home, my nine sisters didn't seem to ask for much, except the right to grab the bathroom first.

The women's movement hit me at the Life Center when I encountered Millie, a slim, young blonde who moved into one of the houses. She was particularly adamant about language. Every time a guy said "he" and meant men and women, she would correct us. With a bored look, she'd add, "And she?" It was annoying. *What do you think, we're a bunch of dummies?* I tried to avoid her and bonded with the men.

20

Bundling Brothers

Winter, 1973, Philadelphia, Pennsylvania—

The Bundling Brothers Collective of the Life Center comprised about a dozen men, "straight, gay, bisexual, and everything in between," one of them told me, as he blinked. The collective was intent on breaking down the sex-role stereotypes that men grow up with in our society.

"These roles leave us wounded emotionally and out of touch with our feelings," George Lakey,[18] the married and bisexual leader of the group, explained at my first meeting. Around me, members bundled up close together underneath quilts and afghans to keep warm on a wintry afternoon. "We hardly realize that we are locked into rigid sexual orientations that make us treat one another as rivals and women as pawns or trophies."

The Bundling Brothers believed that everyone needed at least three full-body hugs a day. If you didn't get these, you hadn't really lived. By full-body hugs, they meant embracing with bodies touching their entire lengths—genitals and all. It was brief and strong, not passionate. Pretty soon the Life Center men could be identified by the way we greeted each other. For sure, Philly was the City of Brotherly—*and yes, Millie, Sisterly*—Love.

This simple gesture began to exorcise in me years of Catholic uptightness about sex and my body. Even so, I still watched the reactions of other people as we hugged. When I visited my family in Upper Darby, I'd babble on about this new expression of human feelings as though I'd just returned from some South Sea island. My parents watched quizzically.

In this men's collective, I began to know Toby more deeply. Judy and he had recently moved in with each other. It was as though their intimacy allowed me to get closer to each of them safely. But it was Toby about whom I fantasized.

Toby was a Native American. As two of the few non-Protestants in the Life Center, he and I hit it off almost immediately. With his olive skin and long tousled black hair, he reminded me of the freedom I associated as a boy with Indians in Western movies. Maybe such a world would have a place for me and my feelings.

Passionate and intelligent, Toby offered opinions on everything from music to politics to religion. He had been raised in New Mexico's Taos Pueblo in the ways of the Native American religion and viewed Christians, especially priests, with suspicion: "Why do your people see Jesus on the cross as a sign of love and forgiveness and at the same time Christians are intolerant of other spiritual ways?" I didn't know how to answer him, but we kept on talking.

With his degree in political science, Toby volunteered with the Southwest Community Enrichment Service, run by a Catholic Charity sister. He helped mostly Black inmates within Graterford State Prison build links to the local community. I soon joined him in this.

Toby and I used to make fun of the group's mission, "Helping Everywhere on All Levels," and smile at the grandiosity of its rehabilitation dreams. "On all levels!" Every Wednesday, Toby and I went up to Graterford with a van of neighborhood people, wives, mothers, and girlfriends of the inmates, who'd get the two of us confused. I didn't mind. It made me feel closer to Toby. I began to dream about a future with him or someone like him.

Strolling home one afternoon, I stopped. I needed someone in the Life Center to know about my sexual orientation. And Toby was gradually becoming my best friend there. I prayed he would understand.

"Toby, did you ever have part of yourself that seemed strange, something that makes you feel different from everybody?"

"Sure. I'm bow-legged. Did you ever notice?" Toby laughed, and I felt a little braver.

The words tumbled out softly, awkwardly, "Toby…Toby, I'm gay." With his head tilted to the side. I waited while my heart raced. *Oh God, is our friendship over? Is that it, after all we've shared? Please.*

"A gay priest?" he asked incredulously. "On all levels, Paul? On *all* levels?" His laugh saved me. The two of us cackled away, falling into each other. *Oh yes! Oh yes, Lord. We can really be friends.*

We made tentative plans for him, Judy, and me to go to a movie that weekend, and we parted with a Bundling Brothers' hug. Wow. Not since I had come out to Celt on New Year's Eve seven years before had I shared my secret with anyone. With a great sigh of relief, I turned toward the Stone House.

21

My Most Honest Moment

Summer, 1973, Philadelphia, Pennsylvania—

On Friday nights, Toby and I would meet at the Shamrock, a working-class bar on Baltimore Avenue, and quaff pitchers of beer along with our pizza. We'd entertain each other with self-dramatized tales of dealing with intellectual WASPs all day long, even if they happened to be Quakers.

My being a priest, and a gay priest at that, intrigued Toby. Even though he was often critical, he was fascinated by all the Roman Catholic symbols, and especially curious about celibacy.

"So, what's it do for you?" he asked.

"It gives me a freedom, Toby. Imagine if you didn't have to be driven by sex all day."

He told me that he hated it if Judy got out of bed first in the morning and left him alone. "I can't imagine it, Paul. I wouldn't *want* to be free from that."

"No?" I challenged his sureness. We thrived on such jousting.

Toby licked foam from his lip. "No! And y'know something, Paul? I think you run away from sex with your promise of celibacy."

It felt like a punch to my heart. "It has more to do with my relationship with God, Toby." He couldn't dent that traditional explanation.

"And a relationship with God doesn't permit sex?" His chest hair peeked above his unbuttoned sports shirt.

I couldn't let him into my God-space yet. "Celibacy doesn't have to be against sex," I countered, "just different from it." Jesus didn't have kids. Maybe that was why he was strange to his own people.

"Different?"

"Yeah, Toby. Different." I was getting ticked. Questions about celibacy began to stir up sensual vibes in me. Our verbal tussle continued, and gradually developed into a different kind of electricity. *Maybe you could pull me out of my sureness tonight, Toby.*

"Yo, Vera!" He ordered another pitcher. "Hey, relax! It's Friday." He touched my arm, and we got mellower.

On the way home, the summer air was thick with lightning bugs and the smell of roses as we bumped into each other. As we passed a house with a thick hedge, I pushed him into it.

"Hey! Cut it out!" He laughed, then turned and shoved me in.

"Hey! I protested." Toby waited in the shadows, his khaki pants hanging low on his hips.

"C'mon Tonto, help the Lone Ranger!" Toby's hand reached for mine, as though we were about to dance.

"Tonto," he murmured.

"Hmm. Remember him?"

"And the Lone Ranger."

"Keemosabie." We walked the rest of the block in silence.

"See ya tomorrow," Toby announced when we got to his house. Judy was away for the weekend. I thought of my lonely bed back in my room. "Keemosabie need a hug," I said into the dark.

The moonlight on Toby's nose cast a shadow. I couldn't read his expression. He glanced up and down the street before he invited me close. "C'mere."

Suddenly, Tonto was hugging me. When I felt his body curve to meet mine, I did the same. "Oh man." His cheek was warm against mine.

"You wanna stay over?" he asked, stepping back.

My mind raced. "But Sandra?" She owned the house and rented it to Toby and Judy.

"I've got a sleeping bag. You can sleep on the living room floor."

Wanting to remain close to him, my heart sank.

"I've got two bags. We can sleep there together if you want."

I searched Toby's eyes in the dark, the whole world opening up. A spruce tree behind him came into view. Perched there like crows, I imagined all my seminary masters squawking their pointy beaks in unison: "Remember the Rule! Remember the Rule!" while in my right ear, my provincial's voice reminded me, "Don't Paul, don't." My legs began to wobble.

In the tall leaves, the crickets chirped. Quaker mantras came to mind like answers for an exam—*Consensus! Follow your Inner Light!—Even if a single person disagrees!—Conscience!* Sighing deeply, I said, "Okay, Toby, I'd like that."

"Good." He grabbed my elbow. A warm feeling rushed over me as we pushed through the broken screen door into his house.

Except for the time with Nick when I was sixteen, never had I been sexual with a man. Never had a man encouraged me in a way that felt nonshaming. Never had I consciously reached out for what I wanted, for what I sensed might heal my shame:

"Let's take our T-shirts off. I want to feel your chest."

"Me too," Toby said.

He found the sleeping bags in a closet and spread them on the living room floor. We gazed at each other in the streetlight. Soon he laid down on one. With my heart thumping, I only paused a second before I joined him.

Laying my head on his lean muscled body, manly but open to my wanting him…The musky smell of him, the chest hairs tickling my nose, his eyes watching me….

Beginning awkwardly to caress him, enjoying the wonder of his body stretched out for me, and all this feeling as normal as apple pie….

The exhilaration of moving with only my feelings guiding me for once, wanting to burst at such masculine beauty right at my fingertips….

The sound of the crickets, our breathing in unison, my body on its own now. "Oh, Lord…oh!" Reduced suddenly to exhaustion, kissing him softly on his chest….

Assuring him as he lay there with his hands behind his head and eyes closed, "I will not possess you." As though he needed to be reassured, reassuring myself instead….

Later, falling asleep under the covers, my back curved against his belly….

Waking up with the sheet twisted around us, eyeing each other with a grin as we heard Sandra coming down the stairs.

Not sure exactly what he and I said as we parted, knowing it wasn't shame that we saw on each other's faces....

Believing that what had happened was all right and didn't need to be forgotten. We would still be friends.

You've just experienced the most honest moment of your life! It couldn't have been just a dream, could it? Not the way Toby had looked at me. "The Blue Danube" waltz played in my head as I floated past St. Francis De Sales Church on a cloud. Morning sunshine bounced off its blue and gold mosaic dome while children's voices from the schoolyard broke through my reverie. In their long blue habits, Immaculate Heart of Mary sisters, the same ones who taught me in grade school, shepherded the students into lines, two by two...The choir of little voices singing, *"O Lord, I am not worthy...The Bridegroom of my Soul...."* Innocence.

I could never go back there now, even if I wanted to. Another voice inside me mocked, *Now, how are you going to fit this together with your life as a priest?* I did feel shaken, shaken together. My body at last in harmony with my soul. Never had I known such a feeling. On one level, I felt guilty, yet I was no longer a stranger to myself. I wanted to scream: *Hey everybody! I am part of the human race now, do you hear? I'll never be the same again!*

I remembered my friend Jimmy's warning at Sikorsky: *Once you start having sex, you'll never be able to stop.* Maybe I won't. I'll speak about it to my spiritual director and confessor. But for once in my life, I've been my truest self with another human being. Even God must want that.

22

Coming Out to Family

Winter, 1974, Upper Darby, Pennsylvania—

My family was going crazy. The youngest child, Joan, always seemed to be in trouble. After her older brothers and sisters had attended St. Alice's Parochial School with first and second honors. Joan, at the caboose of the family train, was reversing the Morrissey reputation.

Being the last of our fourteen siblings, Joan was pampered at first. She also had to fight for her rights, since she was a perfect lightning rod for trouble around the house and the neighborhood, blamed for anything that went wrong at her grammar school. The Immaculate Heart of Mary sisters forgot our worst escapades and continually reminded Joan that she wasn't like the rest of us little saints.

When her seventh-grade class nominated her to play the Blessed Mother during the Christmas pageant, the sister in charge thought it was a joke and asked the class to vote again. "And this time," she warned them, "remember it is for someone who will be a good model for Mary, the Mother of Jesus." The class took her words to heart and voted for Joan a second time. Exasperated at their rebelliousness, the sister had students from the third grade play the roles of the Holy Family instead.

By high school, Joan's intelligence was apparent. With her dark Irish hair and a cameo face, she was always bubbling with young energy. The drug culture of the sixties and the antiwar rebellion of her older siblings egged her on.

Every Wednesday after dinner, I rode my bicycle from the Life Center in West Philadelphia to our family's home in Upper Darby for a meeting about Joan, who was then seventeen. Mama and Daddy were in their early sixties with five children still living at home, which swirled around Joan's latest escapade. As the priest in the family, and with my experience at the Life Center, I led these discussions.

By now, I had become comfortable acknowledging my sexual orientation with a few friends. My housemates took it in stride. During this period, a reporter for the *Different Drummer*, a grassroots newspaper, arrived to do a story on the Life Center commune. Looking back, I don't know what possessed me. Maybe it was an attraction I felt for the wispy-goateed reporter, Jake. Over lunch after the interview, when he asked what brought me to the Life Center, I told him very naturally, "I'm gay, and I wanted to live with people who could handle that." A week later when the interview was published, it referred to "Paul: A Gay Revolutionary Catholic Priest."

"Can you believe it, man?" a friend of mind said. "They've outed you to the whole city!"

I was afraid. "I'm the only Catholic priest at the Life Center! At Villanova, someone will surely show it to one of our priests, and also at St. Joe's, where my two sisters work! Oh God!" It felt like I was going to have a heart attack. Yet a secret corner of my soul was glad. I couldn't hide anymore.

My provincial secretary was kind but wary, and my priest friend, Tim, from Merrimack backed me. "Don't leave, Paul."

As I pedaled home, I whispered a prayer: *A bomb struck my life, Lord. How could you let this happen? Maybe you wanted it to happen. Maybe I did. Now I've got to tell my family before they read about it in the newspapers. Help me, please!*

Our big semidetached house looked a little shabby. The porch windows needed painting. I had too much going on in my own life to acknowledge that my father was getting old. I needed to keep him in my mind as a rock.

Mama, too, looked more world-weary these days. Dark circles under her eyes. Her hair a little mussed, the makeup not so perfect.

Mama went to the foot of the steps to call the rest of them. "Tom! Joan! Kate! Paul's here."

Our family's weekly meetings seemed like poking a splinter from your finger with a butcher knife. Tonight, though, would be different. The "identified patient" wouldn't just be Joan, I thought, as she slouched in from the dining room.

Kate, Peggy, and Pat came down the stairs. My sisters and I hugged each other. Peggy and Pat sat on the sofa next to me. Kate perched primly in a stuffed chair. Leo wandered in, greeted us, and squatted by the door. To my left, Mama sat in her rocking chair. My mouth felt like a blowtorch had blasted it as I tried to practice what to say.

Soon, Daddy came down. He must have just showered because his hair was still damp. Standing, I reached to shake hands. "How are you?" he asked.

"Good, Daddy." Looking at him, I realized I hardly knew my father, even though he had worked his tail off for me, was faithful to Mama for almost forty years, and had given his life for our family. I yearned for his love, this man who scared me by his strength and discipline, who might be ashamed of me forever if I told him the truth about myself. Oh, if only I could've talked to him about this stuff all these years.

I began. "So, how's everyone's week been?" If I didn't speak soon, there'd be no time left. I nervously cleared my throat. "I've got something to bring up tonight..."—the words blurted out quickly—"and it's gonna make Joan's problems look like nothing." A few swiveled their heads.

"Did you ever have something that you knew about yourself...some scary space you wanted to hide, even from those who loved you...something you felt that, if they knew about you, they would run down the street to get away from you?" My voice began to tremble. I looked at my family, my beloved family before things changed. Might they despise me now?

I threw my head back and looked at the ceiling, my voice gaining strength from the pain. "Sometimes I complain to God... 'I'm not weird enough?'" I paused to look back at them. "'I've got to be *gay too?*'" My head dropped back down with my eyes closed. When I opened them, Kate's mouth was hanging open.

"I didn't know, Paul. I didn't know," she said, running to me. "I love you...It doesn't change a thing." She threw her arms around my neck. Quickly, Peggy and Pat did too. Tears of relief welled up in me, but I brushed them away. I needed to see Mama and Daddy's reaction.

Mama was sitting up in her rocker looking stunned but contained. I bit my lip and waited. "Paul, you are our son. We love you no matter what," she said. *No matter what! Oh God, I needed that. Thank you! Thank you!* "And if you are celibate…" she continued, searching for a way to reconcile my statement with the priesthood, "…what difference does it make?" Her words hung in the air like the echo of a bullet.

What? "Love you no matter what…*if* you are celibate?" *You mean there's a catch to your love, Mama?* I couldn't say so then, but a question had been sown. Having needed my mother's special love for so long, I looked for a glitch, something to doubt in her love that would keep my own love for her at arm's length. But it was the Church's glitch, not my mother's.

I turned to my father. "And what about you, Daddy? How do you feel?"

Flustered, he looked to Mama for a clue. Her face, though trembling, held the family center like a cast iron anchor. "The same as Mama, naturally," he said.

Our gazes met, my father's and mine, searching the space between us. Just a living room but a lifetime. Oh Daddy, couldn't you just for once not have let Mama speak for you? I needed you most of all now to say how *you* feel about me. *Your* flesh and blood. *Your* son. *You, Daddy! You! Not Mama!*

Soon, my parents were standing and coming toward me. The girls were chattering like birds in a tree at dawn. Leo lay on the floor with his mouth agape. I stood.

Done! Out now, no matter what! Sick and tired of trying to be something for them, for anyone. Finally, just myself in front of my family. A great sigh of relief whooshed up from my soul.

Suddenly, Joan burst through the others and grabbed me around the neck. As though I had just handed her a ticket out of Alcatraz, she gushed out her heartfelt blessing, "Paul, now you're one of the assholes of the family like me!"

23

"I Don't Get This Gay Thing!"

Spring, 1974, Pennsylvania Turnpike Rest Stop—

After coming out at the family meeting, I phoned some sisters far away and told them. Tommy, Francis, and Joe lived nearby, so we got together Saturday morning at a Howard Johnson's on the Pennsylvania Turnpike.

Joe was twenty-five, home from Vietnam for three years and building houses out in Chester County; Francis was twenty-nine, a hotshot IBM salesman about to marry JoAnn, an Italian girl from South Philly; and Tommy, thirty-four, a gung-ho ex-Marine was married with four kids. I needed to see their faces even if what I saw might lack some brotherly love.

When I pulled into the parking lot, I spotted Tommy leaning against his Jeep, sipping his coffee. No hunting knife on his belt, I noticed. Good. Tommy loved to posture as the biggest, baddest Republican in Pennsylvania. He'd brag, "If any jerk ever harms one of my girls, he'll soon be singing soprano." We figured he was bluffing because, like Daddy, Tommy always teared up at a sad story.

"Hey, what's up?" he yells as he lopes up to the car.

"Fran's already in there, getting us a table. Joe should be here any minute. Did you hear he's got a new motorcycle?"

"No." I pictured Joe, wind blowing through his sandy locks as he sailed around his pad in Newtown Square. When he came home from the war, rattled and gun-spooked, my sister Peggy and I hitchhiked to California with him. Joe claimed he learned to trust again because complete strangers had picked us up. I've felt close to him ever since.

Just then, Joe coasts into the parking lot like Easy Rider.

"Yo!"

"Hey, you hot shot!"

"Brother!" The joy of brotherhood tingled in my skinny chest. We were close. Every spring, the five of us took canoe trips down the Delaware River with any brothers-in-law and nephews who could tolerate our endless family stories. The three of us pounded one another on the back like gorillas and headed into the diner.

After we ordered, I decided to plunge in. "Umm! I needed to talk to you guys because some things have happened."

Tommy kept it light, "Okay, what antiwar protest do you want us to hook up with now?" I shook my head.

Joe threaded our lives together in our ritual. "Hey, do you remember when we had Nixon's face on a dartboard on the third floor?"

"Ha-ha-ha!" laughed Francis. "Or the time Joe laid down in front of the draft board?"

Tommy joined the ritual, "Yeah, Mama and Daddy had to go to court to testify he wasn't a derelict. Ha-ha!"

Underneath the table, my legs jiggled like a racehorse at the gate. I practiced my words. *I've been going through some difficult times. I need your help. There's no other way to tell you this.* It was so important that I didn't sound like a wimp. Joe leaned closer. "So, what's going on, brother?"

I sipped coffee again. "Y'know those kids in the schoolyard we used to make fun of?" I fixed my gaze on the place mat—*Twenty-Nine Flavors of Ice Cream!* "The ones who played with the girls or lisped?"

"Yeah, like this? 'Thay fella!'" Tommy faked a lisp and flopped his wrist. "Ha-ha-ha!"

I gritted my teeth. "Look! You're my brothers. I'm goin' through some incredibly difficult stuff." My voice trailed off. "It could even have me leaving the priesthood." Their faces dropped, and they leaned closer. I could barely spit the words out. "I'm gay."

Stunned looks. Like when Kennedy died. Memories of queer jokes and creeps who may have come on to them. Flashbacks of bathing together when we were boys. How I ran cross-country and dated. And the priesthood hovering over it all. They'd be wondering: How does being gay fit into that?

Months of anxiety rushed out of me. I was enormously relieved just to have said it and show them that I hadn't betrayed the brotherhood. I didn't want to be alone in this. I'm still me. I began to tell them how I had broken it to the family the week before. In the middle of this, our food arrived. Like starving beasts, the four of us dove into the plates. "Yummy!" We chomped away, unsure what to feel or say. It could've been a Sunday meal when we were all at home as boys.

"But Paul," Joe said, "I know some homosexuals, and you're not like them." Concern riveted his face. "Somehow you are more than that to me."

"Like *them*?" He meant something loving, but I burst out anyway. "It's not *them*! It's individual people like me."

Francis asked, "How long have you known? I never suspected."

Like a prisoner in the witness box, I tried to answer all their questions. Tommy, silent so far, kept stabbing his eggs and stuffing hash into his mouth. I remembered an old joke of his: *Did you hear the one about the faggot and the cop?* "What about you, Tommy?" I asked in fear. More silence. I held my breath. He was the one we'd all been measuring ourselves against since childhood.

Tommy's eyelids were closed, then flipped open: "You-mean-you-like-to-*suck*...?" His unfinished sentence hung between us like a gunshot. We all laughed nervously, even me.

I checked around the room to see if we could be overheard, then shot back, "Tommy, is that what *your* love life is about? If someone says they are gay, why is it that people immediately have them in bed with someone?" I was on a roll now, the adrenaline pumping from some deep well of pain. "Y'know, being gay is about a lot more than sex—just like being straight is." Maybe it was his way of asking if I was sexually active. "Tommy, how do you know so much about it?"

More nervous laughter. More checking around the room. "Hey, keep your voice down," Francis whispered.

"I'm just kidding," said Tommy, as his voice grew softer. He was doing mental gyrations as he swigged some water.

"So, what's it like for you?" asked Joe. "What's going on that we can help you with?" He was trying to smile.

Should I get into it? Oh God, why not? "I've had some sexual activity…not much, but with a friend." Swiveled heads checked out each other's reactions, then turned back to me.

"But that's not the main thing. It's about what I *do* with these attractions, do you understand?" I heard my voice rising from its whisper. "Do I just hide them? Hate them? Find some way to channel this energy for God as I promised? As a priest, I want to be celibate. Yet I know these feelings are part of me." I paused. "And no matter what the Church says, I know they are good."

"Whatever you decide to do, you've got my support," said Joe.

Francis glanced at Tommy, before adding, "Mine too, but I'm worried what could happen to you in the Church. It's so against gay people…against sex even."

Tommy shifted in his seat. "I don't get this gay thing." Red splotches appeared on his cheekbones. "I never could figure out why two guys would want to get it on with each other."

My heart began to sink. *If only I could describe it. The whole array of feelings. It's not so different,* I wanted to say. "I've been reading this book called *The Church and the Homosexual.*" I offered. "It shows how all the scriptural statements about homosexuality are not what we think. Back then, they thought everyone was heterosexual, so it was against *their* nature to be involved homosexually. But, it would be against a gay person's nature to be involved heterosexually."[19] I could see the brothers chewing on that.

"Tommy…" Joe interrupted.

"Wait! Let me finish." Tommy's hand flew up. "I may not get it, but you're my brother, right?" Grinning like some demon, he patted his hip where he usually carried his hunting knife. "If any of these assholes in the Church make any trouble for you, I'll cut their fuckin' balls off!" A moment of shock before the four of us broke up.

Oh Tommy! You crazy man! You asshole! I love you! For once in my life, I was grateful for Tommy's macho soldier stuff.

"C'mon! Let's get out of here," he barked, suddenly standing. Each of them gave me a bear hug as we parted.

24

Breaking from My Mother

Autumn, 1974, Upper Darby, Pennsylvania—

Six months after I came out to my family, I called Bishop McShane, the pastor of St. Alice's. I wanted to celebrate a Christmas Mass at my home parish. Home for a visit, I called him on the family phone. Mama was sitting in the living room—unusual for her, a perpetual motion machine.

As I made the call, I reflected on how our family—and others like us—*was* the parish. It was as though the original religious dynamics of our family life, like the rosary after dinner, had now stretched out to include others. The priests and sisters, the liturgies, as well as the city block of church buildings across the street from us, provided the religious structure that held our family life together. The church was the place where we had celebrated fourteen baptisms as well as our parents' and sisters' marriages and grandparents' funerals.

A church—a parish—isn't just a building or the religious hierarchy who serve there.[20] The Second Vatican Council taught that the Church is primarily "the People of God." It is this very history of human lives, all mixed together in grace and struggle, that the priest offers up to God when he celebrates Mass. When the consecrated host is held up, Catholics believe the priest is lifting the Body and Blood of Jesus to God, the Father. When the congregation says Amen to this, they are saying yes to Jesus's sacrifice, and to all the pain, joy, spirituality, and sexuality in their own lives, which Jesus came to redeem.

"Hello. This is Bishop McShane." *A stern voice.* I knew him as a warm enough man, but I never felt quite at home around the hierarchy.

"Hello, Bishop McShane. This is Paul Morrissey...the Augustinian."

"Yes, Paul. What can I do for you?" *An aloofness...?*

"Um...Bishop, I wondered if I could help you out sometime over the holidays...perhaps celebrate a Mass on Christmas." My heart skipped faster. *A long pause.*

"There is, uh....a problem," he said. I could feel him searching for words. I turned away from Mama in the living room and faced a mirror. Had he already assigned the Masses for Christmas? Heck, I could do it a week later. I wanted my family to see me on the altar as a priest now.

"A problem?" I asked.

"Yes. It's about...ah..." *What's he talking about? He can't even get it out.* Suddenly, I noticed Mama's reflection through the mirror. It was like she had seen a ghost. As though a grenade had been tossed, it suddenly crashed in on me: *You told him, Mama! How could you?* I watched as her face flashed with terror. Whirling around from the mirror to her, my eyes flung daggers. *You betrayed me, you, you!*

"Bishop, are you talking about...homosexuality?"

Whoosh. He exhaled. "Yes."

At that moment, it felt like my life crashed through the floor. The coldest fury I ever knew seized my heart. Glaring in disgust at my Judas mother, I turned my back on her and said, "Bishop, I don't think we should talk about this on the phone. May I come over and talk with you in person?"

"Of course."

"How about next week?" My voice was hollow as an old drum.

"That would be fine." I could hear his sigh of relief. Now, our discussion about this would be on his turf, behind his desk, behind his real feelings.

"I'll call your secretary and make an appointment."

"Good." Click.

Replacing the phone back to its cradle, I paused and exhaled. Turning slowly, I roared like a lion into the living room. Mama gripped her chair arms with horror and a steely resolve. Hovering over her with my fists clenched, rage spurted through my clenched teeth, "You told him! How could you?"

"I had to talk to someone, Paul. There was no one else." *Please, please understand*, her eyes pleaded.

"That *jerk!*" I stormed around the room, imagining how the bishop would now use that information against me.

"I never thought he would use something that I told him in confidence."

"You never thought!" I whirled on her. "Mama, if you ever go behind my back to try to run my life again, I'll…I'll…" Blindly, I slashed out at an umbilical cord I had never had the courage before to cut. I groped to come up with something that would devastate her. "I'll…leave the priesthood! Do you hear me?"

Instantly, remorse rushed to her face. "Yes…I'm sorry…I'm so sorry, Paul." Unable to say another word, I shook my head in silence. Having threatened her with the worst I could imagine—for her? for me?—I didn't know. I had never spoken to my mother, my lifeblood, like that, nor had I ever made a link between my choice to become a priest and what she might desire for me.

When I had calmed down, I went out for a walk. Tears welled up in my eyes, and I realized that I was cutting myself free from more than my mother. But what? The umbilical cord of Mother Church! The claustrophobia…being treated like a child…the rules being more important than being myself!

Returning later, I heard pots banging in the kitchen. Mama was peeling potatoes as I walked up behind her. She gave me the wary look people give to dogs when they've been bitten.

"I'm sorry for the outburst," I offered, staring at the floor.

As I reached to give her a hug, she whispered, "No, you're not."

Later that night, it occurred to me that I wasn't sorry for my feelings, just the rough way I had blurted them out. No, not even that. I wasn't sorry at all. Something was irrevocably different between us now. I needed this distance. If I hadn't been so cruel, I would never have gained my freedom.

When I eventually met with the bishop, he informed me that he didn't think it would be wise for me to celebrate Mass at the parish anymore. His manicured hands were folded in repose on the wide mahogany desk. "Your sisters and brothers have friends," he said. "They would think it a mockery if you…a homosexual… were to preside at the liturgy."

I hadn't thought of that possibility yet and tried to reassure him: "But my sisters and brothers will keep it to themselves." He waited for reality to dawn on me. *If your mother needed to talk…?*

But I knew Leo and Joan's teenage crowd. I went to their parties, had celebrated Mass for them in Grogan's garage because otherwise they wouldn't go to Mass. "But even if they do tell others," I shifted my argument, "don't you think it would be a chance for the Church to educate them?"

He shook his head slowly. It was like I had suggested educating chimpanzees. Sorrow and anger surged in my chest. But again, I did as I always do, remembering Jesus and the hope He gives me. A memory of Christmas past sparked into a bubble of joy:

> Fall on your knees, oh hear the angels singing:
> Oh, night divine, oh night, when Christ was born…

Serenity came over me as we stood and shook hands. I turned briefly to look backward at him from the doorway before leaving.

A month later, the phone rang at the Stone House while I was preparing dinner. "Is Father Morrissey there? My name is Chris Debellis. I belong to a group of Catholics called the Home Liturgy Group.[21] We were wondering if you'd be willing to celebrate Mass for us some Sunday evening."

A home liturgy. I had done that before. It brought the Eucharist down to the participants, helping them understand the original Hebrew meal setting for the Mass. "How did you get my name?" I asked.

Silence. "I read the article in the *Drummer*." More silence. "We're a group of gay Catholics."

Gulp! When fear stirred in my bones in recent years, I had begun taking it as a sign that God was inviting me to embrace my fear rather than just push it away. "Tell me a little more about the group, will you? How many are in it? How long have you been meeting? Do other priests celebrate Mass with you?" Chris breezily informed me about the group. Sometimes they had to celebrate Mass using a TV as the altar; sometimes Episcopalians attended. It didn't matter.

I heard myself saying, "Chris, I'd be glad to celebrate Mass with the Home Liturgy Group." I wasn't alone anymore—*Yay!*

This was Frank Rizzo time in Philly, the mayor who reveled in sending mounted police against people who disagreed with him. A gay rights bill was being debated in the Philadelphia City Council that spring.[22] Emboldened by Black Americans fighting for their rights, gay and lesbian people had begun organizing. Chris DeBellis, along with a young Catholic lesbian named Barbie Grant, and I went down to hear the debate. To show that a part of the Church stood with them, I wore my short-sleeved black shirt with the Roman collar.

All sorts of constituencies were represented. Up front were Evangelical Protestant groups, huffing and puffing, "in the name of God," against approving in any way "perverts and child molesters who are out to destroy society and the family." Equally adamant was a group of gay people, including a few intimidating lesbians. They were part of the gay community with which I was beginning to identify.

TV cameras rolled in to cover the statements by the Black Evangelical preacher, along with a female member of the ACLU and the president of the Gay Activists' Alliance, who wore his leather pants. Then, a gray-haired monsignor from the archdiocese rose to speak. "The Roman Catholic Church teaches that we should all strive to love one another as the Lord taught us....Of course, homosexual people must be treated with all due respect, but we must love the sinner and hate the sin....For the sake of our families and the good of society, our Church stands against this bill that would blur the lines of what our citizens need to hold as moral and ethical behavior." He nodded to the camera and returned to his seat. *Is that what you stand for, Lord?*

George Schwartz, the white-haired chairman of the council, rose in his place at the front of the crowded chamber. Since he was a Jew and a Democrat, we were counting on Schwartz to be sympathetic to the bill. "Thank you, ladies and gentlemen. We are grateful for your heartfelt and often conflicting feelings on this very important bill that will affect the lives of so many disenfranchised people of our city..." Barbie and Chris and I turned to grin at each other.

"I know that many of you are worried at what effect the homos will have..."

"WHAT?" Like gored tigers, a row of gay people jumped to their feet. "WHAT DID YOU SAY!?"

Schwartz dropped his glasses.

"You called us homos!"

Schwartz tried to backpedal fast. "I...I didn't say that...what I meant was..."

Homos! That hateful word used to shove human beings into a sick box. A lifetime of self-contempt transformed into a boiling, challenging rage. *"Yes, you did!"* we shouted.

Pandemonium broke out.

Schwartz pounded his wooden hammer, "Order! Order!"

The monsignor nailed me to the bench with his red eyes. What did I care? My true self was being born, and it felt like a breath of springtime.

The next day, I typed a letter to the editor of the weekly archdiocesan newspaper, *The Catholic Standard and Times*, in support of the gay rights bill. The Bible quote from Deuteronomy "Choose life!" ran through my head.

Bicycling down to the archdiocesan headquarters, excitement pumped through my legs. *Oh David, you must have felt this way when you headed out to meet Goliath!* When I handed the letter to Archbishop Foley's secretary with a smile and a thumping heart, I knew I had passed a point of no return. After praying about it, I had risen at dawn and signed the letter, "Sincerely, Paul F. Morrissey, OSA, a gay Catholic priest."

Part III
WITH

My grace is sufficient for you,
for my power is made perfect in weakness.
(2 Cor 12:9)

25

My Provincial and the Chancery

Autumn, 1974, Philadelphia, Pennsylvania—

"The archdiocese isn't going to publish your letter in support of gay rights, Paul—to protect you," my provincial, Harry Cassel, assured me. He had summoned me to the Augustinian headquarters so that we could prepare for a meeting that the chancellor of the archdiocese had requested regarding my letter. Earlier, he had seemed okay with my coming out in the *Drummer* article, though he may have been confronted with a few nasty comments in the monastery afterward. This was worse, though. Now it was in the cardinal's lap.

I was comfortable with Harry. In his late fifties and my former speech teacher at Monsignor Bonner High School, he was one of a few authority figures with whom I felt comfortable. Ever since LBJ and Nixon had lied about Vietnam, and Pope Paul VI had reversed the recommendation of the Birth Control Commission, it was hard to trust these people. It was as though they mainly acted to keep their own power at all costs, even though they often masked their intentions with nice words about doing things for the good of the people.

More than fifty thousand American soldiers and a million Vietnamese had been killed "for the good of the people." And thousands of priests had been forced out of the Church after Vatican

II; they could no longer put up with the duplicity between what the bishops and the pope said about birth control and what they believed. And they did not want to publish my letter to protect me. *Yeah, sure!*

I leaned back into the comfy chair across from Harry. Even if he was my superior and I was vowed to obey him, Harry was a mensch and a real earthy man. "Paul, what's the difference between a heterosexual celibate and a homosexual celibate?" probed Harry, puffing cherry smoke out of his pipe.

I had just read Donald Goergen's fascinating book *The Sexual Celibate*, in which he made the case for celibacy being a commitment to have only non-genital relationships. Celibacy, he explained, wasn't to be a life without affection. Even celibates have erotic feelings that we are meant to guide rather than erase.

But no one ever talked about this stuff openly before. Yes, a heterosexual's experience of celibacy might be different from that of a homosexual, I reasoned, if only for the reason that heterosexuals grow up learning that their sexuality is good, at least if they get married. When homosexual people awaken to the spirituality of their orientation, it is like waking up from a nightmare. You want to claim your sexuality is good because this is your new experience. But after a lifetime of being taught that it is shameful, the conversion from being a self-hating and ashamed homosexual to a person who accepts his or her same-sex (gay/lesbian) orientation as a gift of God is a process that cries out to be shared with others, especially the young in churches where the shame is taught.[1]

Dodging the issue of celibacy for a second, I wanted to know something even more basic. "Harry, what's the difference between a heterosexual and a homosexual?"

Puff-puff-puff..."I don't know, Paul,"...*puff-puff-puff*..."you tell me."

Oh! I get it Harry. Maybe all you want to know is whether I am celibate. I wanted to assure him that I was trying. "Harry, sometimes I wish I were living out the fantasy that the guys in the monastery imagine I am living."

Puff-puff-puff..."Don't, Paul. Don't!" I grinned at this father figure, who asked me questions my own father wouldn't. I knew he liked me. It was a father's love.

"Don't worry, Harry."

Puff-puff-puff...

By the time I left, he knew I was privately questioning the Church's teaching that all homosexual acts are intrinsically evil.[2] We made plans to meet Monsignor Raymond Flynn at the chancery on the following Monday morning at 10:00 a.m.

As the Augustinian provincial, Harry was my immediate superior and, in dealings with the cardinal, like my protector. But he knew there was only so much he could do if I got into trouble with Church authorities. For him to accompany me to the chancery was a sign of solidarity. Yet I wonder, today, why I didn't seek his and others' guidance *before* I sent such a letter. Why did I expect Harry to just pick up the pieces after I dropped the bomb?

Monsignor Ray Flynn was in his early fifties, a suave and friendly man as front office people usually are. I had heard his name associated with the Catholic Charismatic movement. Charismatic people believe the Holy Spirit is active in the Church and that its "gifts" are freely given to all of us, not just to the ordained. In the early seventies, these enthusiastic believers began to crowd into churches and stadiums to pray in body-swaying, hand-waving styles more familiar to Pentecostal Christians than Roman Catholics, at least in the United States.

The Holy Spirit kept surprising us. The movement even began to cross the boundaries of the other Christian denominations. Why debate differences when you can pray together? Why begin by dividing yourselves over the meaning of the Eucharist when you are finally speaking with people you have been estranged from for centuries? There was an opening to other churches back then that has practically disappeared over the past forty-five years.

This unity of Christians threatened some Church leaders. They didn't want a diluting of the truths of the faith; they also didn't want forms of spiritual power to develop from below that might challenge their authority. The Holy Spirit was a little too wild to trust without the Church's velvet glove of control. In Philadelphia, Monsignor Flynn was appointed to provide this guidance.

The chancery—the very name struck fear in my bones—was the headquarters of John Cardinal Krol, who had ordained me seven years before at Villanova University. He had neither spoken to us nor smiled as we waited in the sacristy that day. But he did look directly into my eyes when I knelt before him to promise obedience.

Krol, of Polish background, was originally a welcome break from the decades of Irish control of the diocese—Cardinal O'Hara, Cardinal Dougherty, Archbishop Prendergast—with huge Catholic high schools named after each of them. After Krol showed his true hard colors—cracking down mercilessly on challenges—even Italians missed the old guard.

Alone in the elevator, Harry and I watched the ministry office signs flashing by: Confraternity of Christian Doctrine, Family Life Bureau, Black Apostolate, and our destination, Personnel. After dealing with the reaction to my letter, Harry was going to request that I be assigned to a ministry serving the gay and lesbian community. As Harry watched the floor signal, he tried to joke. "There's no sign for Gay Ministry, Paul!"

Not exactly in a joking mood, I remarked anyway, "Not yet, Harry." Harry smiled.

Authorities can intimidate me, almost erase me, make me shaky or remove my belief in myself. As a kid, I feared my father and mother might take away their love if I didn't obey. Religious authorities could withdraw God's love for the same reason. Perhaps I joined a system of religious authority to identify with the aggressor.

I tried to stride confidently, let my body calm itself while Harry and I walked the burgundy carpet, attempting to ignore the rogues' gallery of former cardinals and archbishops peering from elaborately framed portraits on the walls.

"Hello Father! Hello Father!" A woman, older than I expected, rose from her desk with a sweet smile. "Make yourselves comfortable," she gestured to some seats. "Monsignor will be with you in a moment. May I get you some coffee or tea?"

There it was, the maddening deference that Roman Catholics give to their priests, a deference we had learned to expect. It was part of the contract of ordination: we'll respect you, treat you as we would treat Jesus Christ. We will feed you in your rectories, bow our heads for God's blessing when you lift your hand, press envelopes with twenty-dollar bills into your priestly hands at Christmas and Easter, even overlook your occasionally boring sermons or curtness when you are having a bad day.

All you need to do is to live like Jesus Christ, especially regarding sexuality. Uphold the Church's teachings unflinchingly even if the laity cannot. Even if you possibly have doubts about them yourself. Most of all, never break ranks with the brotherhood, this magnificent priestly band, this special calling from God that has changed you in your deepest being and left an indelible mark on your soul.

We will love you and hate you for this distance between us, Father. And you may love and hate us for it some days. But God knows that it is for the good of the people. You must never ever forget that, even if it kills you. *Certainly, Father.*

A few moments later, we were ushered into the monsignor's comfortable office. Dark polished furniture. Bright lamps. A painting of Cardinal Krol in a crimson and ermine cape hovering behind the desk. "Harry, it's good to see you again. Father Morrissey, may I call you Paul? Sit down, sit down." The monsignor himself, handsome with his hair brushed, greeted us warmly. I felt hopeful. Harry and he bantered briefly about the Phillies.

"So, Paul, what is the Church's clear teaching on homosexuality?"[3] *What?* Even with his smooth voice and smile, a gauntlet had landed at my feet. Did the diocese care what my sexual orientation meant to me? No, I was a risk. What if people started thinking about priests' sexuality? If priests and laity began discussing the meaning and necessity of celibacy, it would cause far too much commotion.

The Church's clear teaching on homosexuality. Never mind that society and the Church hadn't even discovered that homosexuality was a unique sexual orientation, rather than simply a behavioral act of normal heterosexuals, until a hundred years ago.[4] Never mind that the Church always developed its teachings, such as its belief (against Galileo) that the sun rotated around the earth, its teachings on slavery, usury, and religious freedom, often hundreds of years after condemning initial discoveries and the people who taught them. *For the good of the people,* my future as a priest would be sunk with biblical quotes and church teaching...."*The Church has always taught....*" The monsignor cleared his throat. *Be cool, Paul. Be cool.*

It occurred to me that I never really liked the clergy world. Many rectories chilled my party-loving Irish spirit. How, I often wondered, did I join a profession that hid so many resentments? What anger lies within us when our profession expects us to always be kind? How can any congregant trust their inner doubts and quirks to someone like that?

Oh, there are good brothers in the church, like Harry,[5] but as I awakened to my real self, it seemed that too many priests gave up their individual humanity for the sake of the clerical system. *Am I going to be one of them?*

Just then, Monsignor Flynn leaned forward and folded his hands prayer-like on the desk in front of him. As though to offer me a way to respond, his gold cufflinks engraved with little black crucifixes peeked out at me.

"Uh…we all know what the Church's clear teaching on homosexuality is," I began. I felt like adding "The Church speaks so darn much about it that it hardly needs to be mentioned," but decided not to. The gray eyes in the pleasant face across from me hardened ever so slightly. I felt my hand begin to clench. "What I would like to know is…"—my voice went up and my gaze dropped to rest on his cufflinks—"what is the Church's clear teaching on poverty?"[6] I gazed over at Cardinal Krol in his ermine cape.

Though the diocese had parishes in poor areas, I felt that the Church in Philadelphia at that time didn't really give a hoot about changing the systems[7] that keep many people in poverty. When it came to racism, war, economics, and hot social issues, Cardinal Krol was a bosom buddy of President Nixon. He even invited him for a photo op right before the 1972 election. Instead, the Catholic Church had embraced hardline sexual doctrines for our Catholic identity. Even the Holy Spirit wouldn't want sexuality to come flying in the church window.

At first, the monsignor didn't respond. Harry shuffled his feet. I didn't know from where the question about poverty had come, but I knew it was hopeless to answer his question on homosexuality. I guess the Holy Spirit helped me shift the debate onto a moral issue where I felt self-righteous. Since living with the Quakers, I now spent only a dollar a day for food.

Noticing my gaze on his cufflinks, the monsignor inched his sleeves up to cover them. After a few awkward minutes, he announced, "Your ministry to homosexual people is not a traditional one. Unless you get faculties for a traditional ministry such as a parish or teaching position, you will no longer be able to function legitimately as a priest in the Philadelphia archdiocese." He nodded to Harry as though this was perfectly understood.

Shocked at the swiftness and utter politeness of the guillotine, I froze. "But, but…couldn't we see gay ministry as missionary work?" I tried. Flynn shook his head sadly. It was useless. My brother priest placed his palms together, his morning work done.

You mean that's it? Just like that I can't serve as a priest? What'll I do now? The Scripture quote came to me—"I am not strong enough to dig, and I am ashamed to beg" (Luke 16:3). Maybe if I get down on my knees and plead, "Oh please, please, there are so many out there like me. The Church could make a difference in their lives. They are hungering for Christ. For God's sake, let me bring the gospel to them."

My friend Toby came to mind. "Paul, you can't fight the Catholic Church. It's impossible. In the end, it'll always be more concerned for the majority of its people rather than for an individual, no matter how right that one person may be. That's how it has survived for a thousand years." *Oh God, I'm sorry…I'm so stubborn…all those years of study down the tubes!*

I heard Harry talking. "We will explore the possibility of a traditional ministry and get back to you, Ray." Turning toward me, Harry made as though to stand. "All right, Paul?"

Sure! I could apply for a traditional ministry. I knew that was a dead end because now that they knew I was gay, I'd probably have to swear to mention the Church's teaching on homosexuality in every sermon, or every college classroom. They'd be watching my every step to see if I was orthodox.

"Do we have an understanding then?" The monsignor's voice was smooth, comforting, as an ironic smile spread onto his face. The gray eyes softened for a moment as Cardinal Krol looked on. *An understanding!* The altar boy in my heart flashed with neon anger. Taking it all as a personal rejection, I fantasized ripping off those gold cufflinks and tossing them out the window. Instead, I smiled back at him.

"Certainly, Monsignor," I answered in my own smooth voice. Priests, I had learned, must never show anger. The brotherhood must never erupt into open warfare. What would people think?

"We'll get back to you," Harry said as we stood.

"Good, then." We all shook hands. It was as though we had just clinched a deal on the stock market. Only then did he come out from behind the desk, graciously ushering us into the outer office.

"Margaret, see that Father Cassell and Father Morrissey get a copy of the bicentennial celebrations being planned by the diocese, would you?"

"Certainly, Monsignor."

My anger was becoming more palpable, even though I had forced the issue. As I gazed through my own eyes at the world and Church, I didn't get a sense of Jesus in me—nor in others, for that matter. Was I looking for ways to be kicked out of the priesthood? I didn't feel at home anymore in this clerical system, but I didn't have the guts to leave.

26

A Gay Carpenter

Spring, 1975, Philadelphia, Pennsylvania—

After the encounter at the chancery, I saw that coming out as a gay priest would cause reactions. However, I didn't grasp the big consequences that would be set in motion and would never stop.

My family and friends, the people I served, and especially church authorities would feel conflicted. They would see me in a new way, challenging their view of right and wrong. This is not easy for people, even those who have known and loved you. There would be a huge price to pay. But I was young and felt immortal. A wonderful energy came knowing that I no longer had to hide my sexual side. I believed the Holy Spirit was with me.

At first, I was drawn to people like me—gay and lesbian people who seemed to be the lepers of our time. Because of this, they often chose to live in their own sections of town. Since I felt a call to minister to gay people, I began to go to this "Gayborhood" for my own support.

It was during this period that I decided to move out of the Life Center. There weren't any specifically gay households among the communes. I wanted to be in a space where gay and lesbian people would feel comfortable. One afternoon, after my "bread-labor" job as a substitute public schoolteacher, I saw an ad on a telephone pole advertising for a roommate. Stan Olaffson turned out to be a cute gay guy who loved to dance. Seven years younger than me at twenty-eight, he was an ordained minister in the United Church of Christ, the first openly gay intern hired by the University of Pennsylvania's chaplaincy program.

The apartment at 24th and South Streets was near the gay part of the city. I needed a pal to help me come out socially. Two weeks later, I moved in. Stan and I did not relate sexually. Mostly, we just shared breakfast and some dinners each week. We didn't pray together either. In fact, I felt lost regarding God at this time. I was looking for a different kind of religious community, but I didn't know how to find it. The first time I danced with Stan at the Allegro, a gay bar off Broad Street, I felt the joy of showing affection for a man out in the open. *Yes, this is good! How can God not enjoy it too?* Isn't this affection with men as much a part of being gay as sex? This could be a part of me too, even though I am a priest.

I kept struggling to hold together the sexual and spiritual sides of my life. My former Life Center pal, George Lakey, gave me the news at Allegro one night that the American Psychiatric Association had removed homosexuality from its list of mental disorders.[8] This was big news, which George and I celebrated on the dance floor.

After our meeting with Monsignor Flynn, my provincial, Harry, urged me to consider other dioceses more open than Philly to a gay ministry. "But Harry," I countered, "that's why I should stay here! They already have people doing it there." In the end, he relented. If I promised to do so very quietly and keep him informed, Harry gave me permission to minister to the homosexual community in Philadelphia, even without the diocesan faculties. Thrilled to be breaking new ground for the Church and my order, I was on my way. The next few years proved challenging.

Bob Nugent, a local diocesan priest, and I joined Sr. Jeannine Gramick, a School Sister of Notre Dame, at a restaurant to discuss Dignity, the national Catholic Gay and Lesbian Ministry, which the Philadelphia chapter had joined. Originally founded by an Augustinian, Fr. Patrick Neidor, OSA, in 1969 in California, it felt to me like St. Augustine was atoning for the trouble his sexual teachings had caused over the years. No wonder our religious order was becoming a leader in this movement.

Over our lasagna dinner at the Arches in the Gayborhood,

Jeannine spoke glowingly of Fr. John McNeill, a Jesuit Scripture scholar who had given the keynote address at Dignity's first convention—"Homosexuality, God's Gift." She read to us one of Carl Jung's quotes from McNeill's book *The Church and the Homosexual*, which was published in 1976: "Because of their outsider status in society, gays and lesbians often have deep religious feelings and a spiritual openness that makes them responsive to revelation. Because of this, they are often the ones who bring the church community into a reality."[9] The three of us clicked our wine glasses, "L'Chaim—to life!" We felt in our hearts that we were being led by the Holy Spirit.

In August 1976, the Archdiocese of Philadelphia hosted the 41st International Eucharistic Congress of the Catholic Church. It was an enormous event, attended by major figures from around the world—Dorothy Day, Archbishop Hélder Câmara, and Mother Teresa, to name a few. On the day devoted to "Freedom and Justice for All," the Quaker Life Center community helped the local Dignity chapter sponsor a "Mass for Freedom and Justice for Gay Catholics" on the street outside the Convention Center of the congress. Hundreds of people showed up at this joyous and prophetic event. Sister Jeannine gave the homily. I was one of the concelebrants. Many of the convention attendees stopped and listened with their eyes rolling, including a reporter-priest for *L'Osservatore Romano*. The Philadelphia police provided security.

We felt the spirit of Vatican II urging us into uncharted territory. The streets became our church, as Pope Francis encourages young people today. We didn't have time to worry too much because we were responding to their needs. It was a breathtaking time for gay Catholics, and perhaps not since rivaled in the Church. *Freedom and Justice for All.*

The following year, Bob and Jeannine went on to found New Ways Ministry, a national Catholic ministry to gay and lesbian people; I stayed in Philadelphia to minister to the local chapter. Sometimes, I think I should have gotten a college degree for what I learned among the group of gay and lesbian Catholics in Dignity/Philadelphia. The storefront basement office we rented held only about twenty people. After the word got around that a Catholic Mass was held for gays and lesbians every Sunday evening, crowds showed up. Because I identified with their struggle, I was able to give and receive some of the best sermons in my life there.

Oh sure, sometimes the leather outfits of hustlers or a flamboyant person in drag gave me pause, but these people reminded me of the crowd Jesus used to hang out with. I was happy when a guide dog for a person with vision loss would lie under the altar and thump its tail. At last, I thought, I am doing what I was ordained for. Dignity was where I learned to accept my own homosexuality among the people to whom I was ministering. Every Sunday, I preached how God loves them no matter what. And all the while, I realized that, in God's mysterious way of healing us through others, the lepers were healing the priest. Maybe they did that in Jesus's time too.

I was in it for the ministry. Yet with excitement and a sense of playfulness, "Paul" was trying to be educated as well as "Father Paul." One day, an ad in the *Philadelphia Gay News* caught my attention: "Gay Carpenter Wanted. Club Baths. Start Immediately."

Hmm…Jesus was a carpenter, wasn't he? Maybe I could learn what happens in these places. I called my brother, Joe, who was a skilled carpenter. "Joe, I have a job possibility. Maybe you can help me." Of all my brothers, Joe was the most openly sensitive. He didn't mind giving me a hug or talking about his feelings. "Joe, I need to get a handle on these places where gay people hang out if I'm going to minister to them."

"Yeah, sure…maybe you want to see some sights yourself," he teased. My face went hot.

"No, no Joe! Won't you come if I get an interview? You can protect me—*ha-ha.*" *But you're right, I wouldn't mind seeing some sights either.*

Joe agreed. "But you better not spread it around among the family that I was at a gay bathhouse, bro."

"Never."

On the morning of the interview, with mounting excitement, Joe and I climbed the narrow staircase. A tiny caged-in office with a glass barrier revealed a big gruff guy with wispy gray hair and a puffy face. Grinning to show him we weren't the vice squad, I said cheerily, "We're here for an interview. Rusty told me to come in this morning."

"Oh!" Suddenly he was all sweetness. "I'm Rusty. Are you Paul?" Hairy shoulders stuck out from his black tank top.

"Yes." Joe showed no emotion, but his eyes darted between Rusty and me.

"Come in, come in," said Rusty. The buzzer sounded and suddenly we entered the "forbidden zone." Rusty, with his beer belly hanging over his belt, shook our hands warmly. "So, which one of you is the carpenter?"

"I am," I said quickly. Rusty grinned.

"I'm here to help Paul make an estimate," volunteered Joe.

"We're brothers," I added, noticing the bowl marked "Free Condoms" at the window.

"Oh!" Rusty seemed even more interested now.

"Why don't you show us what you want done?" Joe asked. He didn't realize it, but with his faded bib jeans and boots, my brother looked like the hot guys in the gay magazines. Rusty raised his eyebrows at the double entendre.

"Follow me," he grinned.

The room was about ten by twenty feet and crammed with lockers. Small wooden benches rested in front of them. Joe began to study the room as though it were the Sistine Chapel.

"You see that space up there?" Rusty pointed to an eighteen-inch area between the top of the lockers and the ceiling. I heard a shower start. "I want cabinets built up there."

Within ten minutes, Joe had settled on the style and type of wood Rusty wanted, including the price. I would get a hundred bucks when I had the job completed. I could start the next day. It wasn't much, but what the heck? I'd be making a little cash while I continued my intern project on gay ministry. As we were about to make our escape, Rusty tapped his finger in a campy fashion on Joe's chest. "And-you-can-come-too!" Joe and I practically ran down the stairs.

I started my carpentry job the next day. What would I discover? *Maybe I'll meet a friend.* I put on my cutoff jeans and a T-shirt and trimmed my beard. Joe had told me what to do and I measured and cut pieces with his portable power saw. I hammered away like a pro. Glancing around for Rusty, I saw a middle-aged guy with a white towel under his arm. He nodded at me. Instinctively, I nodded back. He went around to a locker out of my sight.

Bam! Bam! Bam! I hammered. My heart began to thump. *He isn't bad looking. A little heavy, but nice shoulders. And a good head of dark hair.* The locker door opened. I could hear him undressing. Once, he caught me looking his way. Bam! Bam! Bam! I needed to stay focused. As I reached backward for a strip of board on the locker, I caught a glimpse of a hand reaching up to pat my butt.

"Hey! What's up?" The guy in the towel smiled invitingly before vanishing. My mouth hung open like a violated virgin. I wanted to yell, "You can't just do that!"

So that's what goes on here, you dummy. You should've known it was part of the job description! And part of you likes it, right? But is this what you want? I wobbled on the ladder with the hammer in my hand. With a backward glance toward the steam room as I jumped off, I grabbed my tools and went to Rusty with my answer. "I quit."

27

Mama's Death

Summer, 1975, Philadelphia, Pennsylvania—

When you are a priest, it's as if you no longer have a personal life. You give up your life for others in community and ministry—a voluntary contrast to living primarily for yourself that the world fosters as the way to happiness. Creating a balance between my ministerial and personal lives, I felt, would be healthier.

I wanted to talk with my mother about this awareness. More than Daddy, Mama had always seemed interested in my life. Since I had gone away to the seminary, I had drifted away from that closeness. I didn't want her running my life, but maybe I could let her in on some of it. I invited her to see my new pad that I shared with Stan in the city.

At age thirty-four, being on my own gave me a blast of joy and also boggled my brain. Did I have a right to my own place in the world? Was my life really my own? Did I have free will? Could I bear to stand on my own? I grew up with such a communal spirit that I hardly knew who I was apart from groups like my family and the Augustinians. I needed to risk leaving them to gain my own identity. It was a little late now, but my egg was hatching.

My entire spirituality was based on "laying down my life for others" as Jesus did, and as my mother did. But what is God's will? I wanted to find a way to hold both God's will and my will together.

I began to experience how I was different from the groups to which I belonged. In fact, my emerging gay identity seemed to create one more group. I didn't see that at first. If I could get to know my mother as Nora and not just Mama, I could grow up in a relationship to my family.

Mama was going to visit me in the early afternoon when Stan would be leading a university workshop. She and I would have the place to ourselves for a few hours. I swept the kitchen floor and the marble stoop out front. I picked dead leaves off the geranium bush and turned the best flowers forward. I vacuumed the shag rug, brushed ashes out of the fireplace, and set up the logs for a new fire. I flipped on some lamps, then swapped posters to bring some color to the living room. No religious pictures or crucifixes. So what? This is my place. I let pleasure and excitement flow through me. It was almost like I was expecting the pope.

Me. Out on a new road. By myself. Where was this leading me? Would the trouble with the diocese compel me to make some decision about leaving the priesthood? Would they force me out because I had come out publicly? Did I really want a lover? So many questions to wrestle with. And what in the world does God want of me?

A tapping at the door. I lit the fire and imagined Sigmund Freud asking mockingly: *"Your own home! And your first real date here is with your mother?"*

I greeted her with open arms. "Hello, Paul," she said with a cheery smile. Mama was decked out in a skirt and sweater with pearls and high heels. Lipstick brightened her face. She was in a good mood; the crease between her eyebrows was relaxed. She held out a package as she scanned the room behind me. "Here, I brought you an Irish scone. It's still warm."

"Oh, yummy!" I placed it on a table.

"Look at the fire!" she said. "It's lovely."

Judy Collins warbled in the background as I grinned like a chimpanzee for getting Mama out of the house. Spinning around, I gushed, "Mama, can you believe it? *Calm!*" Nothing like home with the constant commotion. "Here, take a seat." I patted the couch. "My roommate, Stan, is at work. He's a chaplain at the University of Pennsylvania."

She glanced around the apartment. "You've done well, Paul," she nodded thoughtfully. "I hope it's what you want." Her words sank in. Mama was concerned with how my living like this would play with the Church and my province. The Augustinians had a rule that, barring circumstances like graduate studies, all should live in community. Living with the Quakers might pass, but to move in with a roommate after coming out as gay would create more than flak, no matter what my relationship with him was. The public perception was crucial, and my mother knew that. *What will the neighbors think?*

I hadn't yet informed Harry that I had moved, but I would soon. "It will be fine with my provincial," I assured her, even though I had my doubts. "There are two floors, and we share the rent. Stan and I have separate bedrooms."

She looked right through me.

"We're just friends, Mama." It was true. I couldn't hide it if it weren't.

"I'm learning how to live on my own. Don't you think it's about time?" My voice sounded testy. Her lips pressed together, and her head slowly bobbed. She knew I could be stubborn. The crease appeared in her forehead. I poured glasses of port wine, and we toasted. *"Sláinte!" Clink.*

"Sláinte!" she smiled.

My mother and I talked about many things—Joan's latest escapades, Daddy's being passed over for younger men at work, my visiting at Thanksgiving, the Watergate investigation. Our words mattered less than having such a special time alone with her on my own turf. In fact, I realized that never in my life had I done so. I imagined how jealous my siblings would be.

At one point, Mama excused herself to go to the bathroom. Waiting, I held up my glass. An inner voice intoned: *No more Mama's favorite son. No more doing what she wants as though it's God's voice. It's your life, so live it.*

"I need to be getting home soon," she said. Schoolkids were calling to one another on the street.

"Let me turn the fire over one more time," I said. *She should know what you're considering; she'll give you an honest answer anyway.* "Mama, what if it is God's will that I leave the priesthood?" I gulped the last of my wine and waited for the roof to fall in.

Mama sat in silence, twirling her pearls. I had said the unthinkable. At that time, for a priest to leave the priesthood was like someone dying. People would whisper, "Did you hear about

Father Paul?" There would be shame at a vision lost, a blessing somehow removed, a holy man of God become simply mortal again. You'd be like Jonah going against God's will.

My mother seemed calm. In a way, I had her trapped. If she protested or showed in any way that she needed me to be a priest more than just myself, then her willful son would rebel and leave the priesthood just to make his own voice clear. Maybe she knew that and dodged the trap. Maybe she just answered from her heart. In any case, Nora Morrissey's guidance, soft and kind, was brilliant.

"If it *is* God's will," she said. She gave no hint that she needed me to be anything. Perhaps I had her all wrong; perhaps she only cared that I would be happy. If I could figure out how to be happy, maybe that was really God's will.

I helped her into her coat and kissed her. I watched as she drove up Lombard Street toward Upper Darby, waving to me in the rearview mirror. My mother. Mama. Nora Morrissey. It was a start. *If it is God's will.* God's will. My will. Father Paul. Paul. If I can figure out how to hold these together, I will be happy.

"I wish I were going in to have another baby," Mama joked as she was admitted to Misericordia Hospital a few months later, the hospital where we had all been born. The family couldn't make sense of her suddenly erratic behavior—she began to forget things and had headaches that were excruciating. Her doctor wanted her to have some tests and told her she could take up to twelve aspirins a day.

"Imagine, Nora Morrissey in a psychiatric ward," she said, puffing on a cigarette. Those were the last words I heard her speak aloud. That night, an orderly found her collapsed by her bed. An emergency operation that I had to sign for because Daddy was home with the four younger kids, revealed a hemorrhaging brain tumor. Over the next ten days, this amazing woman, who had loved and worried us into adulthood, lay in a coma in the intensive care unit. Her head was bandaged, and a ventilator breathed for her while the family prayed, cursed the doctor who missed her diagnosis, and rooted her on as though we were football fans and all we had to do was cheer harder for her to survive. Then one morning, the brain monitor went to a straight line, and it was over.

Mama had died. Unthinkable. The hub of the wheel was gone. The center of our lives. The one who knew all the phone numbers.

How would we survive? All of us fell apart. As we planned the funeral, I wondered if the stress I'd caused her had made her vulnerable to the brain tumor.

My heart cracked. Now I realized that the one person in the world who had loved me unconditionally was gone. "I doubt if I will ever love again," I told my friends. "The pain is too much." I went through my days like a zombie. How could people still lead their lives? Didn't they know Nora Morrissey was dead?

Mama's funeral was held at St. Alice's Parish. I still didn't have formal faculties from the archdiocese, but no one spoke about this. The fourteen of us kids, plus Daddy, lined the aisle to greet the hundreds of neighbors, friends, relatives, and parishioners who had known Mama through the years.

My Augustinian brothers came, including Harry, my provincial. Jim McGrane was my master of ceremonies. At one point—half an hour late—he whispered that we should begin. Yet people were still lined up outside the door and onto the sidewalk. I was at the head of the line, greeting people along with Mama's sister, Sister St. Ephrem, a Sister of St. Joseph. Daddy was at the end, held supportively by Nonie and Tommy. I gave the okay, and the undertakers moved forward to close the casket. "Wait!" Francis whispered something in the head guy's ear. He then motioned to the others, and they all stepped back.

As the last mourners filled the remaining seats, the family gathered around the coffin. It was as if Nora was in the crib now, and we were all looking down at our child. I forget who started it, but gradually we found our strength and sang the old childhood hymn that filled our evenings around the table after dinner:

> Good night sweet Jesus, guard us in sleep,
> Our souls and bodies, in thy love keep.
> Waking or sleeping, keep us in sight,
> Dear gentle savior, good night, good night.
> Good night, dear Jesus, good night.
> Go-oo-od night.

Mama's death sent Daddy into depression. Exasperated, Kate, the eldest daughter still at home, gave him a tongue-lashing. "Look, Daddy, you're just feeling sorry for yourself." Her hoarse voice let out all our frustrations. "Think about us. At least you had a life before you knew Mama. We never did. So, get up…please. We need you now."

In the next few days, Daddy got out of bed and started to live again. I started to live too. My guiding star was gone, but I was grateful that she knew all the different parts of me now. In the emptiness, I began to discover room for others I could love. But how?

28

A Sexual Hell Venture

Spring, 1976, Philadelphia, Pennsylvania—

God's will. What is it? Some people think that everything that happens is God's will. I don't believe this. Hiroshima? A car crashing and bursting into flames? The AIDS epidemic? A failed exam? It may feel helpful to attribute everything to God's will, but that seems to leave out our own free will. Does God pre-ordain everything that happens? If so, our free will is not free, is it? And the opposite is equally strange—the belief that God has no concern for us at all but just watches our free wills play out as they want. Who cares if the world goes to hell? Somewhere in the mysterious middle seems to be the case, where God reverences our freedom and the hoped-for love that arises from that freedom. God is with us and in us, urging us along our best path, yet allowing us to go astray if we insist. We are not puppets. God will not force our love. But will God really let me go to hell? I know how bullheaded I can sometimes be, so if this is the case...*God help me!*

We often pray to do God's will. Jesus taught his disciples the Lord's Prayer, which has been translated throughout the globe. According to modern scholarship, the phrase in this prayer, "Thy will be done on earth as it is in heaven," can more faithfully be translated as "Thy *desire* be done on earth as it is in heaven."[10]

In *Prayers of the Cosmos,* Neil Douglas-Klotz explains, "The ancient roots of the word (for 'desire') summon forth images of a vortex of harmony and generation, of a host of stars swirling through the heavens."[11] This newer meaning was exciting. It felt much more relational to think of God's *desire* in me and in all creation. "Thy desire be done on earth—and in me—as it is in heaven."

There is a groan within me, a desire I feel, especially when I slow down and risk being alone. I notice this even sometimes when I am in a crowd having a good time, or when I am with an intimate friend. It is as though the very goodness of these relationships reminds me of some emptiness within that hasn't yet been filled, even with them. Then I get relief only by going off by myself, into the woods or by the seashore, where I can sense this desire in everything—the giant oak trees creaking in the wind; the hawks or gulls circling overhead; or the waves roaring relentlessly into shore and back out to sea. These things remind me of this groaning in my own heart for something or someone that will give it peace.

St. Paul states that "the whole creation has been groaning in labor pains until now" (Rom 8:22), "for we do not know how to pray as we ought, but that very Spirit intercedes with sighs too deep for words" (Rom 8:26). This is part of our Christian faith, that God groans inside every human being in order to be fulfilled. God *desires* in us, yes, but in hindsight I can also say that not everything we desire is of God.

My sexual desire had mostly been bottled up within me by my upbringing and the Church's teaching on sex. Not that these teachings were simply bad—I'm probably alive today because of them and how they protected me—but in their black-and-white simplicity, they also stifled and hurt me. I had been taught not to respect my own sexual feelings, to stuff this part of myself down, and even to hate it, and to hate others who exhibited sexual inclinations like me.

My eyes were the first place where I noticed my desire. Everywhere I looked, I was stunned by beauty—male beauty, in particular. When people shed their winter coats, suddenly the sight of their bodies made me crazy. As I noticed guys, and girls too with their proud breasts, I saw some of them looking at me as well. *What is this?* To see and be seen this way was what I wanted.

Although I had taken a vow of celibacy, that didn't stop my hormones from surging. *All creation groans.* To maintain chastity, in the seminary we had been taught to pray and take cold showers, to cast our eyes down when we saw someone beautiful lest they captivate our souls. As St. Augustine observed in his *Rule*, which we read every week in community:

> Although your eyes may perchance turn toward a woman, you may not fix your gaze, for it is not by touch or desire alone, but by one's gaze also that disordered affections mutually arise. And when unchaste souls meet knowingly in a mutual gaze, even though nothing is said, and take carnal delight in their passion for one another, then is purity of life lost, even though bodily integrity has not been impaired by unchaste actions.... (4.19–23)

Augustine never mentioned men, but the same dynamic happens. I may as well have tried to hold back the tide. These feelings both unsettled and consoled me. People seem to think that when religious and priests take vows, we just press a button and that erases all our desires. St. Augustine wrote his *Confessions* to show us otherwise.[12] After fifteen years of fostering my separateness from others through my vow of chastity, discovering I was like everyone else in the universe blew fresh air into my thinking.

Everyone has sexual desires, I realized—married people, gay people, unmarried heterosexuals, priests, and nuns. That didn't mean they needed to act on them. I didn't either. However, it wasn't that simple. Realizing that my desires weren't evil made me more open to act on them. How could I stop myself? I began to let my barriers down, rationalizing that I didn't need to get sexually involved, just emotionally.

I longed for a gay friend, and so when I got the chance, I went to gay bars and bookstores. I decided to keep my priesthood a secret, at least initially, from guys whom I met, lest it freak them or me out. There were two worlds—the gay world and the Church world. Each saw the other as the enemy, so each had to disguise itself in the other's presence.

I wanted to be a whole person, accepting my sexuality, but the Church insisted that with my sexual orientation that wasn't possible. Even though the Bible preached "God is love, and those who abide in love abide in God, and God abides in them" (1 John 4:16), the Church drew an exception to my form of love. Meanwhile, the gay community seemed to believe that you *had to be* sexually active, or you were cooperating with this strict view. That position felt equally divisive.

If the ideal was to hold sexual desire and love together, I discovered that I could also separate them. I could respond sexually to someone and not get involved emotionally. And I might befriend people for whom I had little sexual attraction. If I wanted to remain in the priesthood, I realized, I couldn't let sexual feelings and love come together in one relationship. In this way, it seems that celibacy fostered the split and hindered sexual wholeness.

Through this period of my thirties, I desired human love, the kind that poetry and songs describe. *Haply I think on thee*. At least to hold and to be held and experience the emotional care this showed. Even amid the pain that my newly cracked-open heart felt, I could sense a stirring ability to love. This feeling gave me courage, and even an ability to preach more from my soul. Yes, I longed to share my heart with someone whom I could call my own. *Lord, is this too much to ask before I die?*

It was Easter night. After all the liturgies at the parish I was attending in the Gayborhood, I wanted to celebrate. I decided to go to the Steps, a hot spot everyone was talking about. I didn't just jump into this club scene. When I first came out, I didn't know gay bars existed. With a little investigation, though, I found a gay bookstore, Giovanni's Room, and bought some books on gay history. I also saw an ad for a Gay Activists' Alliance meeting, which I attended. After the meeting, I joined some guys going out for a beer at what turned out to be a gay bar. What would I do, I wondered, if someone made a pass at me? And what if someone recognized me as a priest?

This Easter night, my friends were all busy, so I decided to go alone. Excited that I might meet someone, I brushed my long hair until it shone, smiling into the mirror. Around 10:30, I headed out into the cool night air, my face tingling with cologne. When I rounded the corner onto 23rd Street, I began to whistle, "Christ has risen from the dead, alleluia, alleluia."

I was only at the Steps for ten minutes when a Black dude in his late twenties drew my attention. He had been swinging his muscular frame as he danced by himself. Lots of people were watching him, his muscles bulging through his T-shirt under the strobe light. Like a dark Adonis, he caught my gaze before looking away.

"Oh yeah, he could put his shoes under my bed anytime," murmured a voice behind me. A tall, skinny redhead in a tank top and tight jeans gave me a knowing grin. Embarrassed to be caught watching, I grinned and turned away.

In these clubs, those without partners meandered through the swaying throng, bumping and flowing by themselves, oblivious to anything but their own mystical journey. If you saw somebody you were attracted to, you might dance next to him to see if you could catch his eye. Even though I felt self-conscious, I let the music pull me out onto the floor. Soon I was gravitating to that muscled guy. *But what if someone recognizes you?*

He didn't take notice of me right away, but I saw him glancing at me a few times through the mirror. I rocked and swayed in my place, enjoying the bellbottoms whipping on my ankles as I crooked my legs to the beat of the music. When I saw him matching my movements, I began to match his. Soon the two of us were rocking in tandem, one number merging into another, until I could feel the beat of the music inside me. The strobe lights swirled around the ceiling like the Milky Way. The hungry stares of the crowd energized the guy while I began to feel dizzy.

When a spacey New Age melody came on, I pushed my way over to the bar. The club was packed at this point. It was after midnight. Soon the cruising would begin. I hunted out a five-dollar bill and waved it at the bare-chested bartender. "What'll ya have, hon?" he called out.

"Gimme a Bud," I shouted. As he ducked to get it, I glanced back at the crowd and couldn't believe it! Emerging from the crowd, his glistening body so liquid and sure of itself, Adonis was headed right toward me. Catching my breath, I turned for my beer. The bartender smiled as he took my money. Slowly, I raised the drink to my lips, not wanting to give myself away though my heart pounded.

As I placed the bottle down, I saw a dark arm beside mine. His presence oozed toward me. Our arms touched. Soon I turned toward him, and words just tumbled out: "What's your name? Mine's Paul."

His eyes glanced sideways at me for a moment…. "Cal."

I pointed at my beer. "Would ya like one?"

Cal nonchalantly surveyed the crowd, leaning back as though he owned it. When he nodded, I signaled to the bartender for another. He winked at me as I took it. Cal and I sipped our beers as we listened to the music. *"Then come in my room, make me feel all right, feel, feel, feel, feel, feel, feel, all right, all right!...her name is GLORIA!"*

After a few minutes, Cal turned to me. "You got a place we can go?" He took a chug, then stared back at the crowd.

A place we can go?! I don't even know this guy. He could be an axe murderer! For all he knew, so could I. Yet everything about him intrigued me by its difference: his woolly black hair, his swarthy skin, his posture, and leather pants. His scent even. I wanted to touch him, bridge the space between us. His aloofness was drawing me in. I thought of the apartment that I shared with Stan, but answered, "No."

We lapsed into silence, watching the others cruise and pose. A magnetic force from his direction pulled on my insides. I could hardly resist. Hoping to keep him with me, I thought of asking him to dance again. Just when it seemed he had lost interest, Cal, staring straight ahead and draining his bottle, whispered, "I got a van." *A van!* Beneath my damp shirt, like a small hungry sparrow, my heart fluttered into life.

Tilting around to face me, Cal's half-lidded eyes locked onto mine. "Well?" His lower lip, moist and sensuous, jutted forward as he placed his bottle on the bar and stared down at it for a moment. Then without another word he strolled to the exit.

With the old empty space aching inside me, I weighed his strange offer: one night of pleasure against surrendering my hope of being a sexual-spiritual person who is faithful to his vows. One part of me, heavy with desire, screamed to throw caution to the wind. *You're on a leave of absence. Who will know? Go for it!* Another part, fearful and faithful, held back. *Is this what you've come to, Paul?*

I finished my beer. Then I noticed the bartender eyeing me as he washed glasses. As he wagged his head slowly from side to side, it dawned on me that he was telling me, *No, don't follow him!* Maybe he knew the guy as a hustler who might rough me up; maybe he just saw my innocence and wanted to give me advice. Still, flush with the scent of a man who seemed to know what he wanted, I left a tip and hurried out the exit. When I got outside, I looked up and down the street. Cal wasn't in sight.

Then I turned into the alley. At first, I couldn't see in the dark. But as my eyes adjusted, I noticed a cigarette glowing hot. There in the shadows he was, leaning sideways on a big van. Then he opened the side door a notch. With the open door beckoning, I held back, as a lurid local headline from the past flashed in my mind: "Strangled Priest Found in Alley!"

Even so, against my will and despite all my commitments, some feverish desire was luring me down into the promise and risk of a dangerous world. I *wanted* this danger, wanted to surrender to this energy and to discover what searching for sex without love can mean. What the empty space in me thought I wanted. Like a tide, this desire drew me on. Cal jerked his head toward the door. As he cracked the door open further, he leaned into the van. Letting out a deep sigh, I began to follow.

Rowdy cackles of laughter from the street behind us broke into my stupor, and I remembered that it was Easter. Suddenly feeling nauseated, I hesitated, straining with all my energy to move forward. Torn as if by the voices of Augustine's mistresses taunting him long ago, *Are you sending us away?—From this moment shall this or that not be allowed to you forever?—You can't live without us, you can't live without us*[13]—I wavered. My breath came haltingly. I felt like I was swimming through molasses. When Cal flicked his cigarette to the ground and squashed it, something snapped inside me. Dragging my gaze from his, my heart from the power of darkness, I stumbled into the darkness.

What felt like a lifetime later, I was waiting for a trolley to take me home. I brushed away tears with my fists as the song from the club mocked me from inside..."*She's a soul sender, she's a lover... what's her name? Her name is...GLORIA!*"

Why didn't I just avoid a scandal by leaving the priesthood? Part of me seemed to want to tell the Church: "You think gay people are intrinsically disordered? I'll show you what that means!" Often, I felt lost. I knew no mentors in the Church, and there was no one I could talk to who would understand.

Yet, somehow in this entire struggle to be whole, I never completely stopped believing that being a priest—including my desire for sexual integrity as a gay priest[14]—was my lifelong vocation and the deepest fulfillment of my vows. Jesus had called me. Even though I was lost, I believed that you shouldn't leave someone you are sworn to just because you discover something new about yourself. What is God's desire for me?

I needed to integrate my orientation, and I begged Jesus to show me how. I was lost in the swirling vortex of my desires. My family, friends, and religious community held me together as I forged my way through this darkness. I briefly tried psychotherapy, but I couldn't afford it, nor could I trust myself to it yet. Mostly a tiny glimmer of faith kept me going.

Nehwey tzevyanach aykanna d'washmaya aph b'arha
Thy desire be done on earth as it is in heaven.

29

"I Have Chosen the Weak Things"

Spring, 1977, Eastern Point Retreat House, Gloucester, Massachusetts—

I needed to go on a retreat. My prayer life had become shallow, and I was getting into some risky territory. I figured that I had better go on a retreat before I became completely lost to God.

I had never heard of a directed retreat before, but Jim McGrane, a fellow Augustinian priest, had described them to me and encouraged me to make one. Following a style developed by St. Ignatius of Loyola in the sixteenth century,[15] each retreatant was expected to meet with an individual "director" once a day to discuss what had gone on in prayer and receive some guidance. Other than this—eating prepared meals, listening to classical music, watching the ocean, and celebrating liturgy together once a day—that was it. I signed up for the same one that my friend was making in late May 1977.

On the first evening, I was shocked to discover there was to be no talking for the eight days, except with your spiritual director. *What?* I had never been silent for a whole day, let alone eight. The Morrissey family was famous for its garrulous banter. Why would people seek silence for a week and expect to find God's presence in that?

Well, I learned why. As good as our religious traditions are, too much talking and too much togetherness can hide our own souls from us. Plus, God can't get a word if he wanted to. I discovered that silence is a way to be with myself, to know myself,[16] and that in this place, I might get to know God better. I recalled my seminary days and the Great Silence after dinner each night until the next morning. Slowly, I began to enter this practice.

Eastern Point Retreat House is situated on one of the most spectacular stretches of geography in America. The huge mansion hovers on a rocky peninsula that juts out into Gloucester Bay on the North Shore of Massachusetts. The most stunning feature is the huge orange rocks that create fascinating cliffs and hidden perches up and down the ragged coastline. Retreatants can quiet their minds watching the seagulls and tides. Possibly even hear a word from the Creator of such stark beauty.

It gave me a thrill to go out on these rocks at different times of the day. Usually, I would take a Bible and read a short passage, then sit and see what happened. Sometimes, I would imagine the Gospel scene I had just read, passing the time to think of Jesus with a leper or a prostitute and trying to imagine their feelings as they spoke to each other. Occasionally, this would get me in touch with what I was feeling.

For a half hour or so, I would sit in this manner, letting my heart speak directly to Jesus or God. It felt good to tell Jesus of a problem and ask his help. To have someone care for what was going on with me and the world made me feel less lonesome.

"I love you, Lord," I'd tell him. Or I'd express my sorrow over some sins, or for a grudge I had nurtured.

Each day, I told my director about these experiences. Bill Barry was a Boston Jesuit who later wrote a book on spiritual direction.[17] I liked his easygoing style and didn't hold anything back, including that I was gay. It was great having his total attention.

On the fourth day, Bill looked across at me. "When you speak to God, Paul, do you ever listen back?"

I guess you could say that I "listened" for God's response, but mostly I looked in the events of my life to see the result of my prayers. "No," I shrugged.

"Do you think you might want to?" Bill grinned softly.

I imagined God being critical, or he might order me to do something I didn't want to do, such as leave the priesthood. Or something I couldn't do, like deny that I am gay. My knees jiggled. "Listen for what?"

"For what God may want to respond," explained Bill.

I mulled this idea. "I could try."

"Good." He made it seem simple. "Do just what you are doing, except that after you speak to God—wait. Try and just sit quietly and see if God wants to speak back to you."

"Okay," I nodded.

"Good. Well, same time tomorrow."

Soon, I was out on the rocks, calmer and more open than I had felt so far during the week.

It was the last day of the retreat, brilliant, cool, and sunny. Wearing a broad-brimmed straw hat, I hunted for the neat place I had found the day before, a ledge sheltered on three sides with a view of the waves crashing below. Gripping the rock wall, I worked my way across a narrow strip to the ledge, and making a little nest out of my blanket, I squatted down and took a swig of water. All by myself finally. By now, I was craving silence. Perhaps today God would break his silence. I sat there for a long time, stumbling back to the house a different person.

I had been reading St. Paul's Letter to the Corinthians again: "But God chose what is foolish in the world to shame the wise; God chose what is weak in the world to shame the strong" (1 Cor 1:27). I closed my eyes and let my head incline downward toward the incoming tide. *The foolish things of the world, the weak things....*

Sitting, breathing, and listening, I began after a while to feel a presence, a pressure. I pictured myself down in the tidal basin with the stones, seaweed, and dirty foam. *Oh God, I am one of your weak things.* A voice like a rumbling ocean spoke these words deep in my soul, "Paul, you are the garbage of the earth, the refuse..." Taking this in, I felt like a piece of shit. *No, Lord! I can't bear it!* Turned inside out, I wept from the deepest part of my soul. *Oh God, please, please, have mercy on me.* I felt like I was going to die.

Then I heard another part of St. Paul's message, deeply tender: "But don't worry, Paul; I have chosen the weak things of this world that no flesh may glory in my sight." With those words, I felt the hand of God reach down to claim me, choose me. Not for my goodness or perfection but precisely in my weaknesses: "God chose what is low and despised in the world, things that are not, to reduce to nothing things that are, so that no one might boast in the presence of God" (1 Cor 1:28–29).

"Oh God! Oh God, please, have mercy on me," I prayed. The sea crashed beneath me as the sun warmed my face.

One last message came to me: "I will give you powerful words to write."

Later that summer, I was in Chicago for the national convention of Dignity. The next day, I was scheduled to lead a workshop called "Gay Clergy and Religious" with Richard Woods, a Dominican priest. This was the first public gathering of gay priests and religious at a national level. In a burst of energy earlier that year, I had called Paul Diederich, the president of Dignity, and suggested we have a workshop for the many gay and lesbian religious and priests who were usually seen only in their role as chaplains for Dignity. "We need a space where we can be ourselves and support one another," I said. He agreed. The workshop with Rick was the result.

In my room the night before our workshop, I was practicing my opening message. Halfway through, I felt a wave of nausea and sat on the floor. Gradually, I stretched out my arms and legs. Still the nausea. It was one thing to speak to my provincial, my family, or my spiritual director about my sexual orientation. It was another thing entirely to stand before a whole group of strangers, even if they were gay or lesbian, and tell the story of my sexual-spiritual journey.

"How can I do this, Lord? I'm afraid." Silence. Then, softly, the words from my ocean ledge experience came back: *Don't be afraid, Paul. I have chosen the weak things of this world that no flesh may glory in my sight.*

The next day, fifty gay clergy and religious showed up for our first workshop, and forty more people showed up later for our second. There was so much electricity in that room! It was as though centuries of bottled-up feelings were being set loose. For the first time in our lives, diocesan priests, sisters, religious priests, and brothers from all over the country were seeing themselves as not alone. At the end of both sessions, I said, "We can't let this be the end, can we?" I held up a clipboard. "If you would be willing to sign up, I will at least send you the minutes of this discussion." In an amazing display of trust, more than sixty people signed their names.

Back at Philly's Dignity storefront, I spoke with Clare, a lay friend and a member of Dignity. "Clare, do you want to help me start a newsletter?" *I will give you powerful words to write.*

"What about?"

"For gay priests and sisters." I imagined how we could pour out our love for God by reaching out to these people. Our eyes met. Two weak things in a dingy basement in Philly.

Yet the moment she said "Sure!," Communication Ministry was conceived. The angels must have sung.

Communication Ministry, Inc. (CMI) became a source of support, connection, and hope for many gay and lesbian priests and sisters from 1977 to 1993. Its board of directors comprised vowed men and women religious and clergy. We organized retreats, published a monthly newsletter that was distributed internationally, as well as journals that addressed AIDS, seminary formation, and spiritual direction for LGBT clergy and religious.[18] Its purpose was stated underneath the logo: "Communication: a dialogue on the relationship between personal sexuality, spirituality and ministry for the purpose of building community among lesbian and gay clergy and religious." We deliberately made the title of the organization and the newsletter innocuous so that we weren't waving a red—or lavender—flag.

We published letters from readers on various themes. Clare and I hung a large world map on the wall of the Dignity storefront and delighted in putting pink pins in places from which religious sisters and nuns wrote to us, blue ones for religious brothers, and black ones for priests. We had a few red ones prepared for when a bishop joined our mailing list, but none did so unless under a pseudonym.

With CMI as a model, Australia and England started similar ministries and newsletters. Like the American model, these were "underground" efforts. We chose to avoid the publicity that would make us better known but would also bring censure from Church authorities because we were discussing things that were normally kept in the shadows.

30

"What Do You Want?"

Summer, 1983, Fishkill, New York—

As the editor of our *Communication* newsletter, I had the opportunity to offer spiritual direction through the written word, and to do so for a group of people who, for various circumstances, could not seek this where they were.[19] It was an amazing and challenging ministry. I did not want to go against Church teaching, yet I wanted to meet people where they were as spiritual directors are trained to do. Here is a sample newsletter[20]:

> Hello All! Our first letter this month is from a cloistered convent!
>
> First of all, I don't know whether to apologize or simply state the truth. I don't think that I am homosexual, or at least, in the degree necessary to precipitate my awareness. My heart tends to go out to people who have been black labeled by society. I can't help but be intensely aware that all people share the same, basic humanity and that no one's orientations, problems or weaknesses are REALLY THAT DIFFERENT from the common stock!...
>
> Reading the several issues of *Communication*, I was deeply touched by the profound personal sharing. In fact, I had a gnawing gut feeling that this was a sacred sharing among members of a group and that I did not belong as a welcome reader of it. If there's anything that I'd like to share with your group, it's the humor of the situation—I felt guilty

because I am not classified as a homosexual! It's amazing how quickly we feel the emotion of discomfort or guilt, when we think we are outside the makeup of "the group."

There were a number of things in your writings that I could resonate with, but this letter would have to go on much longer. What I do want to include here though is my deepest respect for each of you, respect for the mystery (and I use that word in its sacred and best sense) of the orientation residing in you, admiration for your open honesty, and gratitude that you have the courage to witness to the mystery of Christ in you. You have given up much to serve the Lord; he'll never let you down regardless of the judgments of the "more accepted groups."

What a great encouragement! I am particularly struck by her use of the word *mystery* in our regard. Wouldn't this be a much better way for the Church leaders to look at any sexual orientation—a mystery, a question from God to be listened to rather than a problem to be solved? Our next letter, from Africa, continues this same sort of approach:

Your March issue of *Communication* is your best. Steve's letter and your response make a very beautiful treatment of the question of gayness in Religious Life (or priesthood). Most valuable of all is the way you reveal your own experience of chastity in sexual-genital activity, and as a gift longed-for and begged from God in its final form, celibate. I wish the issue could be put in the hands of every Provincial and formator as an extract (since you may not wish to give the newsletter itself all that much publicity). I think I am excited over the issue because it has helped me put my own journey out in relation to yours, and suddenly understand it. Thanks. I thank the Lord for what he is doing through you for us and for the Church.

Thank you for sharing your response with us. Whether it is pro or con to our ideas, it helps us in discerning our personal journey when we hear from you, our community of faith. To help illustrate this, I would like to share with you a letter I recently sent to a reader I will call Frank.

Dear Frank,

Thanks for your excellent letter, excellent in letting me hear where you are coming from. You say you are thirty-one years of age, a religious priest ordained for three years, and that you are sexually active. Thank you for being so open with me. It helps me risk being more personal with you....

I am sorry you were left confused by my response when you asked me about spiritual direction in a letter you sent a few months ago. You say, "I seemed to dismiss (your) holding on to being actively gay as a not-all-that-important factor in direction." That confuses me, Frank. What I do remember writing to you was the name of a spiritual director I know living near you. I mentioned that he may have convictions one way or another about sexually active gay priests, but if you are both open about your feelings, this shouldn't get in the way of spiritual direction. Did you ever see him? What happened?

You say next that the reason you were confused then was because previous to this, "the tone you had always received from the newsletter was joyously supportive of actively gay religious and clergy." You say you now "sense a shift in perspective." I think you are right, Frank; it also reflects my own struggle *as an editor* and spiritual director who wants to share the "passover" (your word) I experienced a while back while not inflicting it on others. How to do this?...

What transpired in my prayer dialogue with the Lord? Time only allows feeble and scattered memories, but maybe they'll be a start to you, and a start in our own further communicating. In 1977, after five years of coming out publicly (family, friends, my Religious Order); and sexually (at first, casually, then with a lover; and ministerially as a Dignity Chaplain), I made a Directed Retreat, my first. On that retreat, I felt claimed by God to the very marrow of my soul and claimed in my gayness at the same time. I even felt claimed as "the refuse of the earth," but one whom God has chosen to love as he does all "weak" things...lest any flesh should pride itself before him (1 Cor. 1:29).

Sitting at my desk in 1983, I cannot remember God or me communicating anything about celibacy during that retreat in 1977. It was much deeper. I felt like I had been turned inside out in weeping. Later that summer, in Ottawa, I began writing a book, which is still in process. I used to write all morning and all evening, then take a walk by the canal near where I was staying, a known cruising area. One night, after spending some time in a gay bar near the canal, I left after having a fellow ask me why I was there. "Looking for a friend," I responded. "Looking for a friend in here?" he asked with a raised eyebrow.

Under a full moon I wandered along the bushes and benches of the canal. It was after midnight. The hunger inside me kept calling for some food. Who will fill this? Who will touch this ache? I wondered. I forget what happened next, whether I was approached or ignored, but in desperation I finally laid down on my back on the bank of the canal. The moon sailed above me in the trees. It was gorgeous, a true summer night. And I was miserable.

"What do You want?" I found myself angrily addressing God. God in the moon so far above me, the same God who had touched me so deeply with his love only a month before on my retreat. Silence.

However long I lay there I do not know, nor do I remember saying anything more myself. But what I then heard spoken back to me in a way that shook me by its newness was this: "Paul, what do *you* want?" Nothing more. Silence again. Sitting up with a start, I wondered if I had just imagined that. But its effect on me was powerful. Years of back-and-forth feelings—of wishing and resenting at the same time, of wanting it like it used to be and knowing it never could be so again—came to a head inside me.

What do You mean, what do I *want?* You mean I am that free? You mean You don't really demand that I be this or that as a condition on our relationship? You mean that I might really have a feeling about how I want to be that is *inside* of me? A feeling that You care about. That I can admit even if it feels impossible for me? Then I heard myself say to God-in-the-moon words I hadn't spoken in hope or truth for years: "I want to be celibate." Something new happened then. A door opened. I felt tiny and fragile, but fresh. A freshness I can only compare to my First Communion Day. And I felt free. Free at last, oh God.

Getting up from that spot, I resolved to start again with the Lord's help. And I knew in my guts how much I needed His grace to be what I wanted now. Day by day, I thought. I resolved not to walk on that cruising side of the canal anymore. That Autumn, a woman friend and I began to write the *Communication* newsletter.

Thanks again, Frank, for the opportunity to relive my

experiences of being touched by God. I am sure I have not yet savored them to the depths they deserve. Pray that I find ways to communicate them in ways that help, rather than hinder, other people's unique journeys and time with the Lord.

Until we meet,
Your brother, Paul.

In 2009, due to the exploding pedophilia scandal,[21] and the witch hunts of right-wing Catholic organizations,[22] the board of directors of CMI reluctantly decided to shut down the American organization and cease further publications. It was like a death. All Catholic organizations were suspect after this, whether they had anything to do with the abuse or not. All Catholic priests were suspect. Walking down the street wearing a Roman collar felt like a big *P* (for pedophile) was painted on your back. Just when we needed to find support the most, we couldn't. By 2005, the Vatican seemed to imply that gay men were largely responsible for the sexual abuse and could not be ordained.[23]

I wonder sometimes how all of those "Communication" brothers, sisters, and priests have fared. They are in my heart whenever I hold up in prayer the shopping bags full of their letters that I still have—from Spearfish, South Dakota, to a seminary in South Africa, from a convent in Ireland to my favorite, the one postmarked from Vatican City.

31

A Lover or a Friend?

Spring, 1977, Philadelphia, Pennsylvania—

When my sister Kate married Joe "Obie" O'Brien a couple of years after Mama's death, they often took Daddy out to dine with them. One spring evening, Obie casually mentioned that a Parents Without Partners Dance met in a hall above the restaurant. That night, Daddy met Dorothy Carney, a woman who had known Mama and whose own husband had been killed in a hit-and-run accident some years before. Dot, pretty and sassy in the Irish way, had twelve children of her own. A few years younger than my father at sixty-eight, she could even stand on her head doing yoga and would demonstrate it if you asked.

Daddy and Dot began to date. Five years later, he asked her to marry him. In fact, he had to ask her three times! They sold the Morrissey family home. The day we left, the whole clan went through the house at 124 Copley Road and told stories in every room—from the third floor to the basement.

As we prepared to celebrate Daddy's second marriage, with twenty-six children between Dot and him, I felt my father's embrace of a new life was an invitation to seek my own. The wedding was highlighted on the Channel 3 Evening News in Philadelphia. I was the celebrant. Before they processed up the aisle, a young female reporter turned and asked Dot, "Do you have anything to say on such a happy occasion, Dorothy?"

"Yes," quipped Dot, as she arched a thumb toward Daddy, "He's Abraham...and I'm Sarah."

A few weeks later, we helped them move into their apartment at Drexelbrook Arms. I carried in the two-foot-high statue of the Blessed Mother that had graced our family dining room for so many years. "Daddy, where do you want this?" I asked.

Before he could answer, Dot winked and said, "Put that on the dresser in the bedroom, Paul. I want the Blessed Mother looking out for me."

I sensed what she meant. Given the many children they both had, it seemed possible that Daddy's and Dot's former marriages might have equated sex primarily with procreation, or at least would never artificially separate procreation from the love and pleasure of sex. This was understandable because they were faithful pre–Vatican II Catholics, and this was the teaching of the Church. Now I was hoping that their intimacy could provide them with comfort after so many years alone.

During the long period between 1977 and 1987, I had left Philadelphia, earned a doctorate in spiritual direction, and was engaged in my own personal psychotherapy. By 1985, I had moved back into the Augustinian community in the Bronx and had recommitted to my vows. What had become an informal leave of absence ended. I was now endeavoring to have close but celibate friendships. Even so, I kept hoping that I'd meet someone with whom I could share my authentic self.

I wanted to own the goodness of my sexual feelings—what psychologists began to name "ego-syntonic" (self-accepting) homosexuality—and keep my vows. This was very difficult in the Catholic Church that fostered an "ego-dystonic" (self-negating) view of homosexuality where all homosexuals are expected to be celibate because homosexual acts are sinful, or at the very least inclined toward sin.

My hope of integration and peace lay in these celibate friendships with people who accepted their orientation. With my often-ambivalent signals about sexual expression, I am sure I drove some good friends crazy. What I was craving was human intimacy and feeling at home in my body on this lonely earth. I figured that even priests needed that.

One gay friend swore that he was happy just leaning together on a couch. I certainly liked being close. Even so, I eventually broke it off, saying, "You deserve to make a home with someone you love someday. You must want this in your heart, and you know I'll never be able to because I have promised to live in my religious community. So, I don't want to lead you on." How patronizing this sounds to me now. I was really protecting myself.

Bob, a gay diocesan priest, became my closest friend for more than thirty-five years. It helped that we weren't sexually attracted to each other. When I visited him at his getaway in the Pocono Mountains every month or so, we enjoyed praying Evening Prayer together, and then, over cocktails and dinner, sharing our ideas and feelings. We went on wonderful vacations together. Only when he died, however, and I wept over him in his coffin, did I realize how deeply my heart was entwined with his. Even today, when I see the miniature Renoir painting in my room that he gave me years ago, I call out, "Bob, Bob...." I know our friendship continues and that we will meet again in the Lord.

During these years, I still fantasized at times about making a home with someone I loved, even sexually. Yet I couldn't see myself leaving my religious community and the priesthood. Perhaps I was afraid not to have the title of priest to cover up my sexuality. I kept myself safe by the sheer number of friendships I fostered, afraid of where love could lead me.

What a shock, then, when one spring day I fell in love. With a stunning rush of emotion, I realized that I'd never been truly sure of the goodness of my sexual orientation until then. Even more so, how I was loveable with it, not despite it. Now I knew better. Even if the pope tried to convince me otherwise, I couldn't deny my own body and blood.

Summer, 1987, Racine, Wisconsin—

At a gay retreat sponsored by Communication Ministry (CMI), by now an incorporated not-for-profit organization, I met a priest from Chicago, thirteen years younger than me. A member of another religious community, Frankie was Italian. "Siciliano," he bragged as though it were a secret that he'd show me the meaning of sometime. Dark complexioned and solid, he had a mix of rough-edged swagger and unexpected tenderness that could turn me into jelly.

Frankie and I hit it off over the salad bar where our eyes locked, then lingered. His deep brown eyes and dark mustache stirred my interest, and his voice drew me in. What did Frankie see in me? I thought all gay guys wanted someone muscular and manly, the kind I dreamed about. I was always skinny. No matter how much I ate or how many push-ups I grunted through in the morning, all I could manage was a "swimmer's build." As though to make up for this, I had the Irish gift of blarney like my mother, able to talk on the intake as well as the outtake of breath. Such energy and words flowed out of me when I was excited! I was drawn to big galoots who could overpower my almost feminine energy, and say, "Enough now, Paulie. Relax."

One evening during a recreation break on the retreat, Frankie challenged me to a game of basketball. I hadn't played in a while, but it seemed like a good chance to see him in shorts and bump up against each other's bodies. You'd think it was the Holy Grail the way we fought for that ball! Testing each other, pushing and shoving to see what it was like to overwhelm and be overwhelmed. Bumping up physically against each other, mingling my flesh with that of another man in this way, was beautiful. It could even become love, I mused, even though I was forty-eight and he was thirty-five.

Later, as we stood together in an open doorway, gasping for breath as we watched a fierce rainstorm drench the driveway, I began to wipe my face with my T-shirt. Frankie glanced over at me. "You're skinny, Paul, y'know?" My heart sank, the old tapes playing...*but you're tough too,* I reminded myself.

I beamed my Irish smile at him. "You better believe it, Frankie." Sure, he had won the game, but I let him sink that last jump shot to draw him in. "I may be skinny, but I'm strong." We fell silent. I began thinking of the Brazilian rain forests, the steamy fertile life in a jungle, and Tarzan swinging through the trees. Also, Frankie's hairy, sweat-soaked legs.

"I like slim guys," he announced with a grin.

"You do?" My eyes widened.

He flipped the ball to me. "Yeah, especially Irish guys with blue eyes." So long in its desert of loneliness, my heart skipped wildly in disbelief. *Go for it! What the hell!*

"And me?" I flipped the ball back. "I like big Italian dudes."

Frankie's eyes went soft. He then spun around, afraid someone might overhear.

From his sharing so far in the retreat's small groups, I knew that Frankie wasn't as comfortable about coming out as I was. I would have to take the lead while helping him feel safe. As he ran to retrieve the ball, I whispered loudly, "Even Sicilianos!" He strolled back to me, batting his dark lashes up and down. "Especially when they try to bump me with their butts," I added, throwing my head back and laughing. Soon, both of us were bent over giggling like fools.

Somewhere, we heard a door close. Standing up quickly, we glanced around, but we were alone. Soon our breathing returned to normal. I imagined just saying, "Thanks, Frankie," and then returning to my room. My pinky finger had other ideas though. It reached over and linked around one of Frankie's fingers as though it had found its mate. Smiling, the Siciliano squeezed back. We watched the rain pour down, mesmerized while our hearts fell with it. Later in my room when I prayed, I imagined God smiling down upon his two gay priests having the retreat experience of their lives.

When the retreat ended, I drove down to Our Lady of Angels Parish in the Bronx where I was living then. While the trees rushed by on the Hutchinson Parkway, the two of us held hands as we told our stories and fell in love. "Why not stay over at the Augustinian community with us?" I had coaxed him. Frankie decided to add an extra weekend in New York before he returned to Chicago.

As I maneuvered my little brown Honda Civic into the driveway behind the church, I let go of the warmth of his hand. When I had finally nestled the car into its spot, I reached for his hand again and kissed it. With the Franciscan Sisters' convent on one side, the priest house on the other, and the razor-wire-topped chain-link fence we had just locked behind us, we had entered a fortress against the ways of the world. It was now reentry time from our safe gay retreat space, but we had been changed.

Just then, Iggy McNamara, one of the younger priests, burst out the back door. I dropped Frankie's hand like a bomb and opened my door. Iggy was heterosexual. We got along. He knew my story, and we could talk about personal things. I had confided in him that I was attending a retreat with other gay priests.

"Hey Paul, welcome back!" He gave me an awkward hug. "How was it?" Iggy asked, then suddenly exclaimed, "What *happened* to you, Paul? Your face! It's glowing!" My face began to scald. *Yes, of course he sees, you idiot. They'll all be able to see. You can't hide love. Oh God!*

Iggy turned to Frankie. "It looks like it was good for you too… hey, I gotta get to class." Grinning, he ran off.

Seeing Frankie's concern, I reassured him. "Don't worry, he's cool." I led Frankie up the back stairs to the third floor. There in my two-room suite—a bedroom and a sitting room, with its view out to the church and a busy Bronx boulevard below—I learned a new meaning of love. As we slowly stripped off our clothes and stood before each other in our underwear, it was like the long road toward acceptance had finally brought us home. Shyly, we began to inch toward each other, hands open, eyes roaming up and down, and resting in each other's gaze before we felt each other's flesh at last and held.

I drew him down onto my burnt-orange futon. We lay there in the shadows of the huge stained-glass window, while the church bells rang and our hearts beat together. Feeling a man's body up against mine after so many years, the warmth and strength of it, I could have died. It wasn't that I wanted sex as much as to be held. Forgetting my fears, forgetting myself for once, I lay my head on his chest and melted into him.

Love. It felt like pure love. I gave my soul to him, and he gave his to me. We seemed to be held by something bigger. We didn't do anything more than kiss and breathe in each other's being. Cooling down after a while, we sat up and agreed that we would be *amigos del almas*, "friends of the soul." It seemed that to be genital with each other could even wreck the moment. *Could this be a further meaning of Jesus's words,* I wondered, *"This is my Body, this is my Blood for you"?*[24] He must have meant more than simply the bread and wine of the Eucharist and the Mass. It's about love, about giving our bodies and souls to each other, about what we do with the gift of our sexuality if we can ever find ways to speak about it.[25]

Frankie and I wanted to be friends and be faithful to our vows. Maybe we could do so and still love each other deeply. Living in different cities might help. I was no longer in control. It felt like the old me had died because I finally let someone into my heart.

When Frankie returned to Chicago a few days later, we wrote and spoke on the phone often. Whenever it was possible, we got together for retreats or conferences. One of the happiest moments of my life was leaning against him as we sat on the shore of Lake Michigan, gazing out at the waves together and planning a trip to Italy that summer where he intended to come out to his family. We still hadn't expressed our feelings genitally, but it felt like we were getting married. *Mi amigo del alma.*

We never made that trip to Italy. One day in June, Frankie stopped communicating. He didn't return my phone calls. Was something wrong? Was he sick? Had he met someone else, someone younger and more sexual? Finally, a postcard came. It was oblique, but ominous.

> Dear Paul,
>
> I don't want to communicate right now. Nothing bad is happening with me. I just need some time to think. I hope you are all right. I will write when I get clearer.
>
> Peace, Frankie

Oh my god, what is happening? Rashly, I jumped on a plane and flew to Chicago to find out. I went to his rectory, and they said he wasn't home. I left a note, but Frankie never got in touch. I flew home in a deep funk. Eventually, he wrote, telling me he loved me more than anyone he had loved in his life. "I will always love you," he said, "but I realize I want to be in a sexual relationship." He had met someone and might even leave the priesthood so they could make a life together. "I know that you would never do so," he wrote, "and I don't want to be a threat to that commitment. That's why I can't see you now." He signed it, "*Your amigo del alma,* forever. Frankie."

Desperate, I wrote him, at first solicitous, understanding, and pleading, but he didn't write back. He's afraid I'll talk him out of leaving, I thought. I wrote a second letter, angry and challenging, "If you love me, you'd talk this out with me. How do you know I wouldn't leave the priesthood for you?"

But would I? Could I? I walked around New York like a zombie, while the world went on, and my hopes for a life of body and blood love vanished with my friend.... *Pray for us at the hour of our death.* Later, in a little hidden corner of my heart, I began to feel relief. I wouldn't have to make the terrible choice now between a lover and the priesthood.

No matter the pain, I would never wish away the brief relationship we had, or others I have had since in the search for intimacy. These relationships have taught me the meaning of love that you need to know if you are a priest.

Love of God and love of human beings. Love of men and women for each other, and the children that come from such love. Love of women for women, and men for men, and the friendships that bring sweetness into a cold and lonely world. Love of flesh and blood that I discovered and embraced, even if those embraces vanished one day.

During the next year, on an eight-day retreat at a hermitage in West Virginia, I climbed a woodsy mountain to sit by myself at the top. Once I saw a mountain goat in the distance. On the last day, I carried with me the icon of Harvey Milk that Frankie gave me that day in the Bronx when we swore to be "friends of the soul" forever.[26] He had signed his promise on the back as I signed the one that I had given to him. Before coming down from the mountain, I dug a hole and buried the icon, gazing up to God with a silent prayer and a few tears. Not to bury my memory of Frankie, but to let go of his flesh and blood love and move on. I prayed to God to give me the grace to live my vow of chastity faithfully...*even yet.*

32

"We Are the Church!"

1999, Stella Maris Retreat House, Long Island, New York—

During my annual retreat, I confided to my spiritual director, Sister Gail, a Sister of St. Joseph of Peace: "The secrecy never seems to end, Gail. You'd think that by now we could acknowledge it when someone in our religious community has died of AIDS. We're supposed to share all things in common, but some things are too difficult to share, it seems."

Sister Gail leaned close, her Italian voice soothing and personal, just like I had hoped for. Except for that, you would hardly know she was a sister with her gray slacks and pink blouse. "I'm so sorry, Paul. I know you and Tom were very close."

"Tom is the one who took care of Buddy until he died. Buddy was the first priest I knew who got AIDS, and he handled it much differently than Tom." My gaze searched out the window behind her, looking for a bird or some sign of life. "After the initial shock and fear, and him almost dying back in 1990, Buddy decided that he could work to educate people about the sickness. He figured that being a priest with AIDS would wake people out of their denial. He did much good before he died, but apparently Tom either didn't get the message or he missed Buddy so much that he hid his own infection from all of us until it was too late. He never told any of us, even the other priests in the community. It looks like he just stopped taking his medicine. I get angry whenever I think about it!"

Gail frowned. "Yes, I am sure. What was the funeral like?"

"You'd have thought he died of a heart attack or something. Not even our provincial said a word about AIDS. We all just sat there in our white albs, though I wore a red ribbon on mine."

She smiled and nodded, a wisp of gray hair dangling over her glasses. "The charade goes on, probably fueled by the family's desire not to cause scandal. But the scandal is that we all get co-opted, and the illness keeps spreading."

"Yes. But the religious superiors get caught in the middle. They need to respond to what the families want, I suppose. But Gail, this was the *third* member of our community to die from AIDS! Didn't we learn anything from Buddy? Hundreds of priests have died from AIDS.[27] What if someone in your community had an infectious disease and you knew how she caught it? Wouldn't you alert others so they wouldn't repeat it? But sex is so taboo that we can't even talk about it, even if it is killing us."

"Do you ever pray about it?" I knew she would eventually ask that. Unlike most psychotherapists, spiritual directors believe that a person's relationship with God, including prayer, is central to their healing.

"Yes."

Her brown eyes held my gaze, though not in an intrusive way. "What happens?"

I kept silent for a moment. We were entering a sacred zone.

"Sometimes I weep; sometimes I get angry. Gail, you know how difficult it is for me to get mad at other people. I prefer to overlook problems rather than risk conflict. So, most of the time I am too cowardly to get angry, especially with God. He might zap me," I smiled. "Yet sometimes it builds up. When it happens in prayer, it usually comes as a surprise."

"Hmm. Anger can be like that." She brushed the loose hair back and nodded. A tree, its yellow autumn leaves waving, pulled my gaze back to the window behind her.

"Hey, y'know what I just remembered? The time back in 1987 when Cardinal O'Connor threw the gay and lesbian Catholic community out of St. Francis Xavier Parish in New York."[28] It was an unforgettable experience, especially because it was liturgical. The sound of our voices made clear to me that my journey is not just my personal struggle to integrate my sexuality but a struggle of the whole Church.

"I only heard bits and pieces about that. Were you there?"

"Yes. That was a time I got angry in a way I had never experienced before. The whole church congregation was angry, Gail, and yet it was one of the best liturgies in which I have ever participated. It is like there was all this rage that as Christians you are never supposed to feel, let alone show, and here we were all doing it together at a Mass, a Mass of Expulsion."

"Expulsion! Oh my. Is that what they called it?"

"It's what *we* called it. A few weeks earlier, Cardinal O'Connor had issued a directive to the Jesuit pastor of the church, ordering him to stop allowing this group of people, which calls itself Dignity, to use church facilities since he felt they didn't accept the Church's teachings on homosexuality. It didn't seem to matter that this group of hundreds of Catholics and their friends had worshipped at this church for over ten years, or that they were at the same time being devastated by the scourge of AIDS. The Church must be publicly pure, and gay and lesbian Catholics who disagreed with its teachings had to go."

"Hmm, hmm."

"When I think about it, I get mad all over again."

Suddenly, Gail shifted in her chair, squeezing her hands together. "Do you want to talk about it?"

Closing my eyes, I leaned back in my chair. I could still hear the chanting.

St. Francis Xavier Church in downtown Manhattan, which seats over a thousand people, was filled to overflowing with men, women, and children, with married couples, parents, siblings, and friends of gay and lesbian people, Black and Hispanic people, clergy, and laity. A festive pregnant spirit caused an electric current to pass between people as they greeted one another on arrival. Most sensed that this was one of those historic moments—a couple of times in your life—when your beliefs go on record, when you experience the cost of discipleship, even though you would not know until eternity whether you are right. There was a palpable sense of community that can perhaps only be experienced when one is under siege.

"I began to vest, along with the dozen or so other priests who would be concelebrating. The Catholic Church, of which I had been an officially ordained representative for twenty years, was formally booting us and hundreds of faithful Catholics out of our place of worship into the streets. And it was doing so in the name of Jesus Christ.

"Two parts of the service engraved themselves on my heart. The first was the speech John McNeill delivered during the 'rite of expulsion' that followed the Mass. The second was the procession out of the church.

"During McNeill's speech, a rhythmic chant began. Low and erratic at first, it gradually flowered into a full-throated communal shout that filled the enormous church up to its domed roof as though to reach the very ears of God. 'We are the Church! We are the Church!' was the refrain, as though we were at the same time reminding ourselves and the absent cardinal that the church is not a building, no matter how grandiose, or the possession of a few of its people, however righteous. Christ died for all and lives in all, especially those who are reviled as sinners.

"For me, to raise my voice in church was frightening at first, especially because I was raising it in anger as I felt the passion swirling around and within me. Some people in the crowd were raising their fists. The pitch grew louder until it seemed that we would burst. What this really did was to allow the rage that was so often internalized to sever at last the cord that linked our sense of self-worth to someone else's approval. And we did this not just as individuals but as a community of faith. '*We are the Church! We are the Church! We are the Church!*'

"Then, we took this understanding of ourselves out of the church building where we had been nourished and into the city streets. We did this at the conclusion of the ceremony. It was one of the saddest and yet most inspiring moments of my history as a Catholic priest.

"The pastor, a young Jesuit priest, was at the podium describing the sequence of events that had led to this expulsion. He and his Jesuit superiors had begged the cardinal to understand how his action would deeply wound the entire Catholic community at St. Francis Xavier. The gay and lesbian Catholics were fully incorporated members of the parish. They served as lectors and eucharistic ministers, in the soup kitchen, as home visitors for the elderly, and so on. He was fighting back tears as he told the gathering that he had no choice. They must go.

"A woman member of the parish council arose. She told the congregation that she could no longer be part of such proceedings and was resigning from the council. 'He is dividing Christ's Body,' she said of the cardinal's action.

"At this point, the entire assembly was asked to stand. The paschal candle, which stood for Christ's triumph over death at Easter, stood in the sanctuary before a fifty-foot sheet of purple cloth that hung from the ceiling to the floor. All the people lit their candles from it to symbolize our one baptism. Meanwhile, the lights in the church were gradually being extinguished until only a single spotlight shone on the purple banner in the sanctuary. The Easter candle and the thousand little candles that had been lighted from it spread the Light of Christ into the dark corners of the church.

"Drumming began. The rolling cadence synchronized with the pounding in people's hearts. We followed the drummers out of the church building into the streets, while above us in the choir loft, the organ began to play 'We Shall Overcome.' We picked up the old civil rights hymn, tentatively at first, hardly knowing where we were going or what we would do next.

"Outside in the streets of Greenwich Village, hundreds of gay and lesbian Catholics turned and marched abreast toward Sixth Avenue. We were going to the Gay Community Center, several blocks away, that would host our future liturgies. Behind us could be seen the blackened church door, a sorry-looking shell now that its lifeblood was pouring out.

"I could feel my anger turn to sorrow, even to despair. My candle flickered and almost went out in the night breeze. As I guarded it, I looked up and noticed the many people in the apartment windows above us gazing down at this spectacle. One man flashed a thumbs-up sign that gave me hope. *We are the Church! We are the Church!* a small voice echoed within me. And the drums rolled, *But you're out! But you're out! But you're out!"*

"Paul, Paul...this is so powerful. Could you sit up and tell me what you are feeling?" Gail's voice broke into my reverie.

Raising my head, I remained speechless for a while, occasionally looking back and forth at Gail and out the window. *"We are the Church!"* yes, but the mantra plays in your head, *"You're out!"* "It is as though, if you are out as a gay person, the price is to be out of the Church, Gail. I feel angry at that."

Gail nodded, gesturing with her hand to invite me to go on.

"To be 'out' as a gay person is crucial for mental health, Gail—not necessarily that everyone knows, but at least some close confidants. Otherwise, LGBT people must live a charade so that others can feel pure. For the Church to split these two constituencies from each other is a great wound that begs to be healed."[29]

"I agree."

We sat there together in silence. Gail, a woman religious in our Church that doesn't allow them to speak about the gospel from the pulpit; and me, a male religious and priest who can speak all he wants about the gospel if he doesn't speak about sex honestly. Our Church—so obsessed with sex. So scared of it and desperate to control it, but it can't. *God help us!*

33

My Father and Forgiveness

Summer, 1990—

My conflicts continued, inside and out. I needed healing. One example of this was my relationship with my father. Over the years, I discovered that I needed to forgive and be forgiven by him. I barely knew Daddy all the time he provided for me and my siblings. Only in my later years did I start reaching out to him. Was it too late?

I sat next to my father on a park bench across from Lincoln Center in New York. I had planned a fancier finish for his and Dot's visit, but Daddy wanted no part of the French restaurant I had located because they didn't have roast beef. In desperation, I had scanned up and down Broadway. Sunday Brunch signs were everywhere. Eggs benedict, grilled chicken salads, salmon croquettes—but no roast beef! When Dot finally spotted an Arby's, you'd think we had won the Lotto. *"Arby's!"*

I had invited Daddy and Dot to New York for the weekend before my sabbatical.[30] They had stayed with me at the Augustinian house in the Bronx for the past two nights. When I met Daddy in the dining room for breakfast the first morning, he greeted me with, "It's worse than Vietnam here." I had forgotten that he wouldn't be used to the car alarms and ambulance sirens that blared all night long. Laughing at first at his usual bluntness, I apologized, but secretly I was glad he knew I was living in a rough area. I wanted him to be proud of how I was serving as a priest, not think I was living some posh life, better off than he was.

On our way down to Manhattan for Sunday brunch, I drove them through the South Bronx, hoping to stir up a conversation about poverty. Instead, after we passed a few homemade shacks on abandoned lots, Daddy announced, "Let's get out of here. This is making me sad." Dot smiled knowingly at her men, me with social justice visions in my mind, Daddy with tears in his eyes.

In a few days, I would be driving across the country to California on a sabbatical, writing about my ministry as a hospice chaplain for the Visiting Nurse Service of New York City. During those three years, I had learned a good deal about death and dying, noticing the different ways families coped with loss. Suddenly, it occurred to me—Daddy's eighty and I'm fifty. I'll be away for almost a year. He could die while I'm gone.

Since Mama died, I had been reaching out, even writing vulnerable things to this tenderhearted man who hid his feelings behind his gruffness. Maybe we could get closer before he died.

The fountains in front of the Lincoln Center kept tumbling upward. Colorful banners announcing current concerts flapped in the breeze. A few tourists got splashed with some stray drops. *Suppose he dies while I'm away. What would I want to have said to him?*

Daddy and I were sitting about two feet apart, a metal arm rail between us, each in shirtsleeves because of the warm weather. I twisted cautiously and reminded him, "Daddy, as you know, I'll be leaving for the West Coast on Tuesday."

He turned his lion's head of white hair and rested his gray-blue eyes on me, still munching his roast beef sandwich. Smiling, possibly wary as well of all my education and highfalutin church life, he said, "Yeah, take care of yourself out there. Don't get in trouble." He wiped his moustache and looked back at the fountain.

I figured he meant not to rock the boat with the Church about my sexual orientation. Since I had come out to the family over fifteen years before, he and I rarely spoke about that side of my life. Somehow though, I needed that now. I wanted to reconcile, be at peace with him no matter how our relationship had been through the years. I needed my father's love.

"Daddy, I'm sorry that I haven't always encouraged you over the years, but I need your encouragement now." I felt an old fear that he would scold me, but continued anyway, "Sometimes, it's difficult being a priest…even more so, being a gay priest."

Daddy's gaze held mine—had he softened a bit?—while Dot approached, clutching her pocketbook as though it were the crown jewels.

Daddy began to clear his throat. "Well, I've been thinking about that…" His lips trembled slightly as he spoke. "And I don't believe a person can change from being gay. I figure that God made you that way so you can take care of other people who are like that." *That way!* Take care of other people *like that?* Caught off guard by what felt like a curious put-down at first, I sat speechless until I realized he had just offered the acceptance that I had longed for.

"Well!" Dot tumbled into our moment. "Oh, did I interrupt?"

"No, no," I said, still feeling electric from Daddy's words. "We were just watching the fountain."

Dot glanced from Daddy to me, and back again. "Oh."

"Here. Have a seat." I moved to make room for her.

"No. Wait. First let me take a picture of the two of you," Dot suggested. She reached for my camera and placed her purse carefully on the bench beside me.

"Okay, but make sure the shutter is open," I said, before I leaned back next to Daddy with my arm on the rail between us. I noticed a homeless couple on the bench next to us taking all this in.

Dot stepped back by the curb and squinted through the viewer. "Smile! Okay?" *Click.*

I jumped up. "Now let me take one of the two of you, okay?" Dot handed me the camera and took a seat. As I peered through the camera, I noticed that she had chosen Daddy's other side, with no rail separation between them. "Okay?" Dot leaned into Daddy. *Click.*

Dot got up and reached for the camera again. "Let me take one more of you,"

"Dot, that's enough!" Daddy said.

"No, Tom," she insisted, "I want to take one more."

The homeless guy flashed a broken-toothed smile at this little dance as I went to retake my seat. Suddenly glimpsing myself through Dot's eyes, I sat next to Daddy as she had, without the arm rail between us. *It'll be a year that I'll be on the West Coast. Who knows what will happen?* It occurred to me to put my arm around Daddy's shoulder. But no, I needed him to encourage me.

Dot paused for a moment. "Okay now, smile," she cooed. At the very last second, as her finger was poised to press the button, I felt Daddy's arm reach up and rest on my shoulder. "That's good!" *Click.*

The homeless couple strolled by with thumbs up, grinning. "Father's Day, yeah?"

With my heart soaring like the fountain, I beamed, "Yeah."

Seven years later, when Daddy was an invalid being cared for by my sister, Pat, and her family in Delaware, I phoned to tell him about an enlightening men's workshop I had recently attended. There I thought about our separate paths in life—he had to drop out of high school when his father became ill, I plunged ahead intellectually with a doctoral degree. Different perspectives, and now our roles from long ago had reversed. Even while I blessed others as a priest, I too needed a father's blessing. I wanted to build some bridges between us yet, and I didn't have much time left.

"I learned something about fathers in the workshop," I told him, "and my father." The other end of the line was silent. I pictured Daddy's stern jaw.

"Yes, they don't have to be perfect," he snapped.

"You're right."

Then, before we could explore this some more, he broke off, "Goodbye." *Click. What? What was that about? Damn! He probably thought I was going to criticize him somehow.*

So, I wrote him a letter, chiding him for hanging up on me.

Dear Daddy,

How are you? I thought maybe I'd see you at Brother's Weekend. It was good getting together with the guys, but it is hard to really communicate when we are all together. It reminded me of our conversation on the phone recently. I want to pick up on that. "Fathers don't have to be perfect," you said. Guess what! You're not perfect, and neither am I. But it is difficult to try to say some words to you about a little success I had and have you hang up on me. This is because I NEED MY FATHER'S ADMIRATION, and nothing else can substitute. It may be late in life that I realize this and try to get it from you, but if I don't have a real relationship with you now, I never will.

Many times, growing up, I think I feared you more than loved you. I was a kid then, hardly getting any personal time with this big guy, my Daddy, whose voice was so loud and who seemed so strict. Probably with so many of us kids, you needed to be the disciplinarian, but I needed more hugs than being strapped on my bottom. I don't remember getting many hugs from you.

How do I know? Maybe I pushed you away somehow. Maybe you were exhausted from work. Maybe fathers didn't show a lot of affection in those days, especially for their boys. And in later years, I discovered this: Your own father hardly gave you any of these hugs after you were ten or twelve because he became ill, even if he had done so beforehand. So, how would you know how to give one?

I was closer to Mama, you know. Maybe I thought that was important then, I don't know. Maybe as a little kid I thought she'd protect me from your anger. How foolish of me! Little did I know that a boy needs his father to take him away from his mother. Somehow, I didn't want this, or you seemed too weak to stand up to her for me. Maybe you still can.

I am sorry if this is hurtful for you to read. I don't mean to hurt you but to try to find some way for you and me to honestly communicate with one another. Not to pretend we can undo the past, or to beat one another over the head for what each of us might *not* have been for the other. I know I didn't always stand up for you in pride when I had the chance. I am sorry for that because I WANT TO DO SO NOW.

This brings me back to the phone call and what I was trying to tell you—but perhaps you felt I was going to be critical, so you hung up. What I was trying to say was this: When I was a boy, we learned somehow that "big boys don't cry." So, I learned to stuff a lot of feelings down in order to be a "big boy" and hopefully be a "man" someday. Now I am fifty-seven years old, no longer a boy. I am a man, and something more that I grew up learning big boys are not—I am a gay man.

It has been so hard and so lonely learning how to overcome these prejudices, which our society and our Church taught me—"big boys don't cry" and "big boys aren't gay." Guess what, Daddy? Somewhere during these past years, I have discovered—probably while I was weeping—that a man's tears are not weak. To feel pain—one's own and others'—and to be able to weep about it as a man is strength. And guess who taught me that? YOU DID!

I learned how to cry by seeing my father—you!—weep when one of us ran up to you as a kid with our foot or hand broken from a bicycle accident or something. You would get us help, of course, a hospital emergency room or a Band-aid, whatever the injury called for. But first there were the tears—"Holy Christopher, smashed!" you'd say—tears spontaneously coming from a "weak" man, and an "imperfect" man yes, but a strong and loving man too.

I guess I feel that this is what God the Father must be like too, weeping over his children's hurts even as he tries to help them. I want to thank you at this late date for that gift of tears—yours and mine. They are helping me to be the weak man, the imperfect man, the strong and loving man, and somehow the gay and proud man that I am. Thank you, Daddy.

I hope we can pick up this conversation soon. I want to forgive and be forgiven by you. I want to love and be loved by you if that is possible. I want you to be proud of me and me to be proud of you. You are my father. There is no other. I wouldn't want any other.

With love,
Your son, Paul.

I visited him at Pat's and Tom's a few weeks later. As I knocked on the door before opening it, I heard a gravelly voice call out, "Who is it?" *No voice in the world like that. The old man!*

"It's me, Paul." I called up the stairway into the living room.

A shuffling sound. Nervously, I climbed the stairs. Making his way across the living room with a cane was this guy—*my father*—as skinny now as I was and crotchety, but whose embrace I needed more than anyone's. Our eyes met. The cane dropped as he held out his arms. Before I could wreck the moment with a light comment, he murmured, "C'mere. Lemme give you that hug I never gave you when you were six years old." My heart cracked open with joy, and I fell into his bony arms like the prodigal son.

1999—

My father is gone now. He died at the age of eighty-nine, two days before the end of the millennium, slipping away while my brother, Tommy, hooked up a cable TV for him to watch the Philadelphia Eagles fight the Dallas Cowboys for a wild card spot in the playoffs. We had been nursing him that last year at Tommy and Nancy's house in Newtown, Pennsylvania, with the help of an illegal Russian immigrant aide, Vita, and a PowerPoint schedule that had the fourteen siblings driving up and down the East Coast like crazy people, trying to connect with him before the end so we could let him go in peace.

"Tom," Nancy called softly. She waited for Tommy to turn from the TV. "I think he's gone."

"No shit!" Tears brimmed in the ex-Marine's eyes as he kicked aside the Pampers and crossed the room. He took Daddy's thin hand. The face was drawn and pale, the mouth open.

"No breath. Silence. Nothing," Tommy told us later. Yet a peace seemed to come over the bed as the frail body of this titan of our childhood let go of the long struggle. "During a football game would you believe?" cracked Tommy. "Ain't that a pisser?"

Nancy and Tommy fell into each other's arms, exhausted after a year of family chaos, worry, and little sleep, between translating for Vita and wiping Daddy's butt while he screamed because his skin was so delicate.

Once when I was on my knees behind him, helping him in the bathroom, in exasperation, I shouted, "Holy shit!"

True to form, Daddy responded, "That's nice for a priest to say!" I had to laugh. Each of us in our own way learned to appreciate the old man's gritty humanity and his gift of life, being down with him in the body and the blood...and the shit.

"I'm happy for him," Nancy said. "It was rough for him at the end."

"Yeah," Tommy said, "me too." With a great sigh of relief, he went to call the rest of the family.

Afterward, when Dot cleaned out her closets, she gave me—along with some of his sweaters and socks—the letter I had sent Daddy a few years before. "Here Paul," she said in her rueful voice, "maybe you'll want to keep this. Your father slept with that letter under his pillow for a couple of weeks after you sent it." Slowly, I opened its yellowing pages, discovering again what I once wrote him in a moment of need. A grin spread across my face as I read it, receiving back from Daddy his blessing from the other side.

34

The Vocation of LGBTQ+ People

Spring, 2005, New Rochelle, New York—

Children have been on my mind lately, probably because of my age. The fact that my parents are both deceased may contribute to my sense of mortality and posterity. How do we live forever if we don't have children? A strange thing happened to me in this regard recently. I was at home on a Saturday afternoon, preparing for Austin Counseling Center's dinner dance later that night.[31] My car was parked in the driveway, and I was tossing bags and bundles into it. Across the driveway by a hedge, I heard a noise. I looked up and saw one of the neighbor's children on his bike.

"Hi," I called.

A little voice answered back, "Hi." It was Jamie, one of the three-year-old triplets who lives next door. They had introduced themselves to me a year ago, announcing, "We're triplets!" Quickly, the two others, Jennie and Gina, ran over too, with their mother Caitlin nearby.

Gina climbed the bottom branch of the tree. "I'm the oldest," she bragged.

"Wow! That's good." I said.

Jamie countered, "I…I kicked…I kicked my sister in…"—he glanced over at his mother—"…in my mom's belly." His big eyes glowed at this public confession.

"What?" I searched for a decent response.

"Yes, he did." Jennie agreed, nodding up and down.

"Jamie, why did you do that?" I probed.

"Because she was taking up too much room!" He giggled and poked her softly.

"Oh! Poor Jennie!"

"I came out last," she countered, and ran over to give me a hug. Grabbing her little hands, I swung her around in a circle.

"Whee!"

Of course, the others wanted this too. Quickly, I gave them each a spin. "Hey, I gotta go!" I told them.

"Bye!"

"Bye! Bye, Paul!...Bye!"

Then I ran back into my house. As I closed the door behind me, tears began to tumble out of my eyes—*What's this?* It was like their little hands reminded me of my own childlessness, that, as a celibate, I was going through life without that greatest of gifts, offspring. Oh, it hurt so bad not to have a child of my own.

"They're not my children!" I cried to God. The tears wouldn't stop. Dammed-up longing for more than sex or a deep relationship spilled out, but for that most sacred fruit of them—a child. I needed the tears to stop though; I had to give a speech at the dinner dance. Soon a response came from inside of me, *They're not your children, Paul, but the people you counsel in your center are.* And Daddy's words came too: *I think that's why God made you that way. When you help other people's hurting children, they are your gift to God.* The tears turned to laughter then, and I did a lot of dancing that night.

Summer, 2006, Ocean City, New Jersey—

For the past thirty years, my four brothers and I have spent a weekend together every spring. In our younger days, we'd take canoe trips on the Delaware River where we'd camp out on little flea-bitten islands. More recently, we rent a condo at the Jersey Shore near a golf course and abundant fishing. We'd include brothers-in-law and nephews if they were interested. Usually, it is about ten of us, drinking Old Granddad and one-upping one another with foul language as we played poker and pool, raved about the Philadelphia Eagles, Lance Armstrong, the Tour de France, and NASCAR, and occasionally toward midnight, discussed religion and politics. But not too much.

My nine sisters also got together like this, usually at the seashore, probably beginning when our mother died in 1975. They included the sisters-in-law if they wanted to try and get a word in edgewise, but not the nieces because there are too many of them. "Start your own group," they were encouraged. The sisters even had "mini" sisters' weekends leading up to the big one in the spring. A key difference, as I understand it, is that the sisters plan every day's menu, and each takes responsibility for something, while the brothers arrive with golf clubs, fishing poles, bicycles, six-packs of beer, and bottles of liquor. We wait until the last minute to decide whether we'll go out for dinner or have some food sent in. Whoever's the hungriest orders it.

Over a few years, I realized there's another key difference. After these weekends, I still didn't know what was going on with my brothers, nor they with me. I once got up the gumption between action movies to suggest that the brothers might want to take some time while we were together to go around the room and say what was happening with each of us. You might have thought I was suggesting mass suicide.

"*What!?*" screamed Leo, the youngest. "You want us to *share* our feelings—*like the sisters do?!*" he mocked his mutant priest-brother. "Ha-ha-ha!" The room exploded in laughter, and we became even more competitive to prove we weren't wimps. I howled along with the rest, at least halfway for self-defense, even though I knew my brothers loved me.

These weekends are mainly terrific. We realize we are very blessed as a family to even want to get together. These gatherings bond us through the rest of the year. The brothers and brothers-in-law initiate the younger males into how to be Morrissey men, while the nephews keep us abreast of the latest music and computer software. Mostly, these weekends allow a space to talk about male things without the sisters and wives commenting, even if it is bragging about the Eagles and the big fish that we once caught.

Unless I surrender to this dynamic while drinking quite a few beers, I sometimes find myself more silent at these events, which is not my normal nature. It is just that you almost need to get violent to break into the discussion, and of course sprinkle your stories with appropriate sexual putdowns and near blasphemies.

And even though I do root for the Eagles, they aren't my religion unless they are in the Super Bowl.

By the time we all had arrived one Friday night, it was dinnertime. Francis called across the room with a phone in his hand, "Hey, Paul, whaddaya think of this new pope, Benedict XVI? Oh, gimmee five large pizzas, one with extra cheese, one with sausage, two with pepperoni and peppers, and one with mushrooms and anchovies," he muttered into the phone.

"I hear his nickname is 'the German Shepherd,'" cracked one of the nephews.

"He's gonna be tough," I offered, not wanting to give any more reasons for them to discount the Church. "He was the one in charge of keeping the rules for the past twenty-five years," I added.

"I hear he believes that religions other than the Catholic Church are not as good somehow," Joe broke in.

"It's not that they aren't as good," I groped for the pope's precise nuance, "he believes they have grave deficiencies, meaning the Catholic Church has the full truth."

"*We do?* What about the abuse scandals?" a brother-in-law yelled.

"He means that we have all the basic truths, even if people in the Church don't always express them perfectly: belief in Jesus Christ as our Savior, the sacraments, the priesthood," I said.

"What the hell good have any religions been in history?" cracked Francis as he poured himself another drink. "They've caused most of the wars, haven't they?"

"Yeah, Judaism, Christianity, Islam, all patriarchal, monotheistic religions, they've all been trying to prove they are the only way to God..."

"Since they overwhelmed the goddess religions."

"I hear the pope said Buddhism is an autoerotic religion."

"What the hell do the Buddhists believe anyway?" Tommy yelled, all these comments overlapping, no one waiting 'til one thought was finished before the next one was blurted out.

I spoke about the Buddhists' belief in detachment, that desire was the root of all suffering.

"Detachment!" mocked Francis. "You've gotta be kidding. I ask you, what the hell have the Buddhists ever invented?"

"Yuk-yuk-yuk!" We all laughed into our drinks, "Maybe yoga?"

"Our country has invented every damn thing you can think of—lightbulbs, airplanes, you name it," Tommy bragged. "Where would we be if we were all staring at our navels?"

"Ha-ha-ha!"

"The Chinese invented gunpowder," quipped our nephew, Chris.

"Yeah, but we converted it into dynamite," countered Leo.

"And now we ship guns all over the world," cracked Joe.

Since we were bordering on politics in our diverse mix of Republicans and Democrats, we needed to get back to the Eagles. "Wait 'til you see us next year."

On that note, I decided to walk to a supermarket to buy some milk, orange juice, and donuts for breakfast on Saturday morning. As I walked alone through the shadowy mist, I thought of how I often got lost in this male dynamic. Maybe I would do better at the sisters' weekends, but their total communication would overwhelm me too. I was too independent to be with my sisters and too sensitive to feel at home with the aggressive competition of my brothers. All thirteen of my siblings had married; all but two had children.

You're gay. That's why you exist. You are a bridge between these worlds, even if it sometimes leaves you feeling like you don't belong to either. I thought of all the gay and lesbian people in the world, how so many of us work in the helping professions, how we are the cement of the world. What would it be like if we stopped helping the world raise its children for a single day? What would the Church do if gay priests had a sick-out one Sunday a month? *That's why you're here. That's why I created you. Don't ever stop believing in this vocation, no matter what is said of you.*

I remembered the trip to the Southwest I made some years before and the Pueblo dance I had seen. During the main procession, men and women marched in lockstep precision, while other garishly painted figures—koshares—darted in and out among them, trying to throw the procession off balance with their ribald gestures and chaotic movements.

Later, when I had asked the tribal leader about this, he responded, "The whole array is under the one canopy of the Great Spirit. Neither the perfectly ordered procession nor the koshares are complete in themselves. We are one family that all need one another. The perfectly-in-step ones portray the core traditions of our people, while the koshares remind us that we will always be a little off balance. Otherwise, the precision-dancers might believe that they alone are guided by the Great Spirit." *Gay and lesbian people are in this tradition. Humanity is one family, but your vocation is to throw the others off balance. The Great Spirit holds this paradox together.*

I thought of how being gay is a liminal, in-between identity, linking and inviting communion between the sexes, helping them to bridge their differences because we've had to learn how to hold these differences together in ourselves. I thought of my hunger for prayer and where it might come from; how ultimately, people like me are almost compelled to be this same bridge between the human race and the divine; why it is natural throughout history for gay, lesbian, bisexual, and transgender people—queers—to be priests and shamans.[32] Those who can hold together the paradox of either-or, male-female, spiritual-sexual, human-divine have always been God's messengers. And often, because of this bridging role, we don't have children of our own.

Consoled by these images, I bought the fixings for breakfast, wondering whether I was throwing my brothers off balance or whether they were doing so for me. It didn't matter; we needed one another. If only the Church could hold this paradox together—the pope and the Church teaching in the center, even as an ideal—and the people with their conscience decisions weaving in and out, reminding the pope and bishops that they aren't God. I went back through the misty night to our family tribe, imagining how I might swear even more outrageously than the rest of them before the night was done.

35

Goodbye to My Therapist

Autumn, 2006, New York City, New York—

I was saying goodbye to Phillip, my therapist and mentor for over twenty years. Our province was selling our house in New Rochelle, and because I would soon be leaving for a new assignment in Philadelphia, I wanted to sum things up with him.

"So, what's been going on? Tell me about your social life." Phillip grinned, because I usually waited until a session's end to speak about it. I gazed around the familiar room, a space where I had shared so many secrets of my soul. Especially amid the sexual abuse crisis, it was good to have a safe space where I could speak of my fears and hopes without having someone read their prejudices into everything I said. I thought of my gay priests' support group and how it had helped me over the years.

"Well, at our support group meeting last Sunday evening, I summed up where I'm at. 'I need affection,' I told them."

"Yes, we all do. It's very human."

"I also told them that I had recently become good friends with a woman, Anne. Most of them didn't seem to recognize the significance of this for me, that a relationship with a woman is a gift. Anne is divorced and has a son who is forty. She is a Catholic chaplain in a pediatric unit of a hospital. She consoles people who have lost their children while giving birth, something that is called a *fetal demise.*"

"Hmm."

"Anne has shown me that love is a gift, totally unique for each person—to give or hold onto like a miser. It's the greatest thing in the world. I'm learning that you need to be able to ask for it and receive it."

"So, you've found a soul friend?"

"Yes. We take walks around Huguenot Lake. We spend a weekend together at her place every few months or so. We talk about everything—religion, our prayer life, our histories, including, at times, our romantic histories. A martini over dinner symbolizes this freedom. It is surprising that the deep friendship I've prayed for is with a woman. I also think this relationship may be a key to my really being able to give and receive affection with a man sometime."

His eyebrows arched. "How so?"

I reflected for a moment. "With Anne and me, it's not about sex, but it is affectionate. Too often with guys and me, the sexual feelings dominate, whether it's attraction or the fear of it. We never seem to get beyond this to being affectionate. With Anne and me, the affection is primary."

"You mentioned how you've learned to receive."

"Yeah, this seems difficult for priests. We've been taught to be always giving, pouring our life out in service to others, especially those who are the most unfortunate. This works very well to channel sexual desires, even those we may never have learned to accept, but it isn't balanced." I thought of all the hard lessons I had learned through the years."

"So true."

"It seems that some priests were never taught to have an identity other than as a priest, and probably not to love ourselves as sexual beings, whether gay or straight. We were taught that life is either sex within a marriage and family or celibacy and service. We did not learn about our need for good mature friendships."

"Yes. No wonder there was sexual abuse."

"Phillip, many of my psychotherapy clients, single or married, also struggle with this. It's the major reason people come to see me, especially the women. As good Catholics, we were taught that sacrifice is all-important. The sacrifice of Jesus on the cross is central: 'No one has greater love than this, to lay down one's life for one's friends,' states John 15:13. The striking part about this—and I only noticed this when I began to struggle with what to do with my gay feelings—is that it says *for your friends.* Hmmm... *What could this mean,* I wondered?

"It doesn't say to lay down your life for your wife, your husband, your children, your family. It doesn't say the greatest love is to die for your enemies, the poor, or even God. No, the greatest love is to pour out our lives for our *friends.*" My voice reached a crescendo as I finished.

Phillip smiled as he often did when I got emotional. "Yes, there is a mutuality in friendship that needs a healthy sense of self-love before it can happen. And I would add one more thing. To receive love and let it *remain* in you" (cf. John 15:4). Phillip knew how love went through me like a sieve, how readily I could feel the absence of someone's love when they weren't around.

"Y'know Phillip, after our gay priests' support group last weekend, five of us went out to dinner. After we hugged goodbye on the corner, almost immediately an old loneliness came over me. It was as though the friendship feeling I had while I was with them was escaping out of me and back toward them.

"An idea came to me: *Call it back. Call your soul back.* Taking a deep breath, I breathed their friendship back into me—the *spirit* of it, even if their bodies were leaving me. As suddenly as the light changed and the traffic stopped, I felt my soul come back across the street into my body. *Oh, what's this? Wonderful!* I was then able to walk alone to my car in peace because these relationships were inside me now. And I've found I can do the same with friends who are far away too, even those who've died."

I closed my eyes and breathed deeply. "Sometimes during the day, I call their names out: 'Bob...Ralph...Aelred...Mama.'" When I opened them, Phillip was smiling at me. "There's another side of this too: when I'm with friends, I'm also alone in the sanctuary of myself."

"Yes," said Phillip. "The challenge is to respect our need for relationship as well as for solitude, to hold them together in a balance no matter which one wants to predominate. Many of us settle for one or the other."

"I think that being celibate allows me to do this. It allows me to hold the sexual and spiritual parts of my life together in friendships that don't possess me." A silence came over us. "Phillip, I'm sitting here with this inner peace now, a peace I haven't felt for a long time. Maybe I can love and be loved now, or as Anne says, 'Let the beam of God's love in and not be afraid of it.'" We both took this in.

"Good," said Phillip. "Now tell me about your ministry."

"Well, I've been celebrating Sunday liturgy in Brooklyn. Preaching is so challenging—it takes me a week to wrestle with the scriptural readings—but I love it. The people are so hungry to hear God's Word in a way that relates to their everyday lives. You can see it on their faces when you've touched a place in their hearts, and they are so grateful. You can imagine how demoralized they've been by the sexual abuse scandal. Their faith gives me faith, though."

"Yes."

"Phillip, this hunger of the people is why I am willing to give up my counseling practice and move to another city as my religious community has requested. At the most, I see about twenty people a week. The crisis in the church begs for us to try to reach more people."

"Perhaps, but can you reach them as deeply?" I realized I was making a comment on Phillip's choice of ministry. What would I have done without him? The churches needed psychotherapists with faith to help bridge the split between psychology and religion. Yet I had gotten a sense recently that I could bring some of my training into the confessional. So often the Three Hail Marys penance that priests gave out, à la Potsy Kenny, could leave people stuck in their guilt-confession cycle instead of having a chance for integration.

"Phillip, I hear confessions in a midtown parish every week. When I hear the door open and someone comes into the box, I can hear the person breathing on the other side of the screen. Who is it? I wonder. A woman? A man? A young person? Married or single? Gay or straight? A person who skips Mass or a murderer? In any case, one of God's people. You only have a few minutes in the dark to assess what the person says, never mind what they *don't* say, and then respond in a way that either treats them like a child or invites them into Christian adulthood. It's an unbelievable challenge."

"Tell me what you mean."

"So many people who come to confession during these lunch-hour breaks seem to be scrupulous, painfully confessing little actions that aren't so much sins as human foibles and imperfections of a sort that a good act of contrition would reconcile them with God—'I missed Mass because I was sick'—'I had uncharitable thoughts toward my neighbor'—'I swore at a telephone salesman under my breath.' I get the feeling that the deeper issues, the real sins, if you will, aren't even recognized, let alone confessed."

"So, they have to come to therapy to get in touch with these." He quipped.

"I suppose. But when someone seems ripe for it, I try to invite them deeper, even in these five-minute encounters in the dark. For instance, just last week I was sitting in the confessional box, hungry and a bit tired from a restless night. No one had come in for ten minutes or so. It felt a little claustrophobic and I began thinking of taking a bike ride when I had finished.

"I heard the door open when someone entered the booth. I slid open the partition window, and at first there was silence on the other side. 'Yes,' I said. Still silence, though I thought I could detect breathing. I cleared my throat. 'Yes?' Finally, a guy's tentative voice, 'Please bless me Father, for I have sinned.[33] It's been about six months since my last confession.' A younger voice. Thirtysomething maybe. Traditional Catholic from the way he opened. 'Yes?' 'I haven't been going to church regularly...I lie at work sometimes...I'm angry that I didn't get a promotion...a couple times I drank too much...I'm envious of my older brother...I masturbate sometimes.'

"I've got to decide quickly. Do I probe about the anger or the sex? Usually, the last one is the clue. 'Are you married?' I figured I'd get a picture of his relationships, focus on the sexual issue even if delicate. 'Yes.' 'How are you and your wife getting along?' 'All right. But we're so busy. Both of us have jobs and we hardly find time for ourselves.' We were already three minutes into the five-minute standard confession, him probably needing to get back to work. 'How long have you been married? Any children?' 'Two years. No children yet...but we want some.'

He was getting more relaxed, so I decided to probe the issue he raised, squeamish as it often is for guys.

"'The masturbation. What triggers it?' I kept my voice nonchalant. Silence at first. Did he think I was a voyeur? Finally, 'I have trouble getting an erection when I feel under pressure.' A strained voice now. How to keep him calm? How to get him to voice the real problem? 'Yes? Where does the masturbation come in?' 'I…I find pornography on the internet after my wife goes to bed. This just started a few months ago after we were having trouble. I love her but don't know….' He trailed off when another penitent entered the box on my opposite side.

"I'd have to finish this up in a few minutes. 'What kind of pornography?' 'It's not too bad. Heterosexual mostly….' He was whispering now. No time for a full counseling session, but I wanted to leave him with a goal that might help. 'Have you tried to speak about this with your wife at all?' 'Not really. She knows something is wrong, but we avoid it.' I could hear the hurt in his voice. 'Would you think about talking to her?' A hesitation. 'Maybe…I could try.' By the tone in his voice, I knew that I had touched his heart.

"'Maybe you might get professional help at some point too, but why not start with some attempt to communicate rather than split this off from your wife whom you love?' 'I think I could do that…if we get a day off together soon.' He made a little joke. 'Okay then, that's your penance. Begin to speak to your wife about this. See where it goes. Come back and talk about it here again soon if you wish. I'm usually here on Wednesdays at lunchtime. I'll say a prayer for you and your wife, and you say one for me, okay? Now, say a good act of contrition.' 'Thanks, Father…this helped. Oh my God, I am heartily sorry for having offended you…'

"Phillip, I felt so happy when he had left. This is what I was born for, I thought."

Phillip's face seemed to be glowing. "Your ministry with these people is terrific Paul, and it is so needed." He sat up and leaned forward. "But what about your book? Are you going to be able to publish it and still do this ministry?"

"I've been torn by this question, Phillip. It's like my whole priestly life is on the line. If I go ahead and publish, it may cost me my ministry, and if I don't, I may be chickening out on my most crucial call to minister." I paused, for the moment flooded with the fears that had dogged me the past few months as I tried to finish my manuscript. "I want with all my heart to be true to myself, to break out of the duplicity that has caused so many problems."

"Yes." Phillip gazed at me for some moments. Our time to say goodbye had come. "I believe you can do this, Paul. Please keep me informed of your progress." He stood and took a step toward me. "It's been a great twenty-one years."

"Yes, and it feels so important to have you believe in me. Do you remember the Scripture passage I told you about the last time? The one about Elijah giving his mantle to his younger friend, Elisha, before he went up to heaven in a fiery chariot?"

"Yes."

"Thanks for giving me your mantle, Phillip." I smiled the smile of one grateful to have received. "You can give it to others now too." Even though my time was up, he waited until my words had run out, until I stood there with the sun shining. Until I could claim God's presence in my relationships and my ministry in the Church and be sure of it. "I'll miss you, Phillip." My heart swelled.

"I'm a phone call away if you need me." He hugged me, his cheek against my face. I felt his beard stubble like a father's. Like my father. Like God.

36

The Fatherless in Prison

Spring, 2008, Philadelphia City Prison, Pennsylvania—

I have been serving as a chaplain at the Philadelphia Prison for two years. I have learned so much here. The sense of Jesus Christ in everyone is perhaps the most significant (cf. Matt 25:36). To glimpse the gaze of Jesus looking back at me through the eyes of a catatonic murderer is enough to reduce all other ministry to ashes. The most amazing thing is that, when I listen to their confessions, I realize my own need for forgiveness.

I have committed many sins in my life. Sometimes it is difficult to distinguish between what are sins and what is simply my self-growth as I evolve beyond a truncated sense of my call in life. Nevertheless, I ask God's forgiveness and mercy on all of it, the same as I pray for the inmates.

One thing I learned: I have been in a form of prison as a gay priest in the Catholic Church. I am sure that this is not completely true. Some of my friar-brothers might ask, "You have been in prison? It sure didn't look like it!" They may perceive me as "doing my own thing." Actually, I hope and pray that I have been "doing God's thing." I know that will raise some eyebrows.

Prison ministry has brought all these questions and meanings together. I sum up the feelings of the inmates and myself in a poem that came to me as I waited to be let in for some visits one day:

On the street you can be free as a lark,
yet chained in the prison of your heart.

You can be chained in a dungeon dark,
but free as a bird in your heart.

Today, I visited "Jason," a young, slim white guy with a shaved head, at the Detention Center, a sixty-year-old building with tiny slits for windows and no air-conditioning. As Jason and I stood at the entrance to his cellblock before I left him, I asked if he wanted to say a prayer as I usually did. I put out my right hand and he clasped it. He glanced around him at first to see if we were within earshot of the others, then began to pray aloud, "Please, Father-God, forgive me my sins," he prayed similar words very poignantly a couple of times. I then joined him in this prayer for his forgiveness. The prayer tapered off. We dropped our hands. Shortly after I turned to leave.

Suddenly, I remembered how two young inmates had wanted to go to confession the week before, and how they had wanted to confess together. When I had rolled my eyes and asked why, one of them said simply, "We know everything about each other, Father." The other one nodded. So, even though this is not generally practiced in the Roman Catholic Church, I agreed. It was very moving!

With them in mind, I turned back and called out, "Jason...." He was already through the gate and was returning to his cell. He poked his head back and I asked him, "Would you say a prayer that God forgive my sins?"

"What?!" he responded, making a bewildered face. "Priests don't commit sins."

"Yes, we do...." I paused. "Envy, greed, lust, pride..." With his thirty-year-old eyes wide with a question, Jason stared back at me. I looked straight at him without expression. Soon, he nodded his head okay. We clasped hands again, all of this in full view of the other inmates, some of whom were looking out of their cells.

"God, forgive Father any sins he has, please," Jason started haltingly but soon got his groove. "But I know he is one of your good men, so bless him for all the great work he does in bringing us the gospel...show him you care about him...give him a sign."

Wow! My heart melted. I truly felt forgiven, by God and

Jason. We parted with a different sense of ourselves and our path together in faith.

A few days later, I realized that Jason's prayer was the sign. In prison, it seems to me that there is hardly a distinction between inmates and a priest (or lay minister). It is down in such holes in the ground that we realize we are all in need of God together. This realization is our salvation. And Jesus, God's beloved Son, has chosen to be in these places with us. This is the mind-boggling significance of the prayer Jesus taught us to pray with him: "*Our* Father, who art in heaven...." We need one another in our faith journey, a need that God himself took on through Jesus in humility.

On a following visit, Jason sidled up to the bench where I was waiting and sat down next to me. He didn't look directly at me. It often takes a few minutes for inmates to relax around me. Soon, we got into a rap about his hopes and plans when he gets out—perhaps in a few weeks. "I don't want to fall back into my old ways, Father. I've been reading the Bible here and it's helping me. I feel close to God here, not like in the past."

"What is the Bible saying to you?"

"I read the Psalms...." He still looked straight ahead.

"I like the Psalms too...the way the prayers are expressed directly to God."

"Yeah, David's prayers. They're helping me." He turned for a second toward me, then looked away again.

"Do you put the Bible down at some point and say your own prayers to God?"

"Yeah....My cellmate and I do it together."

"Hey, that's so good. And when you get out, it is even more important to pray like that. The temptations are all around you." I faced the front like he was doing.

Then came the stunning part. Jason suddenly said, "Father, see these guys?" He swept his hands around to show me the cellblock full of guys, some on phones, some wandering around, some sitting on benches staring at the TV. "Most of them never had a father they could relate to...." He was fully engaged with me now. "That's why they're here."

Struck by such amazing wisdom coming out of this young prisoner's mouth, I dropped my mouth open. "Yes."

"This causes a loss, an emptiness that we try to fill by drugs, money, girls."

"Yes...how about your father?" I inquired, recalling how he spoke about his father to me in the past.

"My father was in jail...."

"Hmm...look at this book," I said. I proceeded to show him our Adeodatus book with the names of all the children of inmates listed in the back along with their ages, some as young as two months old, one even saying "unborn twins, due in three months."

"See this list? We pray for these kids every week at our support group meeting. Do you have any kids?"

"No, but my girlfriend does...a boy, seven years old."

"Would you want to put his name in our book? We'll pray for him."

"Yes." He reaches for the book.

Before I give it to him, I leaf through the many pages of names. "There are hundreds of these children's names in here, written by the male and female inmates whose kids are being raised by a single parent or in a foster home. Some are being cared for by their grandmothers. We even have a page of the grandmothers' names in here too." Jason takes the book and carefully inscribes the name of the boy. Then I add, "All of these children—and the children of all of those in prison—are estimated to be six times more likely to end up in jail as the average child." Jason stares at me. He is one of these children.

Later at home, I pray for Jason and the others, *Is there a chance for them, Father-God?* I use Jason's way of speaking to God. It says a lot. I find my Bible and search before I find what I am looking for:

> Be a father to orphans,
> and be like a husband to their mother;
> you will then be like a son of the Most High,
> and he will love you more than does your mother.
> (Sir 4:10)

37

Half of My Heart

Summer, 2014, Philadelphia Prison, Pennsylvania—

Migo is a thirtysomething mixed-race guy, sentenced to twenty-five years for a second-degree murder charge. He killed his cousin in a fight over a girlfriend. I am no longer his chaplain since he has been sent to an upstate prison. He is spiritually minded, though not Christian.

He wants to know what my life is like living at the Church. I guess it is mysterious to him and other people. We certainly have a unique friendship. Over the years, we've communicated on many levels. Rarely do we see each other. He's about five hours away and has about ten more years to serve. Yet with all our differences—and maybe because of them—we have maintained our friendship, which is one that I am proud of, even if only by letters through the bars. He wrote:

> Father, an Irish priest in his seventies and a thirtysomething-year-old man of mostly Middle Eastern descent, who's a convicted felon, walk into a bar...
>
> I feel very good. I've been less depressed lately and less afraid. I just wanted you to know that I began this letter in the format of the beginning of a joke, but it truly does amaze me of the bond we share (at least to me) on such a deep level. We couldn't be any more different or have less in common. Almost forty years difference. You're Irish; I'm

everything under the sun. You're a priest; I'm not religious. You're a gay man; I'm straight. You've devoted your life to God and loving kindness; I've sadly taken the life of one of God's children and have caused too much pain. Yet the things we have in common—we both enjoy writing, exercising, listening to calm and peaceful music, being in the silence and meditating, lovers of nature, dis-likers of evil deeds. We're both brave—I just fought three guys who jumped me after I returned from the shower—and we both love and respect each other.

There's nothing that I wouldn't do for you if given the opportunity. I'd give you half of my heart if half of yours was fading—I truly mean that. I can't help but wish I knew you a little over six years ago. I wouldn't be here if I had. But anyway, let me stop being mushy. I just wanted to let you know I love you.

Hey, I meant to ask you what's life like living at the church? Peaceful? Please tell and be descriptive. Well, that's it for now. I love you Father, friend, brother, mentor, Paul.

Namaste, Love, Migo

My response—

Dear Migo,

The bond we share is tremendous. So many differences, yet so many simple connections. Maybe I trust sharing these things with you because you are locked up! Seriously, a monastery can be a kind of prison. Sometimes our rooms are called "cells." As a gay priest, I sometimes feel like I am in prison. Yet, staying committed to the priesthood is my choice. Your being in prison isn't yours. A big difference. If my heart is fading at some point, I may take you up on your offer to share half of your heart!

You asked what my life is like living at the church. I want to share some of the basics of our life together in the Augustinian order, so you get a clearer picture. As a start, I want to talk about our Rule. The Rule of St. Augustine, which many religious communities around the world follow, is a blueprint for how men or women can live together while sharing "all things in common" as the early Christians did (cf. Acts 2:44). It is a simple booklet, which we read a portion of each Friday morning. It involves concrete ways for people of different backgrounds, social classes, education, and possessions to live in a community dedicated to God. Below are three of the opening admonitions that show the values that Augustinians strive for:

1. Before all else, brothers, we must love God and our neighbor because these are the greatest commandments.
2. Before all else, live together in harmony, being of one mind and heart on the way to God.
3. Among you there can be no question of personal property. Rather, take care that you share everything in common.

These, as well as other more specific admonitions on how to accomplish this, follow in the rest of the Rule, including sections on:

—the care of clothing: "Do not attract attention by the way you dress. Endeavor to impress by your manner of life, not by the clothes you wear."

—how to pray: "The words spoken on your lips should be alive in your hearts."

—going to the public baths: "See to it that there are always two or more of you when you visit the public baths."

—and how to resolve conflicts: "Do not quarrel. But if you do have a quarrel, put an end to it as quickly as possible. Otherwise, an isolated moment of anger grows into hatred 'the splinter becomes a beam,' and you make your heart a murderer's den."

Are you still with me? Some of these are a little strange to understand today. Augustine, a North African, lived in the fourth century. Some of his rules show his society, but they still can connect to today's struggles. For instance, one of the most intriguing sections of the Rule—and one which we friars tease each other about—is the one about chastity. It can be boiled down to: "Do not fix your gaze." In chapter 4 of the Rule, Augustine says the following:

> When you see a woman, do not keep provocatively looking at her. Of course, no one can forbid you to see

> women when you go out, but it is wrong to desire a woman or to want her to desire you. For it is not only by affectionate embraces that desire between a man and a woman is awakened, but also by looks. You cannot say that your inner attitude is good if with your eyes you desire to possess a woman, for the eye is the herald of the heart. And if people allow their impure intentions to appear, albeit without words but just by looking at each other and finding pleasure in each other's passion, even though not in each other's arms, we cannot speak any longer of true chastity which is precisely that of the heart.

And so, Augustine advises that when you see someone you find attractive, don't keep provocatively looking at her (or him). If we aren't just living in a bubble, we know that our religious communities are made up of all varieties of sexual orientations. We can help one another be chaste if we can find ways to talk about these things.

Another dimension of this sexual desire that Augustine doesn't speak to specifically is one we must address if we are to live comfortably in our own skin today. What do we *do* with this drive that God has created in us? Most of us—whether attracted to women or men or both—discover our eyes seeking out beauty without our even trying.

We can try to ignore it—ha! We can indulge it by locking our gaze on these people. We can walk around the streets and malls like scared zombies, with our heads looking at the floor (custody of the eyes?). We can despise it, thinking and teaching others that the desire itself is evil as many notable heresies have done. Our sexual desires can then become an obsession and addiction—even for the church as a whole—overwhelming us at times because we have repressed it.

If we who are vowed religious people can find ways to acknowledge our sexual desires, confide them to others we trust, love our friends and those in our communities, pray with this energy and channel it to serve the needs of others, preach the gospel, love God with all our hearts and souls—we can find meaning and happiness.

As I see it, this is one of the greatest challenges for people today, to learn to see beautiful people and want neither to possess them nor to run away because they tempt us.

We can even whisper "Gorgeous!" or "Wow!"—under our breath mostly—and yet not "fix our gaze," as Augustine says. Better to move on than lock our gaze on others in a way that can imprison us and them, to spread this desire out to include all of God's creation. By so doing, we can learn to enjoy each day by praising God who is Beauty itself, and the Beauty underneath whatever ravishes our eyes....*Gorgeous! Wow! We are made in Your image and likeness, Lord...You must be so beautiful!*

Oh man, I got carried away, didn't I? But you asked! Maybe you wanted something a little more practical, like who cooks and cleans? Do I have a room of my own? How do we share finances? What responsibilities for Mass and confessions do I have? I can get into these at another time, but this Rule we are trying to follow gives you a clue. Maybe you want to join us when you get out! Ha! And if you want to, let me know how you deal with ***your*** desire for beauty.

Okay, my friend? Praying for you and your family.

Namaste! I love you. Fr. Paul

Oh my. Such a gift of friendship to have with this young straight man. It's easier somehow with the bars between us. If I do live into my nineties, how will we relate? He promises to carry me onto the beach then. I imagine lying down next to him on the sand, listening to the waves roll in. What I would really like the most is simply to hold his hand and look at the sky. I can do that on some level now by our letters through the bars. I hope I can really do so when he gets out…both of us finally free of our prisons.

38

"Forgive Me, Dolores"

Winter, 2015, Philadelphia, Pennsylvania—

A woman phoned today and asked for the sacrament of confession. I traveled to her home to do so because Dolores is an invalid and someone I have visited before. Climbing the stairs of the rowhouse in Northeast Philly the next afternoon, I clutched my purple priestly stole under my arm and knocked. "Dolores, it's Father Paul."

As I entered, Dolores hobbled across the living room where another woman helped her lower her extremely overweight body onto the sofa. "You want a cookie?" Dolores asked.

"I'll wait until after confession." I removed my jacket and dropped into a faded stuffed armchair.

"Have it now," she insisted. This was her house, and I was her guest. To get to the point of the visit, confession, I draped the stole around my shoulders.

"Should I start?" she asked, now compliant.

I nodded, and she began this traditional ritual of the church. Mostly, she focused on her anger, assuring me she never intends to hurt anyone—"I just tell the truth." This premise she interrupted often by barking directives to her helper. "Give me my wrap, Stella, it's cold in here...That's my sister, she's a saint...Go to the basement, Stella, I don't want you to hear my sins."

Stella, smiling meekly, shot me a victim's look. I glanced at my watch. I was hoping to be done in a half hour.

"Okay, Dolores, where were we?"

"How about something to drink? A soda? Some water?" I felt myself getting annoyed. "Do you have any gin and tonic?" I teased.

"What?!" Mock horror.

"I'm kidding, Dolores." I took a cookie to show I was still with her. "Can we get back to the confession?" I was almost pleading now.

Just then a phone rang. Dolores found hers. "I got a priest here…he's hearing my confession…Yeah, really! I'll call you back." She hung up.

It's now or never. "Dolores, you were talking about your anger, and how you don't intend to hurt anyone."

"Yeah, I never want to hurt no one…but why are people so thin-skinned? Do they want me to lie?" A phone rang again. *Oh God, it's my phone.*

My brother, Joe. Usually, I didn't interrupt a conversation, let alone a confession, but I needed some distance from her anger. "Excuse me a second," I told Dolores. "Joe, I'm hearing someone's confession. Gotta get back."

"Any good sins?" he joked.

I glanced at Dolores, then Stella. "Lots of them."

As I slid back into my chair, I apologized. "Forgive me, Dolores. I shouldn't have interrupted your confession to speak on the phone."

Puzzled at first, her eyes gradually widened. "It's okay, I forgive you, Father Paul."

Chuckling at the role reversal, I responded, "Thank you, Dolores. It's so great that you forgive me."

Throwing her head back, Dolores chortled for joy. "Oh my god! I feel so powerful! I forgive you…a priest! Stella, come here," she shouted into the kitchen. "Father came to hear my confession and I forgave him. Can you believe it?" Stella drifted toward us with a question in her eyes.

"Can we join hands and pray?" I asked.

"Sit on the walker," Dolores motioned to Stella.

Reaching for both of their hands, I thanked God for making this happen. Noticing that they had joined hands as well, I said the "Act of Contrition," which we prayed together. I snuck a peek at Dolores. The rigid jaw was relaxed. Her anger seemed to have melted. It dawned on me that we may have reached a moment of forgiveness, the object of my visit.

As a conclusion, I placed the ends of the purple stole across both of their shoulders. "Jesus is with us, forgiving us," I told them, then recited the words of absolution.

"Father Paul, this is so..." Dolores was stuck for a word. "Stella, I told you it would be a good experience, didn't I?"

"It is wonderful." Stella murmured.

A peace came over us. We sat in silence, letting it sink in. Before Dolores could start up again, I rose to put on my coat and hat.

"Don't he look cute in that Irish cap?" Dolores asked Stella.

"Yeah," she giggled.

About to leave, I turned back. "You thought I'd forget the cookie, didn't you?"

Dolores's eyes squinted. "But you did forget something," she said coyly.

"Oh, the penance!"[34] I paused, instinctively searching for an action she could do that could interrupt her guilt dynamic. "Your penance is to not immediately jump to guilt when you feel you've hurt someone by your words. If you can, say 'I'm sorry' to them. It'll help some of these thin-skinned people take it less personally...and you as well."

She considered this for a moment, then nodded okay. I leaned to give her a peck on the cheek, almost falling into her lap as I did so.

Walking to my car, I shook my head in amazement at the encounter. "Thank you, Lord. I needed that. Yet, how many more people need to forgive priests...forgive themselves...and even forgive the Church in this New Year?"

39

Same-Sex Marriage

Autumn, 2015, Philadelphia, Pennsylvania—

An unbelievable event occurred this summer. The Supreme Court of the United States passed a law allowing "same-sex marriage." This permits people of the same sex to have the same rights to marriage under the law as heterosexual people. In a way, this changes everything. Now, a little boy or girl can grow up in this country and imagine bonding for life with a person of the same sex. It is mind-boggling to realize what this might mean. Especially for the Catholic Church, which has made its case through its entire history that marriage can only be between a man and a woman.[35] Anything that would question this, let alone suggest same-sex marriage, is a direct threat to the family model on which our country and the world is based. Catholic priests, of course, are expected to believe this and preach it. What am I to do?

First, do I really believe the Church's position? And do I really want to speak about it? How can I not? As in the teaching on birth control, the Church will divide over this. Even while the statistics report that two-thirds of the American people agree with the court's decision, and Catholic citizens in large numbers feel the same, priests don't have the luxury to remain quiet. As I've done in similar crises of faith, I took a walk in the woods to listen to God's voice and pray.

Forbidden Drive, Wissahickon Park, Philadelphia—

It was a weekday, and the trail wasn't very busy. The multicolored tree canopy above shielded me from the brilliant sun. A couple of runners swooshed by. I had my Villanova hoodie on, and one of them yelled out, "Go Cats!" A woman with two dogs approached and we smiled. My mind went to the question of same-sex marriage.

Growing up in a traditional Catholic family, we were taught that marriage only meant one thing: a man and a woman joined for life in a sacrament celebrated in church. No one in our family before me had ever made known that they were gay. All my siblings are married heterosexuals. I have celebrated many of their weddings. No one had ever been divorced. When my mother died at sixty-five, my father remarried. This is what we, and all the Catholics that we knew, did: you got married and raised children, who got married themselves and did the same. I suppose that to even use the term "marriage" regarding gay and lesbian people and their relationships felt like mixing oil and water…at least at first. I began to pray, *So Lord, what do you think of gay marriage?*

Silence.

I glanced up at the trees, woven into one another. Thick ivy vines grew up some trunks, searching for the sun and life. A family on bicycles drove by in the opposite direction. I wondered about the two teenagers. Could either of them be gay or lesbian? How would their parents deal with that? And if they did, would they experience their child's relationship as one of love? Or do they just think of sex when they imagine LGBTQ people, like the Church leaders seem to do? *Is that what you do, Jesus?*

Reaching the stone bridge over the creek, I stopped to look over. The small rocks in the riverbed caused a mesmerizing rippling effect. A newly fallen leaf meandered its way downstream, dodging the rocks until it was free. I thought of Bruce and Tony, two gay friends whom I have known for over forty years. Once, when they invited me to their home for an overnight, I heard them giggling in the next room and was jealous at first. Even when I briefly imagined them making love, it didn't seem especially wrong. It seemed to be normal in a way because of their longstanding commitment to each other. Like married heterosexuals. *What would you teach us now, Lord? And how is it possible to have a conversation about this in the Church?*[36]

As a church, we have wonderful things to share with the world about the meaning of marriage, family, sacraments, God's love, faithfulness, child-rearing, and yes, even sexuality. But if we act as if all the answers are in, we take ourselves out of the conversation.

As I leaned over the stone wall, a thought came: the key is *experience.* If anything influences the opinions of apparently two-thirds of Americans who now support gay marriage, it is people's experience. It used to be that few people knew any gay or lesbian persons—or so they said. Over the past ten years, almost everyone who lives, breathes, and watches television knows someone, even especially a relative, who is gay. That experience changes everything. It is difficult to tell your son or niece that they are expected to be celibate for the rest of their lives when you see them with a loving partner. Certainly, you don't simply experience your gay son or daughter as "objectively disordered." You don't even know what that means, and it shames *you* when you hear the Church use it in reference to your child. People now know gay and lesbian people and their relationships in flesh and blood. If they have eyes to see and hearts to feel, they might even realize that they are blessed by them. *Could this be true, Jesus, that gay relationships can bless us?* I leaned back up and felt that I might be getting an answer from God.

Turning, I began to walk on more briskly. Now in the open sun, I began to perspire. If I hustled, I could make it to the point in the trail where a little curve created a pool where dogs jumped in, paddling after a ball. There I could have the lunch I prepared while I watched them.

We need to discuss the meaning of same-sex marriage and this new law in America if we want to be a viable Church. A way Church leaders might coax ourselves over the barricade we have constructed against same-sex marriage is this: as bishops and priests know, the ones who administer the sacrament of marriage are the couple themselves. The couple marry each other. The celebrant of the marriage is a witness like the rest of those present at the ceremony. *The couple blesses us* by their relationship of committed love rather than the way we ordinarily think about the sacraments—that they have come to receive a blessing from the Church. We are in awe that two people look at each other and say,

"I will love you and honor you all the days of my life, so help me God." It gives us joy and hope to witness this. We want to absorb some of their love and believe in it again ourselves. This is why we dance and kiss and weep and eat and drink at wedding celebrations. In other words, their love blesses us.

Can we imagine that the love of two persons of the same sex can bless us in the same way? I have experienced this. If we allow ourselves to get close enough to experience their *relationship*, we will not worry so much about their sex life. It will take the Catholic Church a while to do this because we are careful and rooted in tradition, not because we are simply sex-phobic. Same-sex marriage can gradually come to be understood, then, not as a threat to marriage as we have known and loved it but as a blessing for the Church, a sign of God's committed love for each one of us, whether gay or straight.

Pope Francis keeps showing us how to go out into the streets so we can minister to God's people where they are. This is a crucial moment for priests and bishops. Will we stay barricaded in our fortresses of orthodoxy or go out to where the sheep smell?

40

A Holy Kiss

Spring, 2020, Philadelphia, Pennsylvania—

I have felt the special call in my singleness[37] to witness to the pain of everyone's aloneness and need for God. My memoir is really about this. The gay dynamics are a metaphor for a more universal human and existential longing we all have for God.[38] The singleness of Jesus embodies this for me, especially his prayer in the garden on his last night and his death on the cross.

I have gotten in touch with the loneliness of Jesus in prayer. It seems to be an image of *God's* longing for us and in us: "It is not good that the man should be alone" (Gen 2:18). It's not good that *God* is alone. Maybe that's why he created us.

Before dinner one night, I went up to my room to pray. I lit some incense and a candle, then took out my Bible and opened it. It fell open to a passage about Jesus's passion:

> He came out and went, as was his custom, to the Mount of Olives; and the disciples followed him. When he reached the place, he said to them, "Pray that you may not come into the time of trial." Then he withdrew from them about a stone's throw, knelt down, and prayed, "Father, if you are willing, remove this cup from me; yet, not my will but yours be done." Then an angel from heaven appeared to him and gave him strength. (Luke 22:39–43)

Jesus was in the garden. Peter, James, and John were with him, asleep in the shadows. I imagined myself in the shadows with them. Looking closer, I wondered: What is Jesus feeling? What is he tasting or smelling? I asked him how he felt about death, whether he was afraid. Was there anything I could do for him? He didn't say words; he was hunkered down in prayer. In his struggle with death, he seemed to have the same questions that I have. I wondered whether leaving life without children of his own pained him. Or was it leaving his friends, especially sleeping ones? Maybe it was the agony of having bet his one life on this way of being single for God and feeling the apparent futility of it? He died while crying out to the Father, "Why have you forsaken me?" (Mark 15:34).

In the garden, did Jesus feel that path of being single left him without a future? What will his future mean without children, without a family? And what about the Church and his disciples? He promised to be with this little flock until the end of time. Weren't they his hope for a future, why he ultimately didn't give up?

I would have left the priesthood years ago for a lover if I depended simply on the official Church for my belief in a future. Jesus believed in his Father, and the flock his Father would continue in his name. I have both loved and hated the Church. Yet it has begun to dawn on me that my anger at the church hierarchy was because they—we!—were often imperfect. I need forgiveness for the times that I have hated the Catholic Church.

I sat back in the shadows and watched Jesus. He watched me, or rather, let me watch. That's all he wanted, "Watch with me." Off in the distance I could just make him out, prostrate on the ground, praying to his Father. I wanted so much to stay awake for him, but a great weariness pulled on my eyelids. Though trying mightily, I kept falling in and out of sleep with the others.

It's the struggle to be true to my call. Sometimes I don't know if I can make it to the end. Yes, my future has to do with God, especially my relationship with Jesus Christ, whom I believe is always with me, even when I experience doubts, or the absence of God like he did. And yes, it has to do with the Church insofar as it means the flesh-and-blood people whom I love and serve, whether they are formally members of the church or not. But I am weak and feel so powerless at times, as though I may give up.

Still struggling to stay awake, I pulled up with a start to see Jesus approaching us. He was clad only in a towel tied around his waist. As he drew closer, I could see that he was utterly bedraggled. His face was hidden in the darkness, but the posture of his body was that of a falling-down beggar.

I began to grasp that the Church, broken and human/divine as it is, is God's *anawim* or "little flock" where I receive the sacraments and sense God's presence in the Eucharist and the people's faith. The Church is this mix of people like me—loving and sometimes hypocritical, saints and sinners, friends and enemies for whom Jesus lived and died. I guess I could even say that I am willing to lay down my life for this little flock of Christ's as he did for me. A good shepherd doesn't flee when the wolf comes (cf. John 10:11–13). This is why I remain a Catholic.

Pity swept over me for him, and forgetting myself, I went forward. He didn't say anything, but I felt him begging me to put my arms around him. As he fell on his knees, I embraced him around his shoulders as he wept.

It all has to do with my experience of being a friend of Jesus now. Being true to this relationship is what I seek, even if I sometimes long for a human lover. Being true to Jesus means believing that I am loved and forgiven by God and by the Church as I am, for *who* I am, and not for being some terrific but false self that everyone might applaud. This is what I was asking my father to accept years ago and what he embraced, *I believe God made you that way.*

This mutual acceptance—*No, we're not perfect, Daddy!*—is what friends do for each other, and what I bring to my friendships. Jesus knows what this is like. He was flesh and blood and had sexual feelings just like we do. John laid his head on Jesus's chest at the Last Supper. Mary washed his feet and dried them with her hair while people objected. So, what is the Church so afraid of? Friendship with Jesus—or the Hebrew version, "Jeshua," as I call him—is the heart of every other friendship I have or long for. It enables me to be a friend to myself, and to "Little Paul" inside me who occasionally still thinks he needs to be perfect to be loved.

I held him that way for a long time and felt gloriously happy. How amazed I was that Jesus, the Lord, desired someone to embrace him, and that I was able to do so as he felt the fright of death approach. After a long while of my holding him like this, he pushed back, then pulled me against his chest. No words were spoken. I glanced up and watched his eyes partly closed. I knew he was thinking of all of us sleeping in the shadows—thinking of how we would get along without him. Smiling then, he leaned down and kissed me, softly and lingeringly—a kiss to last forever.

Occasionally, at prayer, while celebrating liturgy, walking in the woods, writing at my desk, or playing with the children next door, I see Jesus's eyes looking at me—big, smiling, silent. Reflected in those eyes I see a young boy singing his heart out in a choir, a teenager wrestling with a classmate, a guy saying goodbye to his girlfriend. If I keep looking, I see a young man in a habit on New Year's Eve with a friend's arm over his shoulder, a man riding his bicycle to the chancery to deliver a letter to the editor, a father and son sitting on a park bench watching a fountain, and a gay priest holding a friend's hand.

Later that night after dinner with the other friars, I went up to my room. I was bushed. I put on an Enya tape and lit a candle. Taking a swan feather from its place behind the crucifix where I had stuck it a few years before, I raised it slowly above my head like a promise and began to sway, then dance.

In the oval mirror with the antique golden rim, I saw myself: the skinny shoulders, the lined face, the eyes that held so many stories. *I need affection. Big boys don't cry. I have chosen the weak things. C'mere, lemme give you that hug I never gave you when you were six years old.*

I smiled. A true vocation and the courage to follow it.

Epilogue

A NEW EXPERIENCE OF CONVERSION

As a Roman Catholic, I have always been entranced by the Trinity—three Persons in one God. As an Irishman with Celtic history in my blood, the "three-ness in oneness" feels mysterious, dynamic, and true, even when I don't fully understand it. St. Patrick, pictured with a three-leafed shamrock in his hand, is an effort to explain this mystery. The Bible tells us that we are created "in the image and likeness of God" (Gen 1:26–7). There must be a three-ness in us then as well as in God, I believe. This is how I experience my spiritual/conversion journey—as three stages in one journey.

In the classical/traditional understanding of conversion, it is usually described as a two-stage process: a lost sheep is found, a sinner is saved, a person in darkness finds the light at last (as St. Augustine describes himself in his *Confessions*, book 8). In other words, in this model, a person goes from being "Out" (lost/a sinner/in the dark) to being "In" (found/saved/in the light). It is presented as two stages and is an easy model to comprehend.

In my religious and psychological experience, I have grown to understand my conversion in three stages, not just two. The first point of difference is that the initial *two* stages of conversion are *reversed* from the classical sequence, that is, instead of being converted from "Out" to "In," I discovered myself moving from "In" to "Out," from being basically good and part of the community of the church to feeling on the margins. In addition to this reversal, I experienced a *third* stage, so often ignored in the classical conversion model, the reconciliation of the first two. I call this "With."

My experience of conversion:

1. As a baptized Catholic from infancy, I first experienced myself "In" the one/holy/Catholic/apostolic Church. Immersed in a traditional Catholic family, I served as an altar boy and a choir boy, singing hymns to the "Bridegroom of my Soul." From kindergarten through to the eighth grade, I attended a parochial school in which I was taught by religious sisters; *The Baltimore Catechism* is engraved on my soul.
2. This Catholic world (In) included four years of Catholic high school and four years at a Catholic university. It was a moral environment that fostered a good/holy way of life for the most part: weekly (sometimes daily) Mass, praying the rosary as a family after dinner, weekly confession, and retreats. This included modeling and inspiration by the Augustinian priests, my teachers during these eight years, as well as by my family and friends. I wasn't simply an angel—far from it—but I wasn't the devil either. I knew myself mainly as a "We," as a member of a family, a church, a country.
3. To use psychological terms, I was embedded in the communal "undifferentiated unconscious wholeness" that Carl Jung describes as our natural condition before we complete the "first stage of individuation." To reach this point, "midlife" (usually thirty-five to forty-five years of age), a person is developing an "Ego," says Jung. "The primary task of this stage involves choosing a vocation, gathering a spouse, building a family nest, all part of the demanding business of identifying oneself and one's place in the objective world."[1] I was "In."
4. Within this rather secure religious cocoon/bubble/home/ego, I began to search deeper, seeking what some might call my authentic or true self, that is, "Who am *I*?" (rather than *we*) as an individual person before God, even if this awareness of myself stretched me to the boundaries of the Church and beyond. The psyche's main task during this stage is coming to

know one's "other side" that has been left relatively undeveloped or even repressed in the first half of life, says Jung. In doing so, we develop a new center for the psyche that Jung calls "the Self."[2]

5. This likely results in some estrangement from the security of knowing myself as a member of the "We," of being "In." I call this the "Out" experience, an awakening to what is referred to as an adult self and conscience[3]—with pain and sinfulness at times (at least as understood by the Catholic Church). Jung calls this "the second stage of individuation." These are the first two steps or stages as I experienced them. But notice, they are reversed from the "bad to good" path described by many saints (e.g., Paul, Augustine, Ignatius, Francis). I'm not sure of women's experience (see the Reformist Feminist model below).
6. Most pointedly for me, it was my emerging sexuality—in particular, my gay sexual orientation as a priest—that made me realize that I could no longer identify myself as simply "In" the Church as I knew it, or even simply in my family. A key reason for this was that the Church (and my family, at first) did not accept the goodness of my sexual orientation, certainly if I were to express this in actions. At this time, a third stage emerged because I didn't feel able to choose between my vocation as a priest and my sexual orientation. "Must it be either/or, Lord?" I prayed.[4] The third stage is what I call "With." It urged me—and still does—to integrate myself as a priest with my sexual orientation, what Jung calls "the reconciliation of opposites."
7. In these three stages, I have been discovering my true self: not simply choosing to be "Out"—that is, identifying simply with my own ego/will while negating all the spiritual meaning and Catholic identity I had as a youth—but, rather, desiring and hoping somehow to reconcile these two stages, "In" and "Out." In other words, by God's grace trying daily to integrate my Catholic belief in Jesus, even my commitment to my religious vows, and my gay sexual orientation. I want to claim my initial communal

> religiousness as well as my differentness as a gay person, becoming over time "With" the Lord, the Church, and my authentic, true self through all this.

Many LGBTQ+ people today experience their religious/psychological trajectory in this three-stage manner, even if they may not articulate it as such. Indeed, many never seek to integrate "In" and "Out," settling for the freedom and clarity of being their authentic selves outside the Catholic Church or even society. It doesn't have to be this way. If the Church acknowledges people's experience and questions, offering critique, of course, but essentially listening to their experience and accompanying them as Pope Francis urges, we might at least pause the exodus. LGBTQ+ people—and women—likely have a different experience of God that could stretch us. They may have a unique relationship with the resurrected Christ that can begin to convert the Church as an institution. They may be key to saving the Church and calling it to a needed wholeness.

Instead of only seeing the spiritual conversion journey as a two-stage—"before and after"—dynamic, we can open our eyes to the "three-ness" going on in each of us: (1) "In"—before we become conscious of our struggle for an adult conscience; (2) "Out"—the personal and institutional struggle to be our authentic selves; and (3) "With"—the integration of these two parts of ourselves. If we and the Church so choose, this can be a natural part of a healthy adult church. It can be a way for the Church to hear and articulate what the Spirit is trying to say to us today.

As well as my own description of this human path as an "In-Out-With" dynamic, a contemporary model of an alternate way to understand conversion is the "Reformist Feminist Christian Perspective."[5]

TWO PERSPECTIVES ON CONVERSION

Classical Spiritual Conversion. The trigger of spiritual conversion from the classical Christian perspective is an experience that challenges false pride. In such a context, forsaking oneself as the prime authority of one's life can occur. God then shifts to the central authority of the individual's life, and the person becomes obedient to God's will rather than his or her own will. One recognizes God's central commandment to deny the self and love others (i.e., sacrificial love). The archetypal model for such a conversion is Jesus Christ, who is understood as actual God in flesh but who laid down his life to save others.

Reformist Feminist Christian Perspectives. A feminist Christian model of spiritual conversion originated with a groundbreaking essay written in 1960 by Valerie Saiving Goldstein.[6] She argued that Christian formulations of sin as prideful self-assertion, and of grace as self-sacrificial love, are rooted in the experience of privileged white males in Western culture.

Consequently, the traditional Christian depiction of spiritual conversion contradicts the predominant spiritual and psychological experiences of many women whose primary struggle in life is self-negation, not self-exaltation. Namely, the cardinal "sin" of women is in their failure to acquire a strong sense of self and thus assume responsibility for their lives through reasoned and free decisions.[7] Moreover, the traditional Christian emphasis on self-sacrifice as the prime virtue paradoxically may undermine women's ability to develop any core self at all. In short, feminist theologians argue that "women's sin" is precisely the failure to turn toward the self. The feminist model of spiritual conversion echoes the major themes found in the codependency literature in the mental health field.

According to feminist theologians, this type of conversion goes beyond an individual journey toward God. It demands recognition that liberation of oneself requires participation in the struggle for the transformation of the larger social structure of injustice.[8] When the boundaries between self and God dissolve, a person encounters a sense of solidarity and obligation to address all forms of unjust dominance and exploitation.

The archetypal Christian story for this spiritual conversion is the Pentecostal epiphany of the apostles. Jesus's death shattered the apostles' reliance on their relationship with the human Jesus as a source of their identity and direction in life and triggered immobilizing fear. Via a transformative union with the Holy Spirit, the apostles came to see themselves as embodying Christ; this affirmation of their own sacredness empowered them to conquer their insecurities and go out into the world to help others.

In summary, these two Christian models of spiritual conversion represent two sides of the coin of estrangement from God.

"Self-exaltation" and "self-abnegation" are presented as equal dangers to the human psyche. Conversion from pride involves placing God rather than the self at the center of one's life. The pathway to reach this spiritual destination is learning obedience and self-sacrificial love. Conversion from self-abnegation involves placing God at the center of one's life rather than relying on others as the authority of one's identity. The pathway to reach this goal involves learning self-affirmation in union with God and compassionate love. This reorientation establishes a firm sense of self that prevents oneself from being victimized and obliges one to fight for justice for others.

From my perspective, the LGBTQ+ journey for Catholics, and many other marginalized groups, is described in this "Reformist Feminist Christian" model of conversion. As a gay priest, This has been my experience. Can the Church examine this? Can we see in many of our teachings and homilies "the experience of privileged white males in Western culture" (and perhaps privileged white heterosexual males) as described by Valerie Saiving? If we could begin to awaken to this icon and challenge it, the pyramid of our understanding of the Church and ourselves could begin to be transformed into two concentric circles, with outsiders and insiders in dialogue with one another while the Spirit hovers between and overall. IN + OUT = WITH. Pentecost. Trinity. Salvation. Wholeness.

Notes

INTRODUCTION

1. See St. Augustine, *Confessions* (Kansas City, MO: Sheed Andrews and McMeel, 1942), book 10, 175.

PART I: "IN"

1. Omar Khayyam, *Rubaiyat of Omar Khayyam*, trans. Edward Fitgerald, The Project Gutenberg EBook of Rubaiyat of Omar Khayyam, by Omar Khayyam, release date: July 10, 2008 [EBook #246], https://www.gutenberg.org/files/246/246-h/246-h.htm.

2. William Shakespeare, Sonnet 29: "When, in disgrace with fortune and men's eyes," Poetry Foundation, https://www.poetryfoundation.org/poems/45090/sonnet-29-when-in-disgrace-with-fortune-and-mens-eyes.

PART II: "OUT"

1. The Church was a thousand years old before it took a definitive stand in favor of celibacy for priests. This occurred in the year 1139 at the Second Lateran Council when a rule forbidding priests to marry was approved. At the Council of Trent in the year 1563, this tradition was affirmed.

2. Roland Murphy, O. Carm., coeditor of the *Jerome Biblical Commentary*, and collaborator on the New American Bible. President of the Catholic Biblical Association of America, 1968–69.

3. The year that I entered the seminary, 1962, was the first year that our community, the Order of St. Augustine, had psychological tests.

4. See Bishop Geoffrey Robinson, *Confronting Power and Sex in the Catholic Church* (Collegeville, MN: Liturgical Press, 2008), 201, and footnotes 1 and 2 on p. 215.

5. Robinson, *Confronting Power and Sex in the Catholic Church*, 164f.

6. The Seal of Confession forbids any disclosure of a penitent's sins that could identify the person with such actions. In these stories throughout the memoir, I changed persons' names, circumstances, and specific details of their confessional matter to protect their confidentiality and the seal.

7. *Catechism of the Catholic Church*, #1776. "Deep within his conscience, man discovers a law which he has not laid upon himself but which he must obey…for man has in his heart a law inscribed by God…his conscience is man's most secret core and his sanctuary. There he is alone with God whose voice echoes in his depths." (See also #1779 and 1782.)

8. See Peter Cajka, *Follow Your Conscience* (Chicago: University of Chicago Press, 2021), chap. 4.

9. In 1968, references in the Catholic Church pronouncements were to "homosexuality," and "homosexuals." The word *gay* was not used for anyone, priests or laypeople. Even today, the Church resists the use of any terms other than "same sex" tendencies, inclinations, or orientation. In 2024, homosexuality is still not considered a sexual "identity" by the Catholic Church.

10. The *National Catholic Reporter* (*NCR*), founded by Robert Hoyt in 1964, was established to bring the professional standards of secular news reporting to the Catholic Church. It operates outside the authority of the Catholic Church and is governed by a lay board of directors. For many years since, it has been the primary progressive voice for the Church and world.

11. *Humanae Vitae* teaches that all interruptions of the generative process are to be absolutely forbidden, especially abortion, and including direct sterilization, "whether of the man or woman, whether permanent or temporary."

12. You had to be morally against all wars to be accepted in this category by the government then.

13. Erich Fromm, *You Shall Be as Gods* (New York: Fawcett World Library, 1969).

14. Fromm, *You Shall Be as Gods*, 9.

15. Fromm, *You Shall Be as Gods*, 21–2.

16. See Hans Kung, *The Beginning of All Things*, 93. "Creationism," the belief that God directly created human beings (vs. the Darwinian Theory of Evolution) is explained, including its assessment of original sin. See also, Bernard Häring's *My Hope for the Church*, 66. "Adam is not a historical personality who can be assigned a date. He is the embodiment of the entire human race's solidarity in salvation."

17. The Catonsville Nine witness played a key part in the political and religious—especially Catholic—protest movement against the Vietnam War.

18. George Lakey is an international expert on creating nonviolent protest movements for justice, even up to this day with him in his eighties. *How We Win* and *Dancing with History: A Life for Peace and Justice* are two of his latest books.

19. This became a key point in the debate in the Church about homosexuality. John McNeill's book, *The Church and the Homosexual*, 4th ed. (Boston: Beacon Press, 1993), n. 50, became a flashpoint. He will forever be the godfather of the LGBT rights struggle in the Catholic Church. He was forced to be silent for eight years after his book was published. He only broke his silence when then-cardinal Joseph Ratzinger issued his "Halloween" letter in 1986 to the bishops of the Catholic Church on the Pastoral Care of Homosexual Persons, in which homosexual activity was declared "intrinsically disordered" (n. 3).

20. Vatican II played a pivotal role in the life of the Church as we knew it. "The Church as the People of God" emerged as a new image in the councils' documents (in contrast to the institution, the buildings, even the pope and bishops). This tension is ongoing.

21. The forerunner to the Dignity Group.

22. Bill 1275 was bottled up in committee by George Schwartz's vote.

PART III: "WITH"

1. This point is the motivating belief of the whole memoir. See *Fiducia Supplicans*, a recent declaration on the blessing of LGBTQ people, 2024. This breakthrough document by Pope Francis allows blessings by a priest of gay and lesbian people, though not in liturgical settings. Its aim is to turn away from the grace-stifling "the Church cannot bless sin" statement of recent memory and provide an opening to embrace LGBTQ people pastorally, without changing its views on their relationships.

2. To question any of the Church's sexual teachings publicly can be used as a reason to have your faculties to celebrate Mass and the sacraments removed by a bishop.

3. *Catechism of the Catholic Church*, #2357.

4. See Ethel Spector Person, *The Sexual Century* (New Haven, CT: Yale University Press, 1999), 28.

5. This truncated view of the clergy world was my feeling during my early struggle with my sexual identity. A big part of my conversion to stay in the Church and priesthood was to realize that many, including priests and bishops and the pope himself, were allies and brothers serving God with faithfulness as I was trying to do.

6. The Church has a "preferential option for the poor" since the late 1960s. (See Gustavo Gutierrez, the Medellin Conference in Latin America, and especially Fr. Pedro Arrupe, SJ, the general of the Jesuits, in his 1968 statement to all Jesuits around the world. Most clear is St. Augustine's statement, "You possess what belongs to others when you have more than enough for yourself, and it is a kind of theft not to give to those in need what you have more than enough of" (Sermon 39:6). This is certainly shown in action by the enormous number of Catholic missions, ministry and justice endeavors around the world that are specifically working to end poverty. Yet, regarding the specific critique of capitalism's effect in creating huge swaths of poverty in the world, the Church is often ambiguous.

7. The Church, along with other organizations, is just beginning to grasp the role of "systems" that perpetuate economic inequality. See NETWORK, the Catholic religious sisters' organization for social justice in the Church and society. In 2013, Pope Francis stated that "realities are more important than ideas" (*Evan-*

gelii Gaudium 231–33). "Catholic Social Justice is informed by the prophetic challenge offered by the experience of those suffering from injustice: women, communities of color, the economically exploited, and all whose dignity is denied by unjust systems and structures. Catholic Social Justice witnesses the realities in which people are living and listens to their cries" (https://networklobby.org/about/catholicsocialjustice/).

8. In 1973, the American Psychiatric Association removed the diagnosis of "homosexuality" as a mental illness. See Diagnostic and Statistical Manual (DSM-II), 2nd ed./(DSM-III), 3rd ed., (Washington, DC: American Psychiatric Association, 1968-1985).

9. John McNeill, *The Church and the Homosexual* (Boston: Beacon Press, 1976), 146.

10. Neil Douglas-Klotz, *Prayers of the Cosmos* (San Francisco: HarperOne, 2009), 23.

11. Douglas-Klotz, *Prayers of the Cosmos*, 23.

12. See Margaret Miles, *Desire and Delight: A New Reading of Augustine's Confessions* (New York: Crossroad, 1992).

13. St. Augustine, *Confessions*, 8.11.

14. Sexual integrity, as I understand it, means that a person accepts his or her sexual orientation and tries to be honest about it as much as he or she can, internally and within relationships. Above all, it means that a person tries to live with the experience of being loved by God in his or her sexual identity. This applies to me, living as a priest as well.

15. Eastern Point Retreat House, run by the Jesuits, offers many kinds of retreats. One style that many priests and religious men and women opt for is called a directed retreat. Among other things, it consists of a withdrawal from regular ministry, a practice of silence (and refraining from involvement with computers, phone calls, and other kinds of communication) throughout the day, a meeting once a day with a retreat director, and regular spaces of individual contemplative prayer. The goal is to "listen" to God, that is, "Where is God in my life (or not)?" and "What may God want to communicate with me?" Whatever happens during each of the eight days is what one shares with his/her director. *The Spiritual Exercises*, a pattern of prayer developed by St. Ignatius of Loyola, is generally the framework for the retreat.

16. "Let me know myself; let me know Thee," *Soliloquies*, St. Augustine, book 2.

17. William A. Barry, SJ, and William J. Connolly, SJ, *The Practice of Spiritual Direction* (New York: HarperOne, 2009), and his earlier book, *A Friendship Like No Other* (Chicago: Loyola Press, 2008).

18. One journal title among many was: "Nurturing the Gift: Gay and Lesbian Persons in Seminary and Religious Formation," *Communication* 11 (Autumn 1988), private collection.

19. See Paul F. Morrissey, OSA, "Spiritual Direction for Gay Clergy and Religious: The Integration of Spirituality and Sexuality through the Written Word," Doctor of Ministry diss., Weston College, Cambridge, Massachusetts, 1982.

20. *Communication* 6, no. 9 (1983), private collection.

21. In the early 1990s, an exposé in the Catholic Church, and society, revealed a pattern of sexual abuse by priests, bishops, and even some popes, as well as others in positions of authority. (This exposé extended to sexual abuse perpetrated wider in society as well—the Cub Scouts, other religious organizations, school systems, the military, and police—but none was investigated with such rigor as the Catholic Church.) This had been going on for decades and included the cover-up and denial of such activity. The scandal has resulted in an exodus from the church by some of its members who were either victims of this activity or who were shocked and disgusted by it. Others withdrew their financial support to the churches, and further financial costs continue in the form of legal payouts, in billions of dollars, to victims. This is well documented in all media sources and continues to this day because the scandal still has never fully been dealt with. See Fr. Paul Morrissey, OSA, *The Black Wall of Silence* (Dog Ear Publishing, LLC, 2015).

Since 2004, the Augustinians and other religious communities and dioceses have established "Safety Plans" that spell out clearly what "sexual misconduct in a ministerial relationship" means, including how to prevent it, report it, and respond to it. These guidelines are continually updated. Also—and not very easy to deal with as a priest—there is the constant threat of being removed immediately from ministry if any allegation is made against you, even if it is from thirty to forty years ago, unless and until it is investigated, and you are cleared by an investigative board. This has grievously injured many priests and religious who have suffered the public suspicion such removal creates in peoples' minds, under the broad-stroke approach to preventing such abuse.

22. At least one of these organizations infiltrated a private conversation of some of the CMI members and exposed them to their superiors. This resulted in their suspension from ecclesial positions and duties. The private conversation was not endorsed by the CMI organization—nor was it related to child abuse but the threat that their public disclosure led to the disbanding of the entire organization by its board of directors.

23. In 1961, a Vatican document had stated that homosexual men should not be ordained. By 2005, another document ("Instruction Concerning the Criteria for the Discernment of Vocations with Regard to Persons with Homosexual Tendencies...") more specifically stated that men "with deeply rooted homosexual tendencies" cannot be ordained. This was seen as an official answer by the Catholic Church to sex scandals involving priests, including sexual abuse. Some right-wing groups, including some bishops and cardinals, stated clearly that gay men were responsible for the sex abuse crisis in the Church. This has resulted in a deep problem within the priesthood and the Church, even though it was largely disproved by an official study, "The John Jay Report" (2011), that asserted that the more notable problem was the lack of transparency and accountability by many bishops. For a more complicated—and debatable—rationale for not ordaining homosexual men to the priesthood, see Pope Benedict XVI's *Light of the World* (2010). In this interview-turned-book, the pope claims in a sexually charged way that homosexual priests cannot carry out "the spousal meaning of the body" as heterosexual priests can in their "gift of self to God."

24. Jesus's words instituting the Eucharist, and the priest's words of consecration at the Mass. See Mark 14:22–24.

25. See the website www.touchedbygod.net for a discussion about sexuality as a gift of God.

26. In 1977, Harvey Milk of San Francisco was one of the first openly gay persons to be elected to public office in California. A visionary and famously open gay man, he argued and worked for LGBT and other minority rights. Along with the mayor of San Francisco, Milk was assassinated on November 27, 1978, by a disgruntled former city supervisor, Dan White. Milk had been receiving death threats and recorded several versions of his will "...to be

read in the event of my assassination." One such tape contained the famous line: "If a bullet should enter my brain, let that bullet destroy every closet door."

27. Pamela Schaeffer, "Breaking Silence: Priests with AIDS Eager to Talk," *National Catholic Reporter*, April 18, 1997, https://natcath.org/NCR_Online/archives2/1997b/041897/041897a.htm.

28. This was a historically key moment for the gay Catholic community, especially in New York City. On October 31, 1986, the Congregation for the Doctrine of the Faith had issued "A Letter to the Bishops of the Catholic Church on the Pastoral Care of Homosexual Persons." In it, they used the infamous terms of "objectively disordered" and "intrinsically evil" regarding gay/lesbian people's sexual tendencies and actions. Effectively, this was experienced by the LGBTQ community as naming them as evil. Catholic churches were told to discontinue hosting liturgies for the gay community. Thus the "expulsion" liturgy in the New York City parish that hosted Dignity.

29. See James and Evelyn Whitehead, "The Shape of Compassion: Reflections on Catholics and Homosexuality," *Spirituality Today* 39 (Summer 1987): 126–36; also, James Martin, *Building a Bridge* (New York: HarperOne, 2018), in which he offers new pastoral ways—including specific prayers—for the Church and the LGBTQ community to begin to live together in one faith community.

30. I had planned my sabbatical to write about my hospice work in New York City. My first memoir, *Let Someone Hold You: The Journey of a Hospice Priest*, was written during this time. Originally written with my gay identity acknowledged, my editor recommended I remove this to facilitate it being published. I revised it—thirty years ago—it won the Christopher Award and the National Catholic Press Award.

31. Austin Center for Counseling was founded, in 1994, in the Bronx and New Rochelle, New York. The Augustinians of our province purchased a house in New Rochelle with an office that allowed me to charge regular fees; this allowed us to serve poorer people in the Bronx who could not pay for counseling. We had to sell this house for financial reasons ten years later, and I had to move to Philadelphia.

32. See Mark Thompson, ed., *Gay Spirit: Myth and Meaning* (New York: St. Martin's Press, 1987).

33. This is a conglomerate of many confessions. No one in particular.

34. In the sacrament of confession (Reconciliation), the penance is to give the person an action to make restitution and help to heal the sin confessed, as well as to acknowledge the grace in being forgiven. I felt that to offer her a way to interrupt her instinctive anger/guilt cycle might begin to do so.

35. See John Boswell, *Same-Sex Unions in Premodern Europe* (New York: Random House, 1994), xxi.

36. Pope Francis has consistently urged the bishops and laity of the Catholic Church to "pastoral accompaniment" of the faithful, mirroring the way Jesus encountered people, rather than starting with moral doctrines that exclude them. See Cardinal McElroy, "Can Divorced and Remarried Catholics and LGBTQ People Receive the Eucharist?," *America*, March 2, 2023, where he addresses a key question the Synod in Rome discusses in 2023 and 2024.

37. Sometimes, I use the word "single" or "single for the Lord" to claim my relationship with Jesus as the key meaning of my vows.

38. See Ronald Rolheiser, OMI, *The Holy Longing: The Search for a Christian Spirituality* (New York, Doubleday, 1999), 192–212, "A Spirituality of Sexuality."

EPILOGUE

1. See Wayne Rollins, ed., *Jung and the Bible* (Atlanta: John Knox Press, 1983), 36.

2. Rollins, *Jung and the Bible*, 36.

3. John J. Shea, *Adulthood, Morality, and the Fully Human* (Lanham, MD: Lexington Books, 2018), 219–50, "Spirituality and the Fully Human."

4. Shea, *Adulthood*, 7n14.

5. See Annette Mahoney and Kenneth L. Pargament, "Sacred Changes: Spiritual Conversion and Transformation," *Journal of Clinical Psychology* 60, no. 5 (2004): 481–92, doi: 10.1002/jclp.20007.

6. Valerie Saiving Goldstein, "The Human Situation: A Feminine View," *Journal of Religion* 40, no. 2 (1960): 100–112.

7. For further elaboration, see Judith Plaskow, *Sex, Sin, and Grace: Women's Experience and the Theologies of Reinhold Niebuhr and Paul Tillich* (Lanham, MD: University Press of America, 1980).

8. See Rosemary Radford Ruether, *Women and Redemption: A Theological History* (Minneapolis: Fortress Press, 1998).

Discussion Questions

1. Can you relate to any of the three parts of the book: "IN," "OUT," "WITH"? Explain.
2. Were there any moments in the book that caused you to stop and recall moments in your own life? Can you describe one of those moments and how you felt?
3. Do you ever pray about your sexual feelings, needs, and hopes? Do you find this helpful? What do these sexual emotions tell you about your relationship with God?
4. As a member of the Church, did reading this memoir give you a sense of hope?
5. After reading this book, have you changed your understanding or idea of priests and religious and their role in the Church?
6. In reading the author's interactions with his parents and family, do you recall any of your own interactions with your parents and family? Can you describe one of those interactions?
7. In reading the author's interaction with his superiors and church authorities, do you recall your own interactions with authority figures in your life? Can you describe one of those interactions?
8. After reading this book, do you think that Church teachings about sexuality need to be developed and discussed more? What aspects do you suggest?
9. Do you think sexuality is a gift of God? Why?
10. Did this book and/or discussion change your image of God? Explain.